Death, American Style

Death, American Style

A Cultural History of Dying in America

Lawrence R. Samuel

ROWMAN & LITTLEFIELD PUBLISHERS, INC.
Lanham • Boulder • New York • Toronto • Plymouth, UK

Published by Rowman & Littlefield Publishers, Inc.
A wholly owned subsidiary of The Rowman & Littlefield Publishing Group, Inc.
4501 Forbes Boulevard, Suite 200, Lanham, Maryland 20706
www.rowman.com

10 Thornbury Road, Plymouth PL6 7PP, United Kingdom

British Library Cataloguing in Publication Information Available

Library of Congress Cataloging-in-Publication Data

Samuel, Lawrence R.
Death, American style : a cultural history of dying in America / Lawrence R. Samuel.
pages cm
Includes bibliographical references and index.
ISBN 978-1-4422-2223-6 (cloth : alk. paper) — ISBN 978-1-4422-2224-3 (electronic)
1. Death—Social aspects—United States—History. 2. Death—United States—History. I. Title.
HQ1073.5.U6S26 2013
306.90973—dc23

2013002960

∞™ The paper used in this publication meets the minimum requirements of American
National Standard for Information Sciences Permanence of Paper for Printed Library
Materials, ANSI/NISO Z39.48-1992.

Printed in the United States of America

Gently, o'er a perfum'd sea,
The weary way-worn wanderer bore
To his own native shore.
—Edgar Allan Poe, "To Helen," 1831

Contents

Introduction

"Life, not death, is the great mystery."
—Anonymous

Death, American Style is the first comprehensive cultural history of death and dying in the United States from the 1920s to today. (With all due respect to Jessica Mitford, her classic *The American Way of Death*, both the original 1963 edition and the 1998 revised edition, were primarily exposés of the American funeral industry.)[1] Given that death is one of just two certainties in life, it is amazing that it has taken this long for someone to tackle the subject from a historical and cultural perspective. (Plenty of books have been written about taxes.) This book thus fills a large gap in our literary landscape, offering new and unique insights into an area to which everyone can somehow relate. Because the subject is enormous in scope, *Death, American Style* focuses on the role of the end of life in the United States over the past century or so. It is immediately after World War I (and the 1918 influenza epidemic) when we entered the modern age of death, I argue; the traditional ways of perceiving and coping with the end of life were left behind for good because of these two traumatic events. Death increased in volume and intensity through the twentieth century and into the twenty-first, its trajectory not a straight line but filled with twists and turns. Without doubt, the biggest curve was the cost of living longer, healthier lives; the end of life is now often a prolonged period carrying a heavy emotional, ethical, physical, and financial price.

The major theme of this book is America's uneasy relationship with death and dying through the twentieth century and up to today. Over the past century, death and sex battled it out to be the number one unmentionable in America; these two topics were most reflective of our shame and embarrassment when it comes to all corporeal matters. But death has surged way ahead of sex on a "forbidden quotient," I think most would agree; the former is now firmly ensconced as this country's leading source of uneasiness, discomfort, and apprehension. The notion of one day disappearing is contrary to many of our defining cultural values, I propose, with death and dying viewed as profoundly "un-American" experiences. The rise of the self has made it increasingly difficult to acknowledge the fact that our individual selves will no longer exist. Death and dying became almost unmentionable words over the course of the last century, topics not to be brought up in polite conversation. Although we have recently made some progress in reconciling the fact that life is a finite resource, we remain very unprepared for the approaching tsunami of death as the largest generation in history begins to die off in great numbers. Americans need to individually and collectively come to terms with mortality if we are to avert a major social crisis over the next couple of decades, I propose, something few people are thinking or talking about. I am not optimistic about this happening, and I conclude that the emerging "death-centric" society will be a period of considerable turmoil, perhaps equivalent to that of the countercultural 1960s and 1970s.

The breadth and depth of death as a subject is truly astounding. Not just the end of life, death is woven into many aspects of it, especially some of its most memorable moments. Indeed, a good number of our seminal, defining experiences have to do with the loss of a loved one; these events often stick with us for the remainder of our own lives. Death is really about life, if you think about it, a constant reminder to make the most of the time we have. The social and cultural dimensions of death and dying are equally compelling. Death is as good as any way to read the values of a society at a particular point in time, a central component of any civilization. Our cult of celebrity can easily be detected, for example, by our keen interest in the deaths of famous people (especially when they occur under suspicious circumstances, like that of Princess Diana or Michael Jackson). The death of minor celebrities is often the lead headline on Yahoo's news; in fact, this is just one of the ways we "contain" our fear of mortality by turning it into pop culture fodder. The popular skull and crossbones motif in fashion (inspired by the *Pirates of the Caribbean* movies) is another way we publicly display (and mock) death as a cathartic release for our underlying dread of it.

On a deeper level, death is a rich, metaphysical stew combining elements of philosophy, psychology, religion, anthropology, and sociology; its close relationship with theories about the afterlife makes the subject yet more intriguing. Science and medicine are of course at the heart of death, so much so that some have argued that their unstated purpose all along has been to solve the "problem" of dying. Death has also served as a go-to theme in popular culture, with Americans having an insatiable appetite for the long good-bye as long as it is not their own. More than anything else, however, death is personal, highly charged, with some of the strongest emotions we can feel. Fear, guilt, and, yes, happiness can be found in the dynamics of death, with only love transcending the emotional impact of losing an important person in one's life. Grief is naturally a big part of any study of death; that it is not just a powerful emotion but can be expressed in an infinite number of ways is evident from some of the stories told here. That there was and is an "art of dying" has also served as a common theme, reflecting the (particularly American) idea that death, like life, is something to master. Likewise, "dying well" or achieving "a good death" frequently pops up in the narrative, with many sensibly proposing that planning for the end of life is at least as important as planning for any other stage of it. We learn that those who did master the art of dying saw death not as a stranger or the enemy but as an essential, natural part of life. Death is not a separate entity of or epilogue to life but an integral dimension of it, in other words; such a view offers our best chance to increase the likelihood of dying well.

Meanwhile, the fact that each of us will become the dearly departed remains a major problem for America and Americans. We are entering an unprecedented period of death; this only exacerbates the problem. Americans' fear and loathing of death poses major consequences for the future; the fact that our life spans have been dramatically extended over the last century does not make the impending arrival of death any easier. In fact, many if not most of us are dreading the day this most unwelcome guest will knock on our doors, as our youth-oriented society casts death as a threatening foe or adversary. With the biggest generation in history already in or rapidly hurtling toward its sixties, America is on the brink of becoming a death-oriented society, I contend, something that we are not at all prepared for. Baby boomers are especially unready for this day; their individual and collective deaths may become one of the most important chapters in American history. Already a topic few people like to talk about, death is especially alien to a generation priding themselves on thinking and acting young regardless of their age. Baby boomers will continue to resist their mortality, I believe, making its arrival on a massive scale over the next couple of decades nothing short of traumatic. By putting death in historical perspective, however, *Death, American Style* can hopefully serve as a resource for some to come to terms with the inevitable.

If there is one single idea that summarizes the literature devoted to death and dying in America over the last half century or so, it is denial. In fact, all of the major historical works dedicated to the subject argue in some manner that denial of death is an important dimension of the twentieth-century American experience—a rare consensus among intellectuals operating within a particular field. Geoffrey Gorer's brief 1955 essay "The Pornography of Death" and 1967 book *Death, Grief, and Mourning*, Herman Feifel's 1959 *The Meaning of Death*, Jacques Choron's 1963 *Death and Western Thought*,

Arnold Toynbee's 1969 *Man's Concern with Death*, Richard G. Dumont and Dennis C. Foss's 1972 *The American View of Death*, Ernest Becker's 1973 *The Denial of Death*, and Philippe Aries's 1974 *Western Attitudes toward Death* and 1981 *The Hour of Our Death* all focus on or at least address Americans' and other Westerners' inability or refusal to acknowledge their mortality. In his *Inventing the American Way of Death, 1830–1920*, James J. Farrell made the interesting case that there were three periods in the history of American death and bereavement that reflected changes in the nation's way of life: "the living death" (1600–1830), "the dying of death" (1830–1945), and the "resurrection of death" (1945–present). John S. Stephenson's 1985 *Death, Grief, and Mourning* also looked at how Americans cope with death, usually not very well. In her 2003 *Aging, Death, and Human Longevity*, Christine Overall explored the social and moral implications of our determination to live as long as possible, a goal that often denies the realities of aging and death. Gary Laderman's 2003 *Rest in Peace* is largely a retort to Mitford; his insightful defense of the modern funeral industry is also in some ways an examination of our difficulties in facing our own demise. Finally, Lucy Bregman in her *Preaching Death* of 2011 showed how the focus of Christian funeral sermons gradually transformed from loss to celebration; this, too, is perhaps a reflection of our lack of ability to permanently separate ourselves from someone who is close to us.[2]

In Michael K. Bartalos's 2008 *Speaking of Death*, however, he and his cocontributors claim that Americans now have a "new sense of mortality," an idea that has gained some traction in recent years. "Denial is a much less notable aspect of the American 'death system,'" Christina Staudt argued in her essay (titled "From Concealment to Recognition"), thinking that "we have gone from ignoring and hiding mortal matters to, increasingly, recognizing and exploring the final stage of life." After peaking in the postwar years, our denial of death has eased, these scholars claim, with Americans getting increasingly comfortable with the prospect of no longer existing.[3] I disagree heartily with such a view, of the belief that Americans' repression of their own end of life remains very strong. In fact, compared to the "Greatest Generation" who, because of having to face the harsh realities of the Depression and World War II developed a somewhat pragmatic perspective of death, baby boomers are in a near panic when it comes to the subject. As the eternally youthful generation, the very concept of old age and death is alien to boomers, something that I believe will cause big trouble in the not-so-distant future. In her 2011 *Never Say Die*, Susan Jacoby shows how the marketing of what she calls "the new old age" is an appealing concept to many Americans, especially baby boomers, because it obscures the unavoidable realities of decline and death.[4] And in her *The Mansion of Happiness*, Harvard historian Jill Lepore convincingly argues that through the nineteenth century, life was viewed as circular ("ashes to ashes, dust to dust"), while in the twentieth it became more linear, the root cause of our problems in dealing with death.[5]

A spate of books about death and dying have been published the last couple of years, a clear reflection of our intensifying anxiety surrounding the subject. When viewed together, these books give us a good look at the state of death and dying in America and reveal our struggle to come to terms with the unknowable. Self-help books such as Louis LaGrand's *Healing Grief, Finding Peace* are growing in number as more Americans seek out coping strategies after losing a family member or friend. A host of other new books, including *Living Life Dying Death, No One Has to Die Alone*, and *Saying Goodbye*, are resources to help people care for a dying loved one, as their titles suggest, something most of us will do at least once in our lifetime. Almost inevitably, there is more and more literature devoted to the grieving process for a pet, this, too, reflecting our lack of skills in confronting any kind of death. Jon Katz's *Going Home* is one such book designed to help pet owners say goodbye to their feline or canine friends, a process frequently as difficult as bidding farewell to someone of our own species. And in Jessica Pierce's *The Last Walk*, the bioethicist makes the case that companion animals, just like humans, deserve a "peaceful, respectful, and meaningful" end of life, something more difficult than it sounds in our death-phobic times.[6]

Self-help is meeting practical advice in books such as Janet Boyanton's *Alone and Alive*, a guide for widows to deal with the death of their husbands. As both a widow and estate planning lawyer, Boyanton is well qualified to answer the common question "What next?" by helping those who have lost their spouse both grieve and move on with their lives. As a guide to (the often shady) funeral services industry, Joshua Slocum and Lisa Carlson's *Final Rights* is equally practical for those who recently lost someone and needs to negotiate what Mitford called "The American Way of Death." If it were up to Bernd Heinrich, there would be little need for many of the services the funeral business provides. In his *Life Everlasting*, Heinrich, a physiological ecologist, suggests that nature would be better off if humans, like animals in the wild, could become part of the ecosystem once we became dead matter. We can learn a lot from "The Animal Way of Death," he argues, and, by doing so, find greater meaning in what he calls the "web of life."[7]

Not just those with some expertise in dying but well-known authors of both fiction and nonfiction are increasingly tackling what is perhaps the most difficult subject to write about. In *The Inevitable*, twenty writers, including Joyce Carol Oates and Diane Ackerman, take a creative approach to a bevy of death-related areas such as near-fatal accidents, out-of-body experiences, suicide, AIDS, and graveyards. Consistent with where American society and, especially, death, are headed, the essays are more philosophical than religious. Personal reflections on death is well on the way to becoming a literary genre unto itself, and one that is destined to only grow in the years ahead as more of us attempt to make sense out of the end of life. In *At the End of Life*, twenty-two family members and health professionals tell their personal stories about witnessing someone die, shedding light on some of the most important issues involved in the difficult process. Cheryl Eckl's *A Beautiful Death* explores the process of dying through the lens of her husband's death, turning what most would consider a tragedy into a love story and spiritual journey. Memoirs of one's own impending death can be seen as a literary subgenre all its own. In his *When I Die*, Philip Gould takes readers on his journey toward death from cancer, finding that journey, perhaps paradoxically, life affirming. Christopher Hitchens's equally uplifting *Mortality* was written after the well-known journalist (and atheist) was diagnosed with stage IV esophageal cancer, and it was published after he died at age sixty-two in December 2011. Hitchens chronicled his illness in half a dozen articles in *Vanity Fair*, the basis for the book, offering readers a host of truly eloquent (and hilarious) reflections on dying.[8]

Even more compelling, perhaps, are recent books whose authors promise the possibility of some kind of eternal life. In his *The Modern Book of the Dead*, Ptolemy Tompkins conjectures that the human soul has a long and rich future after dwelling for some time in this life, good news to those worrying that this is the end of the line. The rise of science drummed out the millennium-old belief in a life to come, he suggests, our current views of the hereafter "hopelessly vague" compared to those of ancient civilizations. Dr. Eben Alexander, a neurosurgeon who has taught at Harvard, announced he experienced a "completely coherent odyssey" while in a coma, believing he visited not just the afterlife but, specifically, heaven. His bestseller, *Proof of Heaven*, no doubt offers much comfort to many of us who fear death, especially the notion that there will be no form of life after this one. *Heaven Is for Real*, a number-one best seller of 2010, also reaffirmed individuals' faith in an afterlife, although skeptics saw the near-death experience described in the book (by a young child) as entirely consistent with hallucinations triggered by medication.[9]

Death, American Style covers a wide swath in its exploration of the nation's contentious relationship with the end of life. While Americans have for decades been in deep denial about the reality of death (especially their own), the subject has nonetheless received a lot of attention. Much thought has been given to what dying feels like; for example, the question of whether it is peaceful (or euphoric, as some claim) or painful is much debated. Wondering what death itself is like has also been on our minds, part of our longing to know the unknowable. Elaborate theories regarding such have served as the backbone of religions and civilizations throughout history, of course; the story of death is a major component of the story of life. While traditional portrayals of the afterlife have usually been extreme, imagined as either nirvana or nightmare, it is the idea of death as a black void of nothingness that has more recently been deemed most terrifying. In a society in which one's identity is so reliant on achieving things and keeping busy (regardless of what one actually does), idleness and loneliness have emerged as our version of hell. Those who had a close brush with death were routinely asked to tell their tale, any insight into what may lay beyond eagerly sought. What to do if one knew one was dying is another interesting part of this story, such knowledge almost always considered more of a blessing than a curse. Death and dying are far harder on loved ones than oneself, we learn, our own impending doom frequently leading to a higher level of consciousness and a deeper appreciation of life. In the best of circumstances, the death of a loved one often serves as a unique, if extremely painful, opportunity to grow as a human being; one's view of the world is typically changed (for the better) after going through the intense experience.

That death and dying have been problematic in America is not surprising given the number and range of challenging issues that continually spring up. Whether doctors should tell those dying the truth was much debated, for instance; the answer is still not fully resolved. In the 1980s the American Medical Association (AMA) declared that it was a patient's right to know the truth about a terminal condition, contrary to the organization's previous stance that it was the physician's "therapeutic privilege" to tell or not tell a patient of his or her terminal condition. The declaration certainly made a difference: in the 1970s about 10 percent of doctors told the patient of a terminal condition, while today it is close to 90 percent. (Interestingly, in Japan today doctors tend to tell the family but not the patient.) As well, the "right to die" with "dignity" was too close to euthanasia or mercy killing for some, especially given the presence of a small but dedicated group advocating "assisted suicide." The rise of organ transplants also threw a monkey wrench into the dynamics of death; a body was now seen as a valuable commodity rather than something to be quickly disposed of. With time of the essence when it comes to transplants, the definition of death became that much more important, with who would live and who would die another critical part of the equation. Children posed a special problem when it came to death; if and how to tell them about it was a continual concern of parents. If adults could not understand death, children certainly could not, some reasonably observed—not much consolation when a family member died. Given that it was inevitable, however, was it really necessary to give serious thought to death and dying, some wondered? Since we could not do much about death anyway, it was silly to dwell on it, the more practical argued, a position perhaps difficult to contest.

According to some scientists, however, there was a distinct possibility that death might not be inevitable. Science was frankly befuddled by death, the fact that it results in the destruction of an individual organism a perplexing problem. Was death a flaw in nature's design or a brilliant mechanism to ensure the survival of a species? Similarly, was aging simply a bug in our genetic engineering or an essential evolutionary strategy? Until relatively recently, science viewed aging as a disease; this, too, made death and dying one of nature's most enigmatic mysteries. Answering such questions was made even more difficult as the definition of death continued to change, a direct result of advances in medical technology extending the boundaries of life. For centuries, death was considered to have occurred when the heart stopped beating and lungs stopped breathing, a certainty discredited by intervention (or "rescue") medicine. Parts of the body lived longer than others, scientists and physicians discovered; that certain parts could be sustained virtually indefinitely made the concept of death (some argued it was a "process," others an "event") decidedly more gray than black and white.

The pursuit of immortality and "radical life extension," as dramatically increased longevity became known, was always lurking in the shadow of death. Perhaps man's ultimate dream, the possibility of living forever, gained traction over the past century as advances in science and technology made death appear more "solvable." Victory over aging and disease was increasingly believed to be within reach as the keys to human life were gradually revealed. Today, immortality remains one of the grand ambitions of science, with nutrition, gene therapy, or more radical measures such as cryogenics or the integration of man and machine considered possible solutions to the "problem" of death. The average life span of Americans rose from about forty-five to roughly eighty over the course of the last one hundred years, reason enough for some to think that equivalent strides in the twenty-first century are conceivable. "Why not 100, 150, 200, or many more years?" "anti-agists" are asking, with future discoveries in science and technology to keep human longevity spiraling ever upward. "We will soon achieve almost unlimited lifespans and the eventual 'death of death' in the coming decades, even if it still sounds incredible today," says José Cordeiro, one of the directors of the international think tank The Millennium Project. He and his colleagues are convinced that "physical death will ultimately become optional and the nature and meaning of human life will be changed forever," quite a prediction given there is no real evidence of achieving such a thing.[10]

If the science of death is a riddle, the psychology of it has been one of our greatest conundrums. Others died, not us, most of us liked to think; that it was difficult or impossible to conceive of our own deaths was perhaps some kind of survival mechanism to prevent it from actually happening. Rather than just being a biological impulse, however, our denial of death could be a psychological condition rooted in Freudian theory. Americans repress the idea of death, our fear of it is so great that it lies buried deep in our subconscious. (The word itself is a major turnoff, as I quickly discovered when I told friends the subject of my new book.) Fictionalizing death through violent (and wildly popular) entertainment helps us keep it at bay, an over-the-top, stylized version serving as a safe substitute for the real thing. We have, in short, a neurosis when it comes to death, most of us displaying the classic signs of such a disorder (e.g., anxiety, depression, hypochondria) whenever we have to confront the subject in real life. Besides the complex psychological issues, there are practical ones that further complicate things. We are woefully misinformed about what is likely to kill us, overestimating the dramatic (e.g., airplane crashes and acts of terrorism) and underestimating the routine (chronic diseases, car accidents, or falling down the stairs at home). (The "big three" causes of death remain heart disease, cancer, and stroke.) We are incredibly knowledgeable about the most trivial matters—which celebrity is dating which other one, when the newest, latest technological gadget is coming out, or who is leading the American League in ERA—but have little or no idea about when or how we will probably die.

That death is a scientific and psychological puzzle is understandable, but it is our own failures in the area of dying that have proved most worrisome. "We don't die well in America," Bill Moyers observed in 2000, something readily apparent in any examination of the end of life in the United States.[11] Our exclusive focus on life has made death simply not one of our priorities, something for which we are all to blame. Doctors' lack of training in the area of dying and their commitment to preserve life at any cost, the institutional nature of both modern medicine and the funeral industry, religious leaders' own discomfort with the end of life, and families' reluctance to let their loved ones go are just a few reasons why death is so problematic in this country. It was in the mid-1960s that Americans came to believe that medical experts often made the experience of dying worse, Allen Verhey suggested in *Christian Century* in 2011, the process no longer really a "human event." Subsequent legal battles, public policy decisions, and the hospice movement restored some of our right to die a more natural death, accepted thought goes, but there is little doubt that aggressive medical treatments to preserve life are still being used in futile situations and when patients or families do not want them.[12]

More than any single factor, however, it is that death and dying run counter to virtually all of the nation's defining values—youth, beauty, progress, achievement, winning, optimism, independence, and persistence—that accounts for our "dying badly." Our inherent antipathy of death, which we accepted until the late nineteenth century because of its sheer prevalence, became much more pronounced in the twentieth century as the tentacles of modernism reached into all avenues of everyday life. A more secular age, centered around the many pleasures and freedoms to be had in place of a judging God, encouraged an aversion to death and dying. The tools and techniques of modern medicine—antibiotics, vaccines, new kinds of surgeries, transplants, and, of course, machines—allowed us to skirt death, or, more accurately, delay it. Some historians went so far as to say we "conquered" death in the twentieth century, a premature declaration of victory if there ever was one.

The price to living longer lives—living longer deaths—became clear around midcentury with the advent of artificial respiration. Doctors' Hippocratic oath could prove to be, quite literally, a living nightmare, the vow to sustain life a much different idea when put into practice two-thousand-plus years after the Greek physician conceived the pledge. As our quality of life rose, our quality of death declined; the pain, suffering, and cost of dying were something no one could anticipate. As the lines between life and death became fuzzier, the trade-off of living twenty, thirty, or forty more years became more evident. A good half of those extra two, three, or four decades could be very unpleasant, one's sixties, seventies, and eighties often filled with the challenges that come with old age and chronic disease. And while many intended to die at home, surrounded by loved ones, most ended up dying in a hospital, nursing home, or assisted living center. Despite the increasing popularity of hospice, the average American is still likely to die surrounded by strangers, in a druggy haze, hooked up to machines, and, too often, in pain, the result of doctors' reluctance to prescribe heavy painkillers. If the American health care system is broken, our way of death is completely wrecked, the result of decades of sticking our heads in the sand when it comes to dying.

Given the trajectory of death and dying over the past century, none of this should come as much of a surprise. Previously on intimate terms with death, we consistently distanced ourselves from it, the once familiar presence now hidden, isolated, and contained. Not that long ago a neighborly, communal, and familial affair, death became professionalized and institutionalized, just another part of our service economy. Rather than the most natural thing in the world, equivalent to birth, death became seen as a mistake of nature. Death had become, rather perversely, an inconvenient disruption of life, the result of something gone terribly wrong. Insurance companies, armed with precise statistics and actuarial tables, helped to turn death into a rational and predictable event, extracting much of its spiritual power. Less than defeating death, we "forgot" about it, one can say, a classic case of "out of sight, out of mind." The better we got at avoiding death the better we got at ignoring it, the subject something we pay little attention to until we are forced to. And like anything unknown and unfamiliar to us, we now feared death more than ever, the end of life perceived as an abstract idea disengaged from everyday life.

The terms of this Faustian bargain are becoming clearer and clearer. We are essentially no longer equipped with the tools to cope with death when it appears, which of course it inevitably will. We are surprised when it takes place, an ironic thing given that it is the only certainty in life. Like our national debt, perhaps, we have borrowed against our future, our living for the moment, making our dying that much more difficult when it does come due. More significant, being disconnected from death has removed something important from life. Our effort to enhance our lives by ignoring death has backfired; it is, rather, the full awareness that we will die that makes life more meaningful. This is the real cost of our shunning of death, our lives capable of being much richer if we embraced the idea that they will one day end.

Over the past decade or so, more scholarly attention has deservedly been paid to the history of death and dying in America. In their collection of essays, *Mortal Remains*, editors Nancy Isenberg and Andrew Burstein did yeoman's work in pooling a body of knowledge related to the subject of death during the country's first century. While life expectancy in this country increased over the course of the latter half of the eighteenth century (despite the Revolutionary War), we learn, it actually decreased during the decades leading up to and including the Civil War. Infectious diseases such as scarlet fever, typhoid, and tuberculosis spread due to greater geographic mobility, and epidemics were not uncommon in rapidly growing cities such as New York, Philadelphia, and Boston. By the end of the Civil War, the average American was a less-healthy individual and had a shorter life span than the typical colonist. The prevalence of death sparked a fascination with mortality among Victorian Americans, many of them preserving the memory of dead children via what would today be considered macabre photograph albums.[13]

It was thus the late nineteenth century when Americans' current attitudes toward death could be said to have formed. As Drew Gilpin Faust eloquently showed in her *This Republic of Suffering*, the American way of looking at death was dramatically changed by the Civil War because of its "unnaturalness," with dying from disease dreaded even more than from combat.[14] The high rate of child mortality in the nation through the nineteenth century also contributed to making death a heartbreaking fact of life, something provoking deep sadness and grief. Now, however, a growing resistance and antagonism toward death could be detected, a dying or dead body increasingly seen as distasteful and grotesque. Such a view accelerated in the first decades of the twentieth century; death was already beginning to displace sex as the nation's primary taboo. This new, "modern" conception of death was worth examining, a few perceptive social critics believed. In 1912, for example, Roswell Park, a Boston physician, wrote an article for the *Journal of the American Medical Association* in which he argued that death was a field warranting serious study. Although his proposal to create a legitimate field of "thanatology" (from the Greek word *thanatos*, or "death") got people's attention, Park's daring idea was soon forgotten. A book published that same year, Hereward Carrington's *Death: Its Causes and Phenomena*, also raised some eyebrows with its choice of subject matter, but this, too, quickly faded into obscurity.[15] From the 1920s through the 1950s, Americans' denial of death and dying grew steadily, with no place in our progressive, forward-looking age to accommodate the disturbing idea of the end of life.

It was not until the early 1960s that a book dedicated to the subject of death in America made a real impact. Mitford's scathing critique of the nation's funeral industry shocked people by exposing the dark side of what she brilliantly termed "the American way of death." Mitford's best seller would lay the groundwork for a broader examination of the problem of death and dying in the United States in the late 1960s. It would be another woman, Elisabeth Kübler-Ross, who with her then-radical ideas would lead a movement that still reverberates today. Kübler-Ross's work with the dying and her 1969 book *On Death and Dying* revolutionized how Americans thought of death, especially her bold proposition that it could serve as "the final stage of growth." Buoyed by the more open climate of the counterculture and interest in all things "natural," a "death awareness" or "death consciousness" movement was soon in play, with books, articles, courses, seminars, and therapies dedicated to the subject. Most important, perhaps, was the importing of hospice from the United Kingdom and the emergence of "death professionals" committed to the practice. Like many other areas of society, death and dying had left the safe cocoon of postwar America, never to be the same again.[16]

If death and dying came out of the closet in America in the 1960s, they went decidedly mainstream in the 1970s. The 1970s was a good decade for a subject like death to flourish; the economic, social, and political turmoil of the times allowed if not encouraged thoughts of mortality. The pronounced focus on the self also stirred up interest in the topic, with the need to regain control of the process of dying being recognized. The case of Karen Ann Quinlan made death and dying the stuff of watercooler talk, her tragic situation accelerating the emergent "right to die" or "death with dignity" movement. The extraordinary measures being taken to prolong life were too often prolonging death, more Americans were coming to believe, and the living will was a direct result of this new kind of attitude toward dying. Of the many books being written about the end of life during this decade, Philippe Aries's 1974 *Western Attitudes toward Death* was probably the most insightful. Modern industrialization and the rise of individualism in the early twentieth century had led to our becoming detached from death, Aries argued, the decline of traditional religion and depersonalization of medicine other key factors in our increasingly strained and unhealthy relationship with the Grim Reaper.[17]

Death and dying remained a ubiquitous, if less chaotic, presence in the 1980s. The AIDS crisis, New Age phenomenon, and baby boomers reaching middle age helped keep Americans thinking and talking about death, with a legitimate field of "death studies" now established. Besides the unnecessary suffering associated with interventionist medicine (the catalyst for a fringe assisted-suicide movement), it was now the cost of dying that caught Americans' attention. Some 30 percent of total health care costs were now being spent on the last six months of life; the futile extension of dying was, if nothing else, a bad investment. A pervasive search for meaning and purpose in life in the 1990s (a backlash against the materialist 1980s) ensured that death and dying would remain an emotionally charged component of the cultural zeitgeist. Most recently, death has taken up residence on the Internet, with virtual bereavement an ideal alternative for people who have difficulty dealing with grief and loss in the real world. Social and technological upheaval has not significantly altered the "fundamentals" of death in this country, however. Death in America is "still informed by an ancient, persistent, and religiously inspired redemptive ethos which shapes how we understand the value of life and solemnize its endings," James W. Green observed in his insightful *Beyond the Good Death: The Anthropology of Modern Dying*, our contemporary rituals surrounding the end of life rooted firmly in the past.[18] Isenberg and Burstein echoed this idea. "Despite cultural transitions, old themes [of death] are reappropriated," they wrote. "The human condition chang[ing] only very slowly, if at all" when it comes to matters of mortality.[19]

The louder conversation about death and dying during the past half century has not made Americans any more comfortable with the subject. We are certainly talking and reading about death more than we used to, but we remain in denial about its reality, no better off than we were in the 1950s. In fact, a solid case could be made that we are considerably worse off when it comes to accepting death and dying for the natural and inevitable events they are. Fictionalized depictions of death—the vampire and zombie phenomena—are arguably more popular than ever; these stylized versions serve as a safe substitute for the real, much scarier thing. Baby boomers, hurtling through their fifties and sixties, continue to be youth oriented, ignoring or fighting off the effects of aging and physical decline. We should expect no less from the eternally young generation, of course, but this has serious implications. Boomers are taking few if any steps to prepare themselves for their own deaths or that of their siblings or friends, and this is not boding well for their individual and collective future. The huge wave of death that is fast approaching will be emotionally devastating, I believe, our society simply not ready for the historically high numbers of people who will be dying. The immortality and "radical life extension" movement is only compounding the problem, giving people false hope that they may live forever or considerably beyond the average age of eighty years.

Death, American Style tells its story chronologically, beginning at the end of World War I and going right up to today, when the subject of death and dying is arguably more problematic than ever. While I frequently cross paths with spirituality, the intersection between death and religion is much too wide to fully accommodate in this book. As well, I spend little time on abortion, murder, and capital punishment, each of these, I believe, to be dedicated subjects all their own. Likewise, while I regularly brush up with science, philosophy, and psychology in relation to the history of death and dying in America, those especially interested in any of those three areas should seek out the hundreds of resources dedicated to each. Regarding sources, the spine of *Death, American Style* relies on contemporary, popular magazines and newspapers (as a cultural history should), as well as scholarly references. Hundreds of different sources, many of them forgotten, are used, drawing from journalists' writing of "the first draft of history." Secondary sources were prioritized not only because this is a work of cultural history but also because they were typically filtered, vetted, and fact checked and offer a relatively objective and balanced perspective. As well, these sources most effectively address my thesis: how death and dying have had a problematic past in America and why their future is even more troubling. Books and journal articles are used to frame the story and provide valuable context. Death has, of course, played a recurring role in books, movies, and television; this, too, serves as prime fodder in the book.

The first chapter of *Death, American Style*, "Much Ado about Dying," takes readers through the 1920s and 1930s, when the forces of modernism shifted Americans' attitudes toward death dramatically. Chapter 2, "War Department Regrets," tracks the story of death and dying in the United States in the 1940s when another world war reconfigured Americans' view of the end of life. Chapter 3, "Why Can't We Live Forever?," examines dying in the 1950s and 1960s, when death was heavily privatized and contained. Chapter 4, "Living Your Dying," shows how death came out of the closet during the Me Decade by riding on the prevailing pop psychology, self-help, and higher-consciousness movements. Chapter 5, "The Other Side," explores death and dying in the 1980s and early 1990s, when America went through what could be called a collective near-death experience. The final chapter, "Design for Dying," tells the story of the end of life in the United States from the late 1990s up to today as baby boomers began to confront their mortality for the first time. The future of death in America is not a pretty one, I argue in the conclusion of the book, our emerging "death-centric" society something we are not at all prepared for. Still, Americans have an opportunity over the next two or three decades to see dying not as the enemy but as an essential and even beneficial part of living, something *Death, American Style* can perhaps help encourage.

Chapter One

Much Ado about Dying

"It is my opinion that death has been made too much of and, like a spoiled child, takes unto itself undue importance."

—Carolyn Wells, 1933

In June 1921, Vernon Kellogg, a notable biologist, reflected on death after having an experience that was far more personal than his scientific study of it. On a recent train trip from Chicago to Washington, Kellogg spent the evening chatting amiably with a colleague, the pair talking for hours and hours about nature, science, and life itself. The two parted ways late in the night, each having thoroughly enjoyed their intellectual tête-à-tête. In the morning, his friend was found dead in his berth, his sudden departure making Kellogg think about death in a way that he never had before. Biologists typically thought of death in terms of species, with issues such as natural selection and evolutionary progress of primary importance. Humans also were capable of thinking about death in individual terms; however, his colleague's unexpected passing was a much more emotional thing than any scholarly discourse on a species' struggle for survival. "Because a trivial mechanical disharmony prevailed during the night over what had been for fifty years mechanical harmony, he is nothing more to us or himself," Kellogg wrote in *The Atlantic*, an individual's death a frustrating and even preposterous concept for a scientist like himself trained to think of the end of life on such a grand scale.[1]

Kellogg's altered consciousness of death mirrored that of many Americans in the 1920s and 1930s. World War I, along with the 1918 flu epidemic, represented a key turning point in the story of death in the United States, quite understandably, with the sheer volume of people who "died before their time" making many think long and hard about the subject in a way that Americans had never done before. It was "much ado about dying," as *Dial* magazine expressed it in 1923, with major advances in science, especially biology, changing the way Americans felt about death. In the age of modernity, however, death was proving to be a troublesome topic, refusing to obey the laws of logic, order, and rationalism. Instead, it was emotions such as fear and grief that defined death, that our loved ones and we had to die at all now a difficult thing to accept. With the new tools of "modern medicine," scientists and physicians would confront death in a way that was unprecedented, challenging all of its assumptions and very existence.

AN ETHEREAL SPIRIT EXISTENCE

Nothing, in fact, conveyed the transformation of death in American culture between the wars more than the increased interest in immortality. Spiritualism or "spiritism," a subject that had been popular in the United States since the famous (and later debunked). Fox sisters' sensation in 1848, reached a new plateau in the 1920s. Spiritist séances allegedly connecting the living with the dead were all the rage, the Society for Psychical Research was publishing volumes of material on parapsychological goings-on, and so many authors were churning out books on the subject of life after death that it was becoming a literary genre unto its own. Not just those wanting to chat with their Aunt Minnie across the great divide was interested in the prospect of life after death but serious scientists as well. Perhaps in part as a result of his friend's sudden death, Vernon Kellogg posed a series of questions that many other men and women of science were no doubt also pondering:

> Is death really just what it seems, and what the biologist describes it to be, or is it what so many would like it to be, hope it is, and even firmly believe it is? Can the human individual have an ethereal spirit existence apart from, or after, his bodily-machine existence? Is man immortal?[2]

It was clear that scientists like Kellogg were intrigued by and drawn to research being pursued by people who, until recently, would have been the target of considerable ridicule. Inspired by Sir Oliver Lodge's work in England, psychical researchers argued that it was their field that could reconcile the fundamental conflict surrounding death. For centuries, scientists and philosophers struggled with the major contradiction regarding death, baffled by what appeared to be a flaw in the grand design of the universe. How could death be beneficial, even necessary, to evolution but at the same time destructive to the individual? Through death, higher forms of life such as humans adapted to changing environments, biologists pointed out, the replacing of organisms with "new and improved" ones vital to the survival of a species. For a particular organism, however, death was hardly beneficial, a sacrifice for the greater good that suggested that Nature might not be as perfect as we liked to believe. Death was imperative for an entire species but disastrous for an individual, it seemed, a paradox that was inconsistent with the basic logic and order to life. That there could be such disharmony in Nature was disturbing to intellectuals, incentive enough to try to look to alternative theories to solve the mystery of death.[3]

It was only through other sources of knowledge and a wider range of experiences that this apparent disharmony in Nature could be resolved, supporters of "parapsychology" maintained. In short, the "incident" of death could not be the ultimate end of life, they insisted, the individual carrying his or her character and personality into new and different conditions. This was an appealing concept to many serious scientists, offering a theory that could be or lead to a solution to the puzzle that was death. Numerous case studies proved as much, researchers claimed, with rapping from the other side, physical manifestations, and conversations with the dead evidence of the reality of another life. Even better, possibly the worst imagined aspect of death—its loneliness—was not to be concerned about given that one would be surrounded by others in the next world and in occasional communication with people in this one. The jury was still out whether one would have a body in the life beyond, some people (and some spirits, allegedly) making the case for and some against. But just like in this life, unhappiness lay in store for some in the next one, believers agreed, thinking what went around here would go around there.[4]

Given that death was inevitable, at least for the foreseeable future, however, it was worth trying to figure out what it might be like. Writer after writer between the wars mused over the state of death, most of them thinking that it was at worst a neutral experience and at best a quite positive one. Writing in *The Atlantic* in 1923, Sarah Cleghorn explained how her view of death had changed numerous times since she was a child, when her grandmother, sister, mother, and a close cousin all died. It was the near-death of her brother when she was seventeen, however, that made her think differently about the subject. Death was no longer "the black threat over life," as she called it, but rather a fascinating, possibly magnificent, thing to embrace. In her twenties, Cleghorn had adopted reincarnation as "the most congenial notion about death that I had ever had," this despite her friends' nearly universal belief that returning to earth again in another form would be risky if not a punishment. By her thirties, however, Cleghorn had begun to view death as a "pleasurable adventure" and a "more abounding experience" than life, somewhat jealous of very old people who were close to taking the exciting journey. Now in her forties, Cleghorn conceived of death as "a shaft of beaming brightness," our energy dispersed and redistributed around the planet after we died. "Electron with loved electron will meet again, for none are lost, and all are evermore moving," she was convinced, everyone "freer, happier, more fully themselves, more blithely alive, than ever."[5]

Other scenarios of what death may be like were eagerly and seriously entertained. Some proposed that the experience of fainting or anesthesia could perhaps resemble death. The encroaching darkness and drifting off into unconscious of each might be similar to the sensation of dying, some hypothesized, a distasteful but not entirely horrible feeling.[6] Death was most often compared to sleep, however, suggesting that there would still be some kind of existence despite the loss of consciousness. Dreaming could thus be the closest we could come to the state of death, this theory went, offering us access to a world we could not exist in while conscious. Popular thinking (then and now) was that our survival instincts prevented us from experiencing our own death while dreaming; that is, that we were programmed to wake up just before falling off a precipice or getting shot by a Colt 45 in a gunfight at the O.K. Corral. Some believed we would actually die if we died in a dream, just one of many mythologies surrounding this most enigmatic of subjects. This was not true, however, with numerous stories of people dying in a dream and living to tell about it.[7]

One such story was that of "M. E. B.," who told his tale anonymously in *The Atlantic* in 1924. ("We can assure our readers of its entire genuineness," the editor of the magazine noted, that the author held an important post in Asia, adding to its credibility.) One night M. E. B. found himself dreaming of a wild tiger, this obviously resulting from the fact that there happened to be a real one in the area where he lived that was regularly feasting on the local horses, caribou, and elephants. In his vivid dream, the tiger stalked him and his wife, the two desperately trying to get away from the hungry cat. Cornered in a house, M. E. B. urged his wife to escape through the back door while he tried to fight the tiger off with a club. "I saw his wide-open mouth, heard his terrifying roar, was conscious that he struck me a terrific blow with his left paw—and then was overwhelmed with a sensation of great DARKNESS, and knew nothing more," as M. E. B. described the climax of his dream. M. E. B.'s dream was not over, however. "I next became aware of being still existent in a most particular state," he recalled, having "no bodily form whatsoever." He could see what was left of his body on the ground below, rather shockingly, this taken as confirmation that he was dead. M. E. B. shouted out in his sleep, and this made his wife lying next to him wake him up from the nightmare. Was it just a bad dream, M. E. B. wondered, or had he in his unconscious state gained insight into what death was really like?[8]

Like dreams, hypnotism was believed to offer a peek into the window of death. Along with spiritism, hypnotism was quite popular in the 1920s, part of the time's fascination with psychology and, especially, the unconscious. After being instructed to enter a deep sleep, those hypnotized were sometimes told to "leave" their body, some of whom were able to do it. As in M. E. B.'s dream, the hypnotized would then imagine they were floating above their physical bodies, a strange and wonderful feeling that might be similar to the state of death, the more paranormally inclined proposed. Could immortality be like this etherealness, the mind existing apart from the brain? If so, death was hardly something to be feared or dreaded, those who had such an experience happily reported; the indescribable joy of being liberated from one's body was something to look forward to. In fact, the hypnotized were often reluctant to go back to their familiar lives, with nothing on this mortal coil to compare to being freed from one's physical self. Some kind of spiritual presence also seemed to pervade this other world, those brought into such a state disclosed when awakened, all the more reason our antipathy toward death was unfounded.[9]

If being under anesthesia resembled the sensation of dying or death itself, many of those who had experienced the former were quite open to experiencing the latter. During surgery and while recovering from an operation, the anesthetized typically described a feeling of "floating out," as if they were in a boat going farther into a body of water. This was an immensely pleasurable experience, so much so that they were reluctant to regain full consciousness. Some who went through this later reported that they woke up only because they were somehow aware of grieving relatives holding a bedside vigil. Not wanting to put their loved ones through such misery, they turned around and came to shore, as they described it, this requiring a great deal of effort. "I was convinced that I was making an enormous sacrifice; I thought so at the time, and now, when years have gone by, I think so still," said one woman who made such a return journey for her sister's sake. One did not have to have inhaled a heavy dose of ether, however, to be receptive to going off into that good night. Who had not laid on the ground under a tree on a beautiful summer day and felt oneself being transported to a wonderful place that did not seem to be of this earth? Was this what death was like? If so, it was not something to fear but rather something to look forward to, an intoxicating feeling that one was free from worldly troubles and had become part of a cosmic entity. Let me lie here forever, those who had such an experience thought to themselves, death now a welcome proposition if it was anything like this.[10]

The most compelling accounts of how it felt to die, however, were told in the first person by those going through the actual experience. One such account was by Hugh Lonsdale Hands, a British physician who committed suicide "to escape from an intolerable burden of debt and threatening insanity," as *The Living Age* reported in 1931. Hands left a few notes and letters in which he explained why he was doing what he was doing, outlined his wishes for his possessions and his body after he was dead, and, most interesting, described the sensations of dying by poison. "I have come to the end of my tether," he wrote in a good-bye letter to his wife, Sophie, his mounting debts and increasing forgetfulness (the onset of what would become known as Alzheimer's disease, perhaps) the basis for his decision. Hands then locked himself in his office and took a half-ounce of aconite and an ounce of chloral hydrate, each quite lethal if ingested. "Waiting, feeling very happy," he wrote, the knowledge that his worries would soon be over a great relief. Hands became increasingly sleepy but had yet to feel any pain, making him wonder if he should take yet another poison (prussic acid) to get the job done. Hands's "real-time" suicide note soon trailed off, however. "Money is nothing; it is not wickedness," went his final words, the doctor receiving his final wish.[11]

O'ER A PERFUM'D SEA

A double dose of poison was certainly not the way most people would prefer to end their life, but most physicians agreed that dying was not a painful or even unpleasant experience. The event that led to death—pneumonia, drowning, a fatal disease or injury, say—could and usually did involve a lot of suffering as the body fought for survival, but the final act itself was believed to be rather relaxing. Those who had come very close to dying reported as much after being revived and, as important, it seemed to make sense from a scientific standpoint. As the dying person's blood pressure sank lower and lower, his or her brain was less and less able to feel any sensation, physicians explained, our bodies perhaps designed for a merciful end. "The turbulent tidal wave of individual vitality ebbs back toward the sea of universal life whence it came, a recessional undercurrent, flowing on and on into the quiet deepness far below the surging surface," wrote Lester Howard Perry, managing editor of the *Pennsylvania Medical Journal*, making dying seem positively lovely.[12]

Those close to death were not only known to describe this kind of euphoria but also share the news that there was a fuller and lasting happiness to be had in the world beyond. With a weak heart and suffering from influenza in 1925, a nineteen-year-old man from Chicago Heights, Illinois, for example, very much felt like he was being wafted "gently, o'er a perfum'd sea," as Edgar Allan Poe wrote in his poem "To Helen." In no pain and not delirious, the young man was able to contemplate what he thought may be his last moments on earth. "And to my utter astonishment, I found my experience a pleasant one," he recalled five years later, adding that it was "not only pleasant but enticing." The man had no particular yearning to die but, at the same time, admitted that he found this sensation difficult to resist. "I wanted more of this supreme happiness I was feeling," he remembered. "I craved a clearer and deeper draught of this bliss." It was impossible for him to put into words precisely how he felt, but he offered a few ways to characterize the experience. Being near death was "a gradual assimilation by the universe," "a slow but sure entrance into something more vast," and "a constant diminishing of the individual," the man told those who had not had the literal pleasure, descriptions that closely matched those of others who had.[13]

Pleasurable or otherwise, death rarely occurred like it did in the movies, doctors and nurses could attest. "The popular idea of death seems to be that the dying person fights for breath with desperate energy, that he remains conscious up to his last breath, that he gasps out a final heroic message, and that then, leaping up with a climactic contortion and a pop-eyed stare, he achieves a death-rattle like the sound of gravel in a chute, and falls back dead, open-eyed and grinning," wrote Hermine Kane, a nurse, thinking such a dramatic exit was about as frequent as a blue moon. The reality, of course, was far less exciting. A few hours before death, the dying person typically lapsed into a sort of coma, his or her breath gradually becoming slower and more strained. Skin took on a grayish color and lost some of its tension. Eyes were usually closed, mouths open, and bodies seemingly smaller. As the last breaths were drawn, the accumulated liquid in the throat caused a gentle gurgling sound, this the infamous "death-rattle." The heart no longer beating, the patient was "quietly dead," as Kane described it in 1930, the act of dying hardly the stuff of Hollywood.[14]

The anticlimax that was dying belied the lifelong trepidation most people had toward death. This held true for the end of life, with few patients wanting to die even when they were in the direst condition. Like the process of dying, learning one was in extremis would not make good material for Cecil B. DeMille or John Ford. Doctors would typically deliver the news indirectly by saying something like "It might be wise for you to arrange your affairs," the arrival of a priest or preacher confirmation that one was unlikely to make it out of the hospital alive. The appearance of relatives, often excessively cheerful and coming from a considerable distance, was more evidence that things did not bode well. (Short visits were fine, the dying felt, a reminder that they were important, but even they did not want overly buoyant family members overstaying their welcome.) Both nurses and doctors were reluctant to tell dying patients there was little chance that they would recover, however. (Nurses were and are not allowed to tell a patient that he/she is terminal, except now in the state of New York.) "I always tell my doomed patients that they are very sick, but that they will soon be better," Kane confessed, this done for two reasons. First, believing there was still hope made patients more comfortable and, second, it made them easier to care for. The question of whether dying patients should know the truth served as a contentious issue throughout the cultural history of death in America, the answer still not entirely clear.[15]

Kane's many years of experience as a nurse provided interesting insights into dying in America circa 1930. All people died the same, more or less, but that was not true of the relatives of the dying, for example. Family members of a wealthy dying person tended to put on a good show, she had observed, their conspicuous displays of grief more smoke than fire. Relatives of the poor were usually quiet in their grief, however, the loss of their loved one felt more keenly (partly because it could very well mean financial sacrifice on their part). Suicide cases made a good study as well, she had concluded. Those who had attempted suicide but failed no longer wanted to die and, most often, had not wanted to in the first place. Young women who had poisoned themselves because of unhappiness caused by men comprised the majority of this group. Such women, "mentally incompetent" in her view, typically had taken a few pills to become ill enough to make their respective men suffer and to get them to give the women what they wanted. Last words or final requests were another area Kane had given serious thought to. Wives on their deathbed frequently urged their husbands not to remarry, the stated reason being for the children not to have to suffer a stepmother. Husbands, however, rarely mentioned the issue of remarriage, their primary concern not whether or not their wives found another man but, almost always, "money matters."[16]

Kane offered other bits of wisdom into how Americans died some eighty years ago. Grand deathbed speeches could be found in great literature, but not in her ward, where the dying rarely uttered anything of note. Important revelations or voicing regret for past mistakes were also few and far between in her experience, with no urgency to tell someone something of consequence before taking one's last breath. In fact, dying appeared to be not particularly different from any other aspect of living, she had come to see, the protagonist having no sense of detachment from worldly affairs like novelists often imagined. Religion, not surprisingly, was yet another way to classify the act of dying. The devout resisted death more than atheists and agnostics, interestingly, this despite the formers' confidence they would soon meet God and be reunited with those who had gone before them. The worst position to be in when it came to religion was that belonging to those who decided to believe in God and a next life only when they were dying. Prayers and promises said by the suddenly faithful in their final hours constituted "an ignoble spectacle," Kane felt, those of relatives "of a similar wobbly condition" equally unflattering.[17]

Finally, Kane explained why doctors and nurses appeared so callous around death. While nurses did feel some grief when one of their patients (especially a child or baby) died, their job was to care for dying people, not mourn them. It was unfortunate, or perhaps unfair, that relatives interacted with nurses when their sorrow was so great, the highly emotional circumstances not conducive to understanding how anyone could seem so unfeeling. Relatives expected a miracle, Kane believed, and often felt outrage when one was not produced. As far as doctors, they, too, were moved when a patient died but wanted to forget about what they perceived as a defeat as quickly as possible. Physicians could not remain confident and effective if they dwelled on the death of a patient, this the reason they, even more than nurses, sometimes seemed more machine than human. After seeing so many people die, how did Hermine Kane herself want to leave this life? "I should like to be ill for two or three days, knowing that death was near me, so that I could bring myself to a state of conscious willingness to die," she told readers, while admitting that, like almost everyone, "I too shall probably fight to remain and hate to accept the end."[18]

EARLY HOLIDAY

While the last few days or hours of life were rarely extraordinary, at least from an observers' perspective, the knowledge that one had a limited numbers of months or years to live almost always led to a literal life-altering experience. For those who did not have to bear the common discomforts of dying—powerful drugs, occasional delirium, and the physical effects of the illness itself—the approach of death could be a strange, almost incomprehensible experience. Some of those given a year or less to live functioned perfectly normally almost right up to the end, certainly a blessing but at the same time somewhat of a curse. Without the typical signs of dying, those going through the process were generally left with just their doctor's word that death would take place, something that very much affected how one spent the remainder of one's time. In such a peculiar position, Gertrude Carver told her story (titled "Early Holiday") in *The Atlantic* in 1931, fully aware that soon her incurable disease would begin destroying her body. Until then, however, she was going about her business as if there was no problem at all, except in making posthumous plans for her two children. Given plenty of time to do this, Carver used as a guide the instructions often given in a theater program: walk, do not run, to the nearest exit.[19]

While grateful for the chance to put everything in order without having to rush, Carver had mixed feelings about what she described as the "incongruous orderliness" of her situation. "I was either spared or deprived of the conflict occasioned by the practical and individual acceptance of the universal experience," she recalled after being informed of her fatal illness, her impending demise in "the realm of the abstract." After initially feeling self-pity upon seeing a dawn, sunset, or the faces of her children, knowing it could be the last time, she quickly recognized the special privilege she was given to be fully conscious of her dying. "Every thought, sight, sound, touch and emotion becomes burdened with potential finality," Carver explained, her existence imbued with "an almost intolerable value." Just getting up from a chair or walking across the room took on great significance, proof that her body was still, for the moment, working fine. Like most people, Carver had ignored the issue of dying until it became a reality, believing that Christianity's promise of immortality had much to do with Americans' treating death as an illusion. As well, why direct energy from life to something so immutable and impossible to control, she asked, this another reasonable explanation for why most of us did not spend a lot of time thinking about death.[20]

Because it was entirely real for her, however, Carver felt it was important for people to learn how to prepare themselves for death, both their own and that of their loved ones. In fact, Carver believed the subject should be taught in kindergarten, any child not really ready for life until he or she knew the ABCs of death. Learning it later, as everyone who did not die a sudden death eventually had to do, was much more difficult, she argued, and that people would lead better, more heroic lives, another good reason why it should become part of Americans' basic education.[21] Finally, Carver put forth a kind of manifesto about death, making a compelling case that it and life were not opposing forces but rather complementary, symbiotic ones that should be viewed as such:

> Recognizing that we are born pregnant with death, we should be released from our pitiful stubborn attempts at aborting the uncheatable conception. We should know that no man dies as reluctantly as he is born; that life is the shadow of death as surely as death is the shadow of life; that the two shadows and the two realities merge and become inseparable components of experience; that to deny one is to deny the other, to accept one is to accept the full implication and inherent reality of the other; that their mutuality is greater than their difference; that there are as many gradations of dying as of living, but that in their respective crescendos they inevitably meet.[22]

As Carver's rather amazing treatise illustrated, being given a time frame when one was likely to die—three, six, twelve, or twenty-four months, most often—led to a radical change in how one wanted to spend the rest of one's days. We all had to die sometime but, like setting a marriage date, perhaps, having an even general idea of when it would take place made it all too real. (An X-ray usually revealed the bad news.) Some of those who in the 1930s were told by a doctor they did not have long to live compared it to the time they were informed by their bank or stockbroker that they were broke. Many people got such a call in 1929, but the information this time was much more than about losing money. Drastic measures were often considered and occasionally taken. Given a year or two to live, for example, some of those childless contemplated adopting a boy or girl to leave one's things and savings. (Most chose not to after thinking about it for a bit.) For collectors, the thought of having one's Chippendale set of furniture broken up or library of books auctioned off was almost too much to bear, this alone a good reason to have an heir. Others thought about going abroad to die, a way to go out in style. (Again, the vast majority declined.) Many did do a much simpler thing upon receiving their prognosis, however—toss out their calendars, not wanting to see their numbered days tick off.[23]

It was not surprising that those given a fatal prognosis like Carver quickly developed a sophisticated philosophy of life and death. Despite doctors' typical advice to "not worry," knowing that one's time was short naturally brought forth deep, existential thoughts on life and what may come after. One of the first decisions was who to tell, if anyone, the news surely to cause suffering to loved ones. Regardless of whether or not one shared the information with others, the more stoic vowed to keep a positive mental attitude. No complaining or seeking of sympathy, the braver swore, the demanding of special rights or privileges also not acceptable. Likewise, with the clock ticking, it would be easy to withdraw from one's daily routine, but this would be a mistake, some believed. Going into isolation or refusing to take part in the trivialities that made up much of everyday life would be untrue to oneself and to one's friends and family, with no happiness to be found in such a lonely, monklike existence.[24]

Taking such a high road was hardly easy, needless to say, especially for those who did not believe in the immortality of the soul. "To dissolve, to vanish, to be forgotten!—this thought strikes the soul with a terror like the paralysis of sudden cold," worried one anonymous woman in 1935 after being told by her doctor that her cancer could very well return in the next few years. In addition to the panic she felt when thinking about disappearing from the earth, what she would leave behind as a legacy was for her a big concern. "I dreamed of serving humanity, of accomplishing great things, but I have done nothing except to produce children as any woman does," she wrote, disappointed that she had not used her unique talents to make "a contribution to the happiness of the world over and above the average human contribution." In a way, this woman felt fortunate that she was able to realize what she felt were her shortcomings, only her shaky prognosis affording the liberty to see her life as a whole. "The average person like myself needs a shock to make him realize emotionally as well as intellectually that the time for accomplishment is limited," she explained; that she gained this perspective in the prime of her life was a blessing of sorts.[25]

The much greater probability that one would die sooner rather than later could prompt questions worthy of Socrates or Nietzsche. Which was more "real," the outlook on life one previously had when things were normal, or this new one brought on by the awareness that death was fast approaching? Had one suddenly "woken up," or was this altered state of consciousness a strange reaction to the worst of news? Whatever the answers to such weighty questions, the focus of someone in such a position tended to shift from petty wishes to more significant pursuits. Dying was like becoming an adult, it could be said, each process demanding an ability to forego immediate, momentary satisfactions in order to realize ones offering longer-term, longer-lasting satisfactions. Wasting time on any number of things—selfish desires, disliking people, being bored—now seemed ridiculous, as other things—gaining serenity, giving happiness, enjoying anything sensual—took priority. Every action that one took was considered meaningful, as any of them could be one by which he or she was remembered, some of the dying believed. Even the faults of friends were now somehow delightful, a reminder that they—and oneself—were still happily alive.[26]

According to those who could be considered experts in the art of dying, the greatest achievement possible was to see death not as the end of life, but as an equivalent, completely neutral entity. Portraying death in mythology or literature as the evil counterpart to life was certainly an effective dramatic device, but it was not a very good lens through which to view either. Why did life have to be good and death evil? Could they instead be seen as different kinds of energy in the universe, as Carver implied? Ideally, those who had come the longest way in reconciling their own demise came to see death and life as alternative expressions of the same force, separate but equal points on an identical plane. From this perspective, there could be no life without death and no death without life, the two mutually dependent upon each other rather than polar opposites. Such a viewpoint offered the greatest chance of "dying well," as the expression went, a belief in heaven not the only way to leave this life with a smile on one's face.[27]

A RENDEZVOUS WITH DEATH

Another, more practical part of dying well was to "set one's house in order," as the saying went. Told by one, two, or three doctors they had an "incurable malady," the more foresighted dedicated themselves to taking care of what had to be taken care of before they died. Arranging sometimes tangled financial matters (and paying off debts) was usually the first task, especially if one was the breadwinner for a family. Ensuring financial security for one's family got a lot more difficult in the 1930s, the Depression having reduced or wiped out the savings and investments of many Americans. Having the family keep the home was the biggest priority, with those having some money left usually setting up a monthly allowance. Leaving one's wife to figure out a financial jigsaw puzzle or allowing executors of the will to do it was often viewed as the worst-case scenario, neither believed to be well suited for the job. The other financial objective was to make as much money as possible in the limited time remaining. For those who did not earn a set salary, taking any and all jobs that came along was not unusual, some of these much lower in both pay and status than what one was used to. Working not just cheap but fast was paramount since time was of the essence. Given the weariness and pain that typically came along with an "incurable malady" (a failing heart or cancer, most likely), this effort was nothing short of heroic.[28]

Other aspects of setting one's house in order were less altruistic. Getting rid of things that could later prove damaging to one's memory or to others still alive was often next on the ultimate to-do list. Letters and other papers, photographs, or objects with a story that one's spouse or business associates did not and should not know about had to be destroyed, the "clearing out of one's desk" not just metaphoric but quite literal. Failing to do this ahead of time, men on their deathbeds were known to ask friends to handle the tricky situation. Under the pretense of consoling the wife, buddies going beyond the call of duty found a way to sneak into the study of the dearly departed, jimmy the desk lock, pocket the naughty material, and set them on fire after leaving.[29]

After this rather unseemly but necessary business, those whose sand was running out of their hourglasses set out to gain closure with certain family members, friends, and colleagues. (This was especially challenging when one was keeping the fatal illness a secret.) Should one try to make peace with enemies or with those with whom they had bad blood or a long-standing grudge? Individuals were divided on this matter, some wanting to go to their grave with a clear conscience and others having no problem whatsoever leaving this life knowing there were people who disliked or hated them (and vice versa). Those who regretted not bidding farewell to once close, now dead, friends with whom they had lost touch made it a point, however, to reconnect with past chums before they themselves died. Finally, there was the matter of making peace with God. If and how this took place varied greatly based on a large number of factors, one's religious faith, of course, being the most significant. Should sinners ask for forgiveness now that they were about to meet their maker? Again, people were split on the issue, some thinking it was in their long-term interests to do so, others believing it would be disingenuous, and still others convinced the whole idea was a complete waste of time.[30]

Individuals who had "a rendezvous with death," as one of them put it, went through quite an array of feelings when they got the news. Comparing the experience to past close brushes with death was natural, everyone concluding that this one was not at all like the others. Many men told in the 1930s that they had months to live had served in the Great War; that they had survived it was viewed as somewhat of a miracle given the numerous opportunities to have been killed. As well, this situation lacked the adrenaline rush that came with being a soldier, no sense of patriotism or adventure this time around. Upon first learning of their terminal condition, some people felt as if they died right there, right then, and that they had to go through the actual process was just an unpleasant formality. "Somehow I had been condemned to linger on beyond the grave, like some forlorn earthbound spirit who is neither of one world or another," wrote one man in such a tough spot in 1937, believing a sudden, instant death would have been a far better fate.[31]

After the initial shock, it was normal to blame others for the cruel hand that one had been dealt. One's parents were largely at fault for passing on "tainted blood," some rationalized; that their parents had brought them into this world only to be cut down in the prime of life was an even bigger injustice. God, too, had done one no favors, this senseless act confirmation that life was a random series of events and there was no order to the universe. Since this was apparently true, why not spend the rest of one's time in a completely reckless, hedonistic manner, comfortable in the fact that there would be no repercussions? A good idea, perhaps, but one rarely put into actual practice. "I contemplated all manner of indulgences, though I went through with none of them," continued the same man, explaining that he was "too miserable to cope with the intricacies of such activities."[32]

Resigned to die much like one had lived, many of those heading toward their rendezvous with death made some sense out of the senseless situation. What had been really lost was one key consideration, the fact that we all had to die someday, making the circumstances seem less tragic. Was having months, rather than years, to live so terrible? Some people lived longer and some shorter; the length of time less important than its quality. Another way to rationalize a premature death was to frankly face how much more one would have achieved in life. Most of us, after all, were and are not destined for greatness, the hard truth being that the world will keep spinning fine without us on it. Admitting all this was a big relief, something those of us without a death sentence hanging over our heads might keep in mind to keep things in perspective and to help us stop being so hard on ourselves.[33]

It was ironic, to say the least, that complete happiness was found by people only when they learned they were dying. The knowledge that one had just months to live, that there was essentially no future for them, could bring with it a feeling of pure freedom. Thinking and, typically, worrying about tomorrow made today less enjoyable, those with a terminal condition found, a discovery as surprising as their fatal prognosis. Neither joy nor peace of mind could be realized in a life defined by constant struggle; that most of us consciously chose this path is a conundrum. To not have to fret over both personal problems and world events (especially in the tumultuous late 1930s) took some of the weight off one's shoulders, the fear of death apparently much less than the fear of life. Individuals going through this process swore that if they could live their lives over again, they would spend much less time pondering the future and much more time relishing the present. Most of the future these people were so concerned about would never arrive, after all, the many hours invested in trying to create it a sad waste of time. Better late than never to wake up from this slumber, however; had it never happened would be the real tragedy. Time was and is always short, of course, a lesson to be learned for those of us concentrating on what may or may not be rather than what is.[34]

Perhaps an even more challenging situation than being told one would soon die was when a husband or wife was told confidentially by a physician that his or her spouse would. It was not unusual for doctors to share such bad news with a spouse but not the patient in order to "protect" the latter and "keep his or her hopes up" despite the death sentence. In this case it was the spouse who bore the burden of not knowing if a particular moment would be their husband's or wife's last, quite an agonizing experience. Spouses were told to make their husband or wife as comfortable as possible while he or she "convalesced," a difficult-to-keep secret given their awareness of the negative prognosis. Oddly, perhaps, spouses often took the death of their loved one very hard when it finally did take place; nothing was able to prepare them emotionally for what they were told was sure to happen. Although they no doubt had good intentions, doctors' decision to allow husbands and wives to carry the weight of their loved one's approaching death was clearly a mistake, neither the spouse or the patient benefiting from the deception.[35]

Accounts from people who had been placed in such unfortunate circumstances served as warnings to others lest their marriage be all but ruined. Spouses were forced into the uncomfortable position of having to live a double life, they later explained, talking frankly with the doctor but playing a role with their husband or wife. Couples who had had no secrets throughout their marriage suddenly had a big one, a wall built in a relationship where there had been none for years or decades. Not just a spouse but occasionally the whole family of someone with a terminal disease presumably knew what was going on, except the person dying, a bizarre situation that was hard on all parties involved. That the spouse who was dying often suspected as much made it even stranger, he or she thinking it was him or her that was keeping the secret to protect a loved one. If and when told, the dying husband or wife often felt great relief, ironically, the whole charade a bad idea from the start.[36]

Once a widow or widower, the grieving often had to endure annoyances and irritations that went beyond the loss of their spouse. Letters of condolence would typically pour in, again well intentioned but doing little or nothing to help heal the wound. The religious were apt to eagerly seize the opportunity to offer prayers, even if they knew the griever was not among the faithful or believed in any kind of life after death. Even worse were the range of insensitive comments made by those thinking they were doing some good. Time will soften the blow, many advised, a nice idea perhaps but of no consolation at all at the present. Being reminded of what a good person their wife or husband had been also offered little or no comfort, the spouse who obviously knew the deceased best not really requiring this information. Some friends and relatives were bold enough to suggest that the deceased was better off dead than living as an invalid, a harsh remark even if it happened to be true. An even more tactless observation was that the spouse "had lived long enough," or that the dearly departed had chosen "a good age" to die, as if he or she had a choice in the matter. The impact of all this consolation upon the griever could be profound, but hardly in a positive way. Some surviving spouses began resenting people who were older than their husband or wife, especially if they were hale and hearty. Others, angry over their loss, could be cruel, wanting to spread the misery around. Still others became overwhelming indifferent, no longer caring about significant world events or important local affairs. That the globe continued to revolve without their husband or wife seemed unequivocally unfair and unjust, these people clearly not ready to accept the death of their best friend and partner in life.[37]

Grief for a loved one could be and was expressed many different ways. At first, spouses might imagine their husbands or wives to be in the next room, so much so that a quick look was required to make sure their loved one was not there. Rainy days were typically the worst, not just because of the gloomy weather but also due to the disturbing image of their loved one getting wet in the ground. The term *widow* or *widower* took some getting used to, a feeling that whoever said it must be talking about someone else. After some time, surviving spouses half expected to meet their dead husband or wife in the street, again the reality of the situation not fully set in. Meeting a person of the opposite sex whose voice or gestures resembled that of their dead spouse could be a powerful experience, even making them think (for a short time, usually) they could be in love with him or her. Getting a new dog or cat after losing a spouse was not unusual, the quadruped filling some of the void without the commitment of another husband or wife. (Dogs were known to search a house for their dead master for months, the scent of his or her clothes enough to make the poor things howl in canine grief.) Finally, passing by a particular place a couple had visited together could bring back happy memories or a flood of tears, sometimes at the same time.[38]

A strong spiritual connection, whether traditionally religious or otherwise, was typically of immense value when coping with the loss of a loved one. It was our understanding of death, rather than the act itself, that was problematic, the spiritually inclined insisted. "From our pitifully narrow human viewpoint, it is really impossible to see how an event may fit rationally into a majestic scheme of cosmic destiny," wrote a mother who had recently lost her son under mysterious circumstances, his death part of an incomprehensible divine plan. (The body of the twenty-one-year-old law student was found in a nearby river three months after he inexplicably disappeared.) We were able to see just a tiny part of the "majestic scheme," the woman explained, and this is the reason so many people mistakenly concluded that there was no grand design or guiding purpose to life and death. The soul existed in each of us before and after it took up temporary residence in our bodies, believers in a greater power held, making death more of a transition process or change in venue than a final destination. In fact, the next phase of existence was likely superior to the most recent one, making death a kind of blessing. Any religion, creed, or philosophy that assigned a higher purpose in life was thus helpful in the grieving process, with no better way to make sense of the death of an individual than a firm belief in God and the infinite.[39]

This was especially true for many Christians. In fact, true Christians did not subscribe to many of the standard conventions surrounding death in America, a direct result of their belief in immortality, or the eternal nature of life. More religious Christians disliked the word *death* itself, for one thing; its negative connotations (finality, destruction, morbidity) were antithetical to their belief system. Similarly, deeply devout Christians preferred to not think or speak of the dead in the past tense. Rather, their loved ones had moved into a different phase of life, still a constant presence in their own lives. The distinction between "this world" and the "other world" thus was not really necessary, life crossing both geographic and metaphysical boundaries. Finally, the focus on the body in a casket (versus the spirit) at modern funerals was also misguided, the Christian faithful felt, the reason many of them chose cremation over burial. The only difference between this life and the next was that the spirit had a body in the former, Christians maintained, immortality a fact rather than a hope.[40]

DEATH IS NOT A NECESSITY

For all but the most religious, however, death remained a messy business, painful for loved ones and calamitous for individuals. Death was well on the way to becoming, in a word, unacceptable, driving some scientists to try to do something about it. Anything was believed to be possible in the science-obsessed 1920s and 1930s, the forces of modernity to change the world for the better. It was thus a virtual certainty that, as scientists discovered more about the keys to life, they would also begin to want to know much more about death. Why did humans die? Was dying necessary? These two questions occupied a fair number of biologists between the wars, the answers hardly clear. One theory at the time was that "Man" died because he was a complex organism, with many things that could potentially disturb a body's delicate balance and cause it to fail. Death was certainly an inconvenience, in other words, but it was still better being a human than a protozoon or plant that could live forever.[41] Many began to challenge this theory, however, proposing that future advancements in science will show that humans were not necessarily designed to self-destruct. Serguei Metalnikov, a well-known biologist at the Pasteur Institute in France, for example, was one scientist not so sure we should jump to the conclusion that death was absolutely necessary. "Old age and death are not a stage of earthly existence," Metalnikov wrote in a 1924 book called *Immortality and Rejuvenation in Modern Biology*, arguing that immortality was a fundamental property of all living organisms. Because the human body was made up of single, simple cells that were capable of living forever, it, too, did not have to grow old and die, he maintained; death was thus not a natural event but something abnormal and accidental.[42]

Other scientists agreed that, should a fatal disease or injury not come one's way, we could potentially live forever. Just as minute organisms and plants continually replaced their cells with new ones, so could we, meaning we would never grow old or die. One kind of bacterium was known to divide into two over and over again; this was another way human immortality could perhaps be achieved. Naysayers correctly pointed out that the cells of human organs did not become an egg and divide like single cell organisms; this was the major obstacle to such a thing being realized. But who knew what the future held? Great medical discoveries were being made in the 1920s (insulin and penicillin, to name just a couple), and the possibilities of tomorrow were even greater. Scientists were already imagining scenarios that would eventually be known as cloning, whereby new, healthy organs were created out of failing ones. Another idea was that relocating organ cells from the body to a laboratory might be conducive to their reproducing indefinitely. This had already been done, in fact, with chickens, the ideal conditions of the lab allowing their cells to live for years and years. Could the same thing be done with humans one day?[43]

From an evolutionary perspective, one could go as far as to say that death did indeed appear to be an anomaly. Evolution was essentially about change, all living things continually transmuting themselves and shifting from one form to another. It could even be said that the only constant in the biological world was change, both in terms of species and individual units of life. Where, then, did death as the disintegration of a life-form fit in? Was it an exception to the rule of evolution? The self-destruction of anything alive certainly seemed like a repudiation or betrayal of nature given the determination of a species or an individual to survive and evolve, an idea prompting scientists to look beyond the possibility of an afterlife to solve the mystery of death.[44]

American and European physicians and scientists avidly published research that challenged prevailing assumptions about death. In 1928, for example, two German doctors found that the hearts of eighteen people who "showed every sign of being dead" remained active for an average of ten minutes, begging the question of when death actually occurred. The electro-cardiograph, a relatively new invention, was adding to the evidence that the body died "piecemeal"; that is, one organ at a time. That there was not a single instant of death was a major revelation; the traditional belief held for thousands of years that life ended when the heart stopped beating and lungs stopped working was apparently wrong.[45] The fact that the heart still beat for a few minutes after physiological death was itself an important, possibly revolutionary finding. "It might be possible to recall a man to life—to raise him (in a manner of speaking) from the dead," a story in a German news-paper told readers after additional research in this area was published by the Berlin Medical Society.[46] That's precisely what was believed to happen to John Puckering, an English gardener, a few years later. During an operation, Puckering's heart stopped for four-and-a-half minutes, enough time for a brief visit to "the other side of the Styx," as *The Literary Digest* reported the story. A large crowd of happy people populated the afterlife, according to Puckering, including an old friend who had died seven years earlier. Before Puckering had the chance to catch up with his chum, however, the doctor massaged his heart, injected adrenaline into his body, and performed artifi-cial respiration, thus bringing him back to life. Many of what would eventu-ally be called "near-death experiences" would be reported in the years ahead, these glimpses into the great beyond taken as evidence that there was another world waiting after this one.[47]

The shifting definition of death made it that much more important to know when someone was positively, absolutely dead. Sir Bernard Spilsburg, medical expert to Scotland Yard, agreed with the growing consensus that a stopped heart or absence of breathing was not definitive proof of death, as revival was possible in each case. Only by opening an artery to see if it bled, as should a healthy one, revealed whether someone was alive or not, he argued in 1930, such a test requiring quite a bit of medical skill. While perhaps the most accurate method to determine death at the time, it was rarely used. Only those afraid they would be buried alive requested such a test, Spilsburg explained, the fact that opening a major artery would likely cause death another issue that made it not very practical among the living.[48]

Through the 1930s, all kinds of experts in their own field chimed in about the possibility of physical immortality. "I am willing to say it quite plainly: Death is not a necessity," wrote William Malisoff in *The Forum* in 1938, challenging the assumption that all men were mortal. Malisoff, a chemist, made it clear he was not talking about spiritual mortality, insisting that it was the body that could survive indefinitely rather than just the soul. Like others who argued that dying was not an absolute rule of nature, Malisoff was actually referring to aging, with death still entirely likely to result from an accident or disease. Aging was in fact the thing that killed most people, meaning conquering it would lead to many lives saved. Longer longevity was proof that the human body's clock could be tinkered with, the idea that we had a finite number of days to live simply wrong. Because humans could not conceive of their own mortality, at least at an unconscious level, Malisoff theorized, the mind was perfectly agreeable with the notion to never grow old. It was the body that served as the saboteur, wrecking the mind's best-laid plans for eternal life. If physicists, biologists, and chemists like him joined forces (and billions of dollars diverted from defense), however, a solution to the aging problem could be found (something still believed by some). The answer resided somewhere in diet, hormones, and drugs, he proposed, calling for scientists to unite in a war against aging and, thus, death.[49]

Some scientists viewed the dream of a body living forever as pure hogwash, however, seeing death as entirely natural and inevitable. "Death is immanent in life," Alexis Carrel, a physician with the Rockefeller Institute and author of *Man, the Unknown*, told the New York Academy of Medicine, "the necessary outcome of our mode of being." All the scientific research and money in the world would not lead to a full victory over aging, he argued; the chemical changes that constantly took place in tissues and blood are irreversible. "Man will never conquer death [because it] is an essential characteristic of our self," he explained to his colleagues, the end of life "not an extraneous accident" but a complete necessity.[50]

THE SILENT WATCHER

As scientists debated the possibility of immortality, anyone and everyone alive faced the universal question of how to confront the necessity of death. Ideally, as people like Sarah Cleghorn maintained, dying would be a rich experience, the final hurrah of a life well lived. "For really it is the crowning adventure of life, and we ought to come to it like a first-nighter to his seat, waiting with cheerful eagerness to see what sort of a new play it is going to be," agreed Edward S. Martin, the editor of *Harper's*, in 1923. Unfortunately, that was not often the case, with poor health, low spirits, and sad observers raining on death's parade. As well, living to a ripe old age came with the heavy price of seeing most or all of one's friends die, this for Martin also "mak[ing] dying a good deal less enjoyable than by rights it ought to be."[51]

Interestingly, the fear and dread of death that most of us carried for most of our lives seemed to ease when death actually approached. Those who knew they were dying often felt a sense of calm and peace, exactly opposite of what one might expect. Rather than feel a need for haste, to try to do as much as possible in the short time they had left, these people were in no particular hurry, as Gertrude Carver attested. Individuals in such a position explained that the minutia of everyday life no longer seemed that important, happy to not have to be occupied with all the things that kept us so busy much of the time. Problems that caused considerable concern when innumerable years lay ahead were now viewed as insignificant and easily solvable.

Again, it was also nice to not have to be continually striving toward a goal, these same people reported, both their ambitions and self-importance much diminished when death appeared on the horizon.[52]

Before death appeared on the horizon, however, the fear of it was believed to be ever present in our minds, either consciously or unconsciously. Bertrand Russell, the famous British intellectual, asserted we had three options when it came to coping with the fear of death. The first was to simply, or not so simply, try to ignore it by not talking or thinking about it. The second was to do the completely opposite thing by spending as much time possible thinking about it in the hope that, to paraphrase the well-known adage, familiarity would breed contempt. The third option, a very popular one, was to subscribe to the idea that death was the end of this life but the beginning of another, even better one. Given the problems inherent with the first two ways to cope with the reality of death, one could understand the appeal of this third option. The first was "sure to be unsuccessful and to lead to various kinds of undesirable contortions," Russell thought, something Sigmund Freud and his fellow psychoanalysts would certainly have agreed with. As far as the second option, "the practice of brooding continually on death is at least equally harmful," he believed; it was not a healthy thing to constantly think of any particular subject (especially one that a person had little or no control over).[53]

Anyone trying to lessen his or her fear of death was thus left with the third path: the belief that this life was a gateway to a superior one. One would think that those who did choose this option would be less fearful of death, but this frequently was not the case. The explanation for this was that religious belief was for the most part a conscious mechanism, while the fear of death resided in the much deeper unconscious. There was, in other words, very little escape from this primal urge, the fear of death something most of us would have to accept and deal with in our own way.[54] Interestingly, it appeared that it was not so much those thoroughly in love with life who feared death so much as those who were on intimate terms with its travails. The happy-go-lucky simply did not have the time or interest to think much about the party ending one day, viewing the whole enterprise of death as a big bore. Death certainly happened to others but would somehow pass them by, such people consciously or unconsciously thought, the end of life more of an abstract concept than a hard reality. The more pensive, however, tended to give considerable thought to death; that it was an unsolvable and inescapable mystery was a source of great frustration and often concern. As well, those who had less reason to love life—the very old or very ill, for example—typically clung to life more desperately than those who had much more to lose, this another ironic twist in a dimension of life in which logic did not seem to apply.[55]

Not everybody believed that ignorance was bliss when it came to the matter of death. "Isn't it probable that sound thinking about it (which includes sound thinking about life) might rob death of its so largely imaginary terrors?," Lee Wilson Dodd of *The Forum* asked in 1931, suggesting that one's sixth decade was the time to begin such ruminating. (The average life expectancy in the United States was at the time sixty years.) For Dodd, the soundest thinking about death was to view it as a "great adventure," the notion that the end of this life was the end of everything too much to bear. "If death be the end there is very little from a human standpoint to be said for the universe," he wrote, "the total scheme of things . . . an unmitigated washout" should this life be all there is. By our sixth decade, he continued, most of us were just getting started, a cruel twist of fate if we had no opportunity to apply our hard-won wisdom in another setting. "I demand for my fellows from whatever gods there be another and a fairer chance," Dodd stated semitongue-in-cheek, the "wretched farce" in which we were all playing tiny roles just not enough. Dodd subscribed to the idea of immortality not because he was a religious man but because of the simple fact that many of us regularly thought of and desired it. "If we have immortal longings in us, Nature put them there, and if she put them there she is likely to satisfy them," Dodd explained, an admittedly not very scientific line of reasoning but a completely logical one, he maintained.[56]

For some, however, a belief in or hope for immortality was more of a problem than a solution. One such person was Clarence C. Little, managing director of the American Society for the Control of Cancer, who believed that death was one of three "vital points" in the life of an individual. Great strides had been made over the centuries in the other two key moments or events— birth and marriage—but death lagged behind, he thought, not benefiting from the same kind of humanistic and scientific progress. "We have not done what we can to encourage humanity to form a kindlier and more merciful relationship with the silent watcher," Little argued in 1931, with hundreds of thousands of Americans currently suffering because of this failure. In keeping with the between-the-wars interest in and argument for eugenics, Little made the case that the hopelessly ill and incurably insane be allowed to be relieved of their suffering, this the thing that would allow death to catch up to the more evolved arenas of birth and marriage. Until then, death would remain stuck in the values of the Middle Ages, neither a truly humane or Christian part of society.[57]

Although his views were controversial, Little's thesis that challenged the medical establishment could be seen as prophetic. Little believed the Hippocratic oath to be an "ancient fetish," its mandate to "not give a lethal drug to anyone if I am asked" more harmful than helpful. The Church only compounded the problem, "its centuries of organized, highly paid salesmanship to penetrate the heart of humanity with an abiding conviction of immortality" perpetuated hopeless suffering. Finally, our own "overpowering, selfish fear" of death made any kind of effort to intentionally cause it out of the question, even if it was in the best interests of the sufferer. A generation later, however, the essence of Little's bold argument would become much more accepted by the medical community, the Church, and ordinary Americans, death closer to the other "vital points" of life. "When that day comes the present barbaric and superstitious methods and customs as regards unnecessarily prolonging human suffering will seem as dreadful and difficult to understand as do the human sacrifices of past civilizations and the tortures of the Middle Ages to us," Little predicted, modern science to ultimately win the day when it came to our primitive attitudes toward and practices of death.[58]

A JOURNEYING TOGETHER

For some, however, it was not that we were primitive when it came to death but too modern. Although immortality remained a dream, we had, rhetorically at least, already conquered death, critics argued, its role in society much diminished. Milton Waldman, writing in *The American Mercury* in 1927, posited that our sense of death—one of the cornerstones of Western civilization, he felt—was not only on the decline in the United States but also on the brink of disappearing completely. In Europe, Waldman concluded after a trip across the pond that death continued to be a prominent theme in religion, philosophy, the arts, and literature, but here in America few people wanted to think or talk much about it. Americans were more interested in spinning the wheels of commerce and too busy making money in the booming stock market to have time for death, he felt, the only ones taking the subject seriously here businesspeople incorporating their companies to avoid estate taxes should they die, people paying their life insurance premiums, and hypochondriacs. Once firmly embedded in the writings of Poe, Whitman, Melville, Lincoln, and Dickinson (over a third of her poems addressed the subject), the concept of death could now be hardly found in American literature; this was a reflection of its downgraded cultural status.[59]

Why and how had Americans, as he expressed it, "forgotten" death? Life in America in the twentieth century was a lot safer than it had been a half century earlier, Waldman theorized, and significantly more comfortable than in contemporary Europe. It was true that the American horn of plenty had greatly lowered the odds of famine, the Machine Age creating abundance for many if not most citizens. "And so he has come to mitigate death in a sense to avert it altogether," Waldman wrote, with few catastrophes the average American could not somehow avert. (His article appeared thirty-two months before Black Friday and the beginning of a twelve-year economic slump that ruined the lives of many.) Given our dismissive attitude toward death, it was not surprising to Waldman that some scientists and physicians had begun to view death as a faulty cog in the apparatus of life that could possibly be repaired. "It is amazing, this firmly-held tenet that the basic immutable law of nature is merely a careless flaw in the organization of things," he exclaimed, our social resistance to death bringing this on. Waldman believed all this to be unnatural and harmful, our "dying less" making us "live less."[60] Whether we recognized it or not, death was, he eloquently stated:

> A desirable corner from which to survey life, because it makes life itself more precious and significant; because it gives poignance [*sic*] to its beauties and delicate shades to its surfaces; because in the end, by accepting the inevitable, it makes for a finer, clearer understanding of ourselves; because it makes us see ourselves against the one background of which we are certain—that of the inexorable law of our common mortality.[61]

From an evolutionary perspective, the "conquering" of death by Americans in the twentieth century could perhaps be seen as a step backward. Versus animals, which were largely ignorant of death, humans took special pride in their keen awareness of the end of life. Writers often compared humans to animals with regard to death, our understanding of it always considered far superior to that of lower forms of life. Animals certainly knew death when they saw it, popular thinking went, but man was able to see it in relationship to himself, a clear sign of our much more advanced cognitive abilities. The consciousness of death at an individual level was one of the principal factors separating us from the beasts, some proposed, this knowledge a defining characteristic of what it meant to be human.[62] Man was also commonly recognized as the only species to kill their own or themselves, something not at all true. Euthanasia, self-sacrifice, and murder were very much part of the animal kingdom, proof that man was not unique in this respect. Male spiders allowed themselves to be eaten by their mates, worker bees attacked drones en masse, lemmings famously leapt into the sea, crows killed fellow members of their flock, and dogs were known to starve themselves from grief, evidence that humans did not have a monopoly on purposeful death.[63]

Just as humans were uniquely capable of conceiving death in personal terms, intellectuals agreed, so did the learning of its existence occur in childhood. Although the particulars, of course, varied, there did seem to be a consistent theme when it came to a child's acknowledgment of death and dying. Lying awake at night contemplating the meaning of the universe, smarter four- or five-year-olds wondered what might await people when this life was over. Already aware at some level that both animals and people died, the child weighed the possibilities based on the many clues picked up from various sources. By age eight or so, the more inquisitive child could very well be beginning to question or even dismiss what he or she had learned in church or from religious parents. Maybe there wasn't a heaven or hell, the child pondered, that there was nothing at all a distinct and much more terrifying prospect. At the very least, death would be a big change from this life, this alone cause for considerable concern. Death was an unsolvable mystery, brighter children concluded early on, an insight likely to permanently shape their view on the subject for the rest of their lives.[64]

M. Beatrice Blankenship had been one such child to think big thoughts about death, so much so that she viewed relationships with people in terms of the level of grief she believed she would feel if they died. Being a young woman during the 1918 influenza epidemic and Great War brought her even closer to death, only her marriage making her focus more on life. When Blankenship's husband died, however, the occupation she had with death when she was young returned, and she did not know how to ease herself from despair. She first tried reading everything she could get her hands on, thinking this would be a good way to get her mind off her loss. This did not work very well, however, so she decided to read only books about religion to confront her grief head on. After digesting piles of literature about Christianity, theosophy, spiritualism, Buddhism, and Islam, Blankenship came to the realization that the only thing that distinguished religions from each other was their conception of death. Each religion and its beliefs about death seemed as valid as another, she felt, with no definitive answers to be found in any of them.[65]

Why did she, and so many others, have so much trouble dealing with the death of a loved one? The lack of religious faith, both hers and society as a whole, was not the only reason. Once a familiar part of life, death was now "a stranger," Blankenship believed, Americans not knowing "how to meet him" when he arrived. Just as Milton Waldman had cautioned, conquering or forgetting about death would likely lead to trouble when it made its presence all too clear. The casting of death as a "stranger" was a direct result of a number of social and economic changes. By the 1930s, the modern ways of death and dying were already much in place in the United States, the old, traditional ways rapidly disappearing from the American scene. Neighbors sitting up with the sick and families gathering around the dying in their own beds were becoming as rare as a horse and carriage, most deaths now taking place in hospitals. Families and neighbors taking charge of the body after death to perform the last offices had also become a relic of the Victorian Age, the mortician now assigned these duties. It was this disconnection with the reality of dying and death that was largely responsible for Americans' difficulty in facing the loss of a loved one, Blankenship surmised, something in the old, traditional ways that served an important purpose. "There were then, it seems to me, a simplicity, an affection, a journeying together to the parting of the ways, which are utterly lacking now that the disposal of the dead is a business or a profession," she wrote in 1934, an observation that still resonates today.[66]

It made perfect sense that Americans' fear and dread of death had risen as they distanced themselves from it. No longer very well acquainted with dying and death as hospitals and the funeral industry assumed control, many Americans found these aspects of life positively terrifying, the fear of the unknown always greater than that of the known. Knowing less about death as they delegated its responsibilities to others, Americans had begun to see it as an unnatural part of life rather than what it really was: arguably the most natural part of life. The more it was shoved away, however, the more it was feared, a vicious circle that was likely to become even more entrenched. One could not resist comparing Americans' cold relationship with death to how other cultures opened their doors to it, sometimes quite literally. (Seating the skeleton of a dead relative at a feast, as Mexicans were known to do, would be grounds for a visit from the police and/or a psychiatrist in the United States.) Americans had apparently lost sight of the fact that because death was inevitable, it was entirely normal; that it was no longer woven into daily life was the root of the problem.[67]

So how did M. Beatrice Blankenship find comfort after the loss of her beloved husband? It was in the sheer commonality of death—that it was a certainty for everyone who was once alive—that offered the most consolation. Rather than any of the myriad of philosophical or religious theories with which she became familiar, it was this simple idea that proved to be the most helpful. Not only was death an experience that united us all, she reasoned, but also just conceiving of life without death was impossible, and vice versa. Blankenship was also convinced that the dead remained part of the universe, the fact that they were no longer in this time or place making them no less a part of it. "This sort of immortality is not as comforting as the conception of continuing individual consciousness, but it does away with the idea of utter destruction and definitely assures a certain continuance," she concluded, happy to have finally found some peace of mind.[68] Over the course of the next decade, millions of others would have to find a similar kind of peace of mind as another world war brought Americans and death much closer together.

Chapter Two

War Department Regrets

"The War Department regrets to inform you . . ."
—Opening words of a "two-star" telegram sent
to next of kin during World War II

In June 1941, Boston medical examiner William Joseph Brickley reported the findings from the unusual kind of research he was doing with human cadavers to the Massachusetts Medical Society. In an attempt to determine the precise time of death, Brickley had been conducting some experiments that might have made Dr. Frankenstein proud. After examining the body of a man who had been executed by electrocution, Brickley was coming to the conclusion that different parts of the body died at different times. A half hour after death was pronounced, Brickley found that the man's arm jerked when hit with a rubber hammer, some nerve endings apparently quite alive. In another case, the heart of a woman who had been declared dead from a brain tumor suddenly started to beat again on its own, something that happened in the unpredictable world of medicine more often than one would think. The woman had no brain activity, however, so was she dead or alive? Brickley believed she should still be considered dead, but many others, including some in the legal system, were not so sure.[1]

Brickley's poking and prodding of corpses was part of a growing effort to definitively answer the question of when human life ended. The answer was not so clear, more doctors were beginning to think, the traditional view based on the stoppage of the heart and lungs being seriously challenged as new things were discovered about the human body. This fundamental scientific inquiry would accelerate over the next few decades as advances in technology forced the issue into the mainstream of American medicine and society as a whole. In the meantime, the orbit of death in America was about to embark on a much different kind of trajectory, as world events intervened with the nation's best-laid plans. The Second World War had a direct and immediate impact on how Americans viewed death, the fact that so many families, friends, and neighbors were personally affected by the premature demise of a member of the armed forces a major factor in this cultural sea change. With death regularly reported in newspapers, described on the radio, and featured in movies and newsreels, however, all Americans were somehow shaped by the looming presence of this most unwelcome visitor. Seventy years later, in fact, the turbulence of the early 1940s still reverberates, the nation to never treat death quite the same way again.

NATURAL CAUSES

Prior to the bombing of Pearl Harbor and the entry of the United States in the war, however, death in America in the early 1940s was a relatively normal, even innocent affair. Before the reports of thousands of Americans and millions of others dying overseas, stories like that of Carson C. Surles made good reading. For the past fifteen years, Surles, a fifty-nine-year-old gas station attendant from Dunn, North Carolina, had been telling everybody he could that he would die in July 1940. That month having arrived, Surles paid a visit to all his relatives, saying good-bye to them and inviting them to his funeral. He then spruced up his cemetery lot and made final arrangements with the local undertaker. On July 28, a seemingly perfectly healthy Surles suddenly announced to his fellow workers, "Well, I guess it's about time I was going home and getting ready," this no doubt eliciting chuckles from the other men. A few hours later, however, Surles delivered on his promise and was found dead. Police officers reported no evidence of suicide or foul play, the attending physician concluding after his examination that Surles had died "of natural causes."[2]

Other fluffy stories dealing with death filled the pages of newspapers and magazines as the 1940s began. "Taps will sound in 1996 for the last of 4,764,071 United States veterans of the World War," went one of them, a forecast of when "Legionnaires," as they were sometimes called, would die. Some 730,000 world war (there was of course no "I" yet) veterans had died by 1940, with another eighty-five or so packing up their troubles in their old kit bags every day. By 1950, around 171 Dough Boys would be dying every day, the Veterans Administration predicted, the death toll to peak in 1970 at about four hundred per day. The last vet would fight his last fight in fifty-six years, officials using mortality rates reported, unable to know the much bigger number of casualties that soon awaited those in the armed forces.[3] (The VA's forecast turned out to be decidedly pessimistic, the statisticians unable to predict the degree to which Americans' longevity would be extended over the next half-century. The last remaining World War I veteran, Frank Buckles, lived until 2011, dying at the ripe old age of 110.)

Besides the occasional story of how or when someone might die, most of the discussion about death in the early 1940s revolved around accidents, especially those related to automobiles. Traffic fatalities continued to rise in direct proportion to the greater number of miles Americans were driving, something that should have been not at all surprising. More Americans were buying cars and more were learning to drive, an increasingly mobile society also elevating the chance of having an accident. Still, the greater number of deaths from car accidents was alarming, making those in the safety business worry about how high the statistics could go. Traffic deaths in 1941 would continue to go up "unless motorists applied the brakes of caution immediately," the National Safety Council warned, attributing some of the rise to "the fact that national activity of every character is on a faster tempo."[4] The Council also felt that "war jitters" could be a factor in car accidents, Americans apparently shakier drivers because of the calamitous events in Europe.[5]

Home fatalities were also a big concern. The number of annual accidental deaths in the home (about thirty-two thousand) was in fact about equal to those taking place on the road, something the American Red Cross considered unacceptable. "Accidental deaths and injuries place an unwarranted burden directly and indirectly upon each person, individually and collectively," the organization said in its 1940 report; most of them were preventable, making them all the more tragic. The number of farm accidents (considered part of the total number of home fatalities) was particularly alarming, that occupation being the most dangerous of all. The Red Cross was on a mission to save lives by preventing accidents from happening in the first place and by offering first aid courses. Enrollment in the organization's nursing program was way up, at least in part because of the country's mobilization effort should it have to enter the war.[6] If there was any good news about accident fatalities, it was in the air. Private flying was now safer than ever, according to the Civil Aeronautics Administration, with nearly a million miles being flown per fatal accident. Plane crashes had been declining for the past five years, something that the agency credited to its own pilot training program.[7]

Car accidents and home fatalities were certainly concerning, but much of what Americans knew and felt about death was about to change dramatically. Nothing, of course, could have prepared Americans for the "date which will live in infamy," the bombing of Pearl Harbor and the country's entering the war, forever altering the culture of death in the United States. It took a full year for the navy to disclose the facts about Pearl Harbor and what was the worst day in its history. Ten warships had been sunk or seriously crippled, with damage done to eight other ships, the navy finally reported; the only good news was that a few of them were able to be repaired and put back into service. About 250 army and navy planes were also either destroyed or disabled, but it was the human death toll that was most shocking. (Initial estimates of both the number of ships destroyed and men killed at Pearl Harbor were quite low, a result not just of the chaos surrounding the event but the government's reluctance to let the enemy know how successful it had been.) Some 2,343 army and navy officers and enlisted men had been killed, the government announced in December 1942, with another 1,272 wounded and 960 others listed as "missing."[8]

The degree of carnage was horrific but understandable given the degree to which the Japanese had prepared for the surprise attack. The Japanese had detailed maps of the position of the ships, precisely timed their strike during a personnel shift, and had apparently rehearsed it all somewhere in the Pacific on a Hollywood-movie-set-like model of the harbor. The firepower of the Japanese was even more startling. Twenty-one torpedo planes, forty-eight dive-bombers, and thirty-six horizontal bombers had attacked the base, making it surprising if not miraculous that just eighteen of the navy's Pacific fleet were hit. (There were eighty-six ships in the port at the time.) Also amazing was that army and navy forces were able to destroy about sixty of the Japanese planes (and three small subs), the belief at the time that the remaining forty-five enemy aircraft would run out of fuel before they could reach the carriers from which they were launched. That the island of Oahu was not taken by the Japanese when they had the Americans reeling was also considered somewhat of a godsend. It was, however, the heroic acts of army and navy personnel that prevented an even worse outcome, the media told ordinary citizens; the fact that some of these men died while defending their country was the beginning of a new narrative of death in America.[9]

DEATH LISTS

Reports of heroic deaths at Pearl Harbor were commonplace, designed to not only recognize acts of bravery but also to boost morale on the home front. In early 1942, for example, the navy issued a memorandum to the press that described the courageous death of one Captain Mervyn S. Bennion, according to an "anonymous eyewitness account." Severely wounded by a fragment of a bomb that hit another ship, Bennion refused to leave the bridge despite repeated attempts by his men to get him to do so. Bennion was more interested in how the battle was going than his own mortal condition, giving orders to his men to go to their stations and get the other wounded off the ship. "He was exceedingly pleased to hear what guns we were able to fire," said the anonymous officer who witnessed it all, stories like this no doubt making others think about how they could contribute to the war effort.[10]

Regularly issued "death lists" from the War Department published in newspapers across the country also helped Americans realize the sacrifices they were making at home were not so bad. The day after Thanksgiving 1942, for example, the army added 145 names of soldiers killed in action or who had died of wounds, this particular list covering thirty-nine states. Where the men had died (Southwest Pacific, Europe, Africa, and the United States) was included in these reports as was, interestingly, their next of kin and his or her address.[11] A typical listing went as follows:

KLEIMAN, Sergeant JULIUS L.; father, Abraham Kleiman, 1617 Nelson Ave., New York City.[12]

Lists of those missing were also made public, although these were not entirely reliable. "In the Navy casualty list printed in the *New York Times* yesterday, Norman F. Dailey, first-class fireman, whose wife, Mrs. Alice Dailey, lives in Rochester, N.Y., was reported missing," went a note in that paper, adding that "this was a mistake, as a later Navy report listed Fireman Dailey as all right."[13]

As after Pearl Harbor, newspapers regularly carried stories of heroism by dying soldiers, flyers, or seamen, again a way to not just honor the dead but make ordinary Americans go all out to "back the attack." "Wounded to the death, Second Lieutenant Joseph R. Sarnoski of Richmond, Va., bombardier of a *Flying Fortress*, shot down two Japanese fighter planes while his life was ebbing away," went one such story reported in the *New York Times* in 1943. Manning the nose gun of his bomber on a mapping mission over Bougainville Island in the South Pacific, Sarnoski and the rest of his crew were fired upon by three Japanese planes. Until he lost consciousness, Sarnoski kept firing at the enemy planes, two of them going down in flames. Sarnoski's plane barely made it back to base and four other crewmembers were injured in the dogfight, but the airmen's mapping mission was successfully accomplished.[14] Perhaps even more extraordinary was the heroic story of Sergeant Howard G. Collett of Thompsonville, Connecticut. Mortally wounded in his bomber, which like Sarnoski's had been hit by enemy fire in the South Pacific, Collett read from his pocket Bible to his fellow crew members as their plane plunged toward the sea. "While enemy machine gun and cannon fire riddled the bomber and killed or wounded every member of the crew, he, knowing the situation to be desperate, read over the intercommunicating system from his pocket Bible, even after gravely wounded," read the citation of the War Department's Distinguished Service Cross posthumously awarded to the gunner in 1944.[15]

Not all deaths of American armed forces were the stuff of a John Wayne movie, of course. Running tallies of all American casualties—those killed in action as well as those wounded, missing, or taken prisoner—were sporadically issued by the Office of War Information (often timed to coincide with national holidays). By July 4, 1943, some 16,696 members of the armed forces were reported dead, the total split evenly between the army and navy (the latter including the marine corps and coast guard).[16] The statistics did not reflect the fact that two out of every three casualties in the armed forces were a result of disease, however, with just one of three from battle. Thousands of soldiers with malaria were being evacuated from battlefields in the South Pacific to base hospitals in Australia, but almost all were surviving as a result of being treated with atabrine (a substitute for quinine). Still, deaths from disease were a lot lower than in World War I, when dysentery, typhus, and yellow fever took many soldiers' lives. Also unlike the last world war, when many injuries and deaths resulted from face and head wounds because of trench warfare, land mines and booby traps were proving to be the bigger danger in this war.[17]

By 1943, the full devastation of the war upon the world's population was becoming clearer. Because of its magnitude, this war was different from all others, experts agreed. Wars in the past were for the most part local affairs, the populations of uninvolved countries not likely to be impacted in any significant way. This war had stretched into the four corners of the earth, however, meaning the demographic makeup of many countries would be impacted, possibly for generations to come. Crude figures suggested that the Nazis had already killed several million Jews, and estimates were that four million Russians had so far died (half of them civilians). The devastation in China was believed to be even worse. Eight million people there may have died as a result of Japanese aggression, some sources suggested, three-fourths of them civilians. Compared with such numbers, the thousands of American deaths due to the war seemed relatively small. This war would affect the population of the United States in other ways, however, as statisticians pointed out at the time. Ten million American men were currently in the armed forces, for one thing, this likely to decrease the birthrate for a while. The disruption of family life, particularly the mass migration of workers to war plants and the resulting housing shortage, was another factor that could seriously influence the country's population. "The outlook is that as the war wears on our rate of population growth may decline rapidly," worried Louis I. Dublin, third vice president and statistician for the Metropolitan Life Insurance Company in March of that year, the potentially fewer number of births more concerning than the greater number of deaths.[18]

Insurance people like Dublin had a keen interest in knowing how many Americans would likely be born and how many were likely to die, especially during unstable times like war. Life insurance policies were generally honored in wars, meaning companies were paying out considerable sums of money to the families of service men and women who died in action. The same had been true during and after World War I, when insurance payments for battle deaths reached $70 million. Some calculated the amount for this war would be five times that figure assuming there were the same number of casualties. Many more Americans now had life insurance (a rare example of death acceptance versus denial, one could say), and the average amount of coverage was higher. Interestingly, deaths in the current war were in mid-1943 running only about half of what they were in World War I (fifty-two thousand Americans were killed in action in 1917 to 1918), even though this one was much larger in scale and scope. (About 418,000 Americans would ultimately die in the Second World War, according to government statistics.) Payments on claims made during World War I typically took a year to get to next of kin but were being made much quicker this time around as the government had gotten a lot better at furnishing proof of death to insurance companies.[19]

Compared to today's life insurance payouts, which sometimes are in the millions of dollars for a single policy, those made during World War II were decidedly modest. Equitable Life Assurance made payments of a little over $3 million to 1,321 families between the bombing of Pearl Harbor and July 1944, for example, with another $1 million going to the families of 266 civilians killed because of the war. (Most of those being crews of merchant ships sunk at sea.) "War deaths" represented just 2 percent of that company's total death claims, but such an amount could mean the difference between making a profit and taking a loss. Well aware of the greater risks during wartime, many Americans were in 1944 taking out yet larger life insurance policies, making sure they did not lapse, and canceling them less frequently. As well, the booming home front economy was enabling Americans to invest more in life insurance, especially given the scarcity of consumer goods to be found.[20]

Insurance companies like Metropolitan and Equitable were no doubt pleased to know that "modern medicine" and prompt evacuation were saving lives that would have been lost in the last world war. Getting hit in the chest by a fragment from a German mortal shell was no longer necessarily fatal, as it almost certainly would have been a quarter century earlier. Wounded soldiers were often on stretchers just a couple of minutes after they had been hit, quickly moved to battalion aid stations to receive initial medical attention. Within an hour they were typically moved to a clearing station to be given plasma, penicillin, sulfa tablets, and new dressings. A few hours after that, wounded soldiers could very well find themselves in an evacuation hospital for an operation using the latest procedures and then a week or so of recovery. From there it was usually off to a large hospital in England for additional recovery time and then, hopefully, back home. Amputations were also way down compared to the last war, both advances in medicine and the army's much improved logistics saving many an arm and leg.[21]

Despite the saving of lives, Alan Devoe believed the war could very well be a wake-up call for Americans when it came to death, possibly ushering in a new era that harkened back to an earlier one. Because we were living in an "age of unfaith," as Devoe wrote for *The American Mercury* in 1942, we had developed a "squeamish aversion" to the death of the body. One did not have to look very hard to find evidence for his claim. Undertakers on the home front were now increasingly called morticians, for example, the latter occupational title not conjuring up the distasteful image of the body being lowered into the ground.[22] Much emphasis was placed on beautifying dead bodies at funerals, this something that many religious leaders found objectionable. "Under the pressure of materialism and advertising and salesmanship, America's funerals have, within the past fifty years, degenerated into a pagan preoccupation with vulgar display and pagan concern for the body, to the almost total neglect of the spirit," said Reverend Josiah R. Bartlett of Seattle's University Unitarian Church. Bartlett believed both "our popular religion" and "our popular bad taste" were at fault but blamed the funeral industry the most for the "marketing" of death in America, foreshadowing Jessica Mitford's exposé.[23]

Devoe pointed to other ways in which modernity had crushed a more authentic interpretation of death. Graveyards had become cemeteries, the latter carrying little of the emotional weight of the former by seeming more organized and "professional." Coffins had become caskets, their beauty and durability (increasingly metal) designed to give the appearance that bodies would not decay. "In our pride and self-cherishing," he continued, it was "an unthinkable humiliation to grant we die like other animals and become only earth stuff as a dead pine tree does." Now, however, newspaper headlines and radio broadcasts were filled with stories of violent death, the subject impossible to make pleasing. "Every rumor is concerned with it, the whole pattern of our days is incessantly dark with its shadow," he thought, the war opening a window of opportunity to once again "acknowledge death as one of the great natural facts, like the sun or the seasons or love or sleep."[24]

CONSIDER THE CHILDREN

That death was one of the great natural facts had special relevance when it came to children. Death had always been, much like sex, a difficult thing for parents to discuss with their children. If adults were reluctant to talk about sex with their children, thinking it would make them lose their innocence (or, worse, want to test out their new knowledge), parents avoided the subject of death because they believed it would make them sad. Children were supposed to be happy, so why bring up the morbid topic of death? The war brought death further into the open, however, putting many parents into the uncomfortable position of having to have the conversation with their kids. "In time of war this question demands an answer," Ellen J. O. Leary wrote in *Parents' Magazine*, noting that the issue of death was now popping up frequently in mothers' discussion groups. Mothers' instincts to protect their children from the tragic parts of life were being thwarted by radio commentators reporting the actions (and often funerals) of war heroes. Kids had a keen sense of things that upset their parents, this making them only more determined to glean any information at all about this mysterious event called death. Older siblings, too, were sharing stories of death with their younger brothers and sisters, this adding to parents' realization that they would have to discuss the end of life with their children.[25]

Parents' trepidation in broaching the subject was often well founded. Mothers were surprised to learn that it was their own discomfort about death rather than their children's curiosity about it that had made the subject off-limits. Moms would find themselves at a loss for words when, passing by a cemetery in their car, their children asked them what this place was for. Kids quickly learned that cemeteries made adults nervous, making them hesitate to ask the next time (and passing on the taboo of death to a new generation). The flip side to this was that parents were pleased to find themselves seriously confronting the issue for the first time, the need to explain death to someone who knew less about it perhaps the only thing to make that happen. The war thus created the opportunity for many adults to face their own fears of death, an unexpected but welcome development. Adults quickly learned that they had much in common with children when it came to death, the fear of the unknown something that defied age. Children were equally pleased to learn there was at least one thing they shared with adults, making them, rather shockingly, human after all. Kids' brutal honesty also forced parents to admit their own latent fears about death involving a loved one. "Aren't you afraid that Daddy will be killed in the war?," more than one child asked his mom, the question frequently relieving the tension in the house due to its sheer directness. Through a conversation about death, then, family ties could be strengthened, just the opposite of what parents had been so worried about.[26]

The bombing of Pearl Harbor and America's entering the war served as the backdrop for parents' increased recognition that they had better be prepared to explain death to their children. (The death of President Roosevelt toward the end of the war was another good opportunity to have the talk with their kids, that the beloved man died of natural causes an easier thing to rationalize than a soldier being cut down by an enemy in the prime of life.)[27] Upon hearing about the bombing on the radio or as dinner conversation, children were beginning to ask their parents if they themselves were in danger of dying. Would bombs fall on them, some understandably wondered?

"Bombs fall only on bad people," went a parent's common response, this of course not true and a bad answer given what had just taken place. Air raid drill rehearsals confused and upset some children; this, too, made them think that the end may be near given what they had heard on the big Emerson in the living room or from other kids on the playground. Again, lying often made the situation worse, the child too smart to believe that, by pulling down shades and turning off the lights, mom was "just getting ready for company." "Children are better fortified for the uncertainty of life when we are honest with them than when we pretend a safety that is unreal," explained Sophia L. Fahs in 1943, one of a number of wartime experts advising parents on how to discuss death with their children. Fahs, coauthor of *Consider the Children: How They Grow*, believed children should be given some basic facts about the war, including how and where it was being fought. Assuring children that they were protected was paramount, as was reminding them that the family would stay together no matter what.[28]

Young children, unable to understand much about the reality of death, often expressed their emotions through imaginative play. Immediately after the bombing of Pearl Harbor, many a battle between the Americans and Japanese was waged on the floors of bedrooms and school classrooms. Toy airplanes dropped blocks on miniature Japanese soldiers, who were instantly killed, only to come back to life in the next play session. Parents and teachers should neither encourage nor condemn such fantasies, experts like Fahs suggested, this a perfect way for children to work out their feelings about war and death. Children choosing to play in such a fashion supported recent research showing that kids thought about death a lot more than previously believed. The general view between the wars was that because death rarely entered the lives of children, they seldom gave it much consideration. Studies now were indicating that death was on the mind of most children five years old or older, the war obviously increasing the likelihood of such.[29]

Unfortunately for most children in the early 1940s, their first encounter with death was in what was arguably its worst manifestation: one group's taking the lives of another. For young people, death could very well be forever attached to aggression, hostility, and violence, psychologists warned. That death could occur on such a massive scale in such a short period of time was itself frightening and potentially scarring to children. More troubling was that we, the good guys, were killing the enemy in droves, that it was in self-defense or retaliation understandable but not getting around the fact that Americans—maybe even Dad—were agents of death. "This meaning of death brings into prominence the savage in human nature, and is the most undesirable form of death for children to face," thought Fahs, the potential of a whole generation somehow damaged by the ordeal of war quite real.[30]

Still, experts were unanimous in believing it was vital that children be informed of their father's death if and when it happened during the war. That was, of course, easier said than done, with no single formula to follow. The terrible task was compounded by a host of variables such as the age of the child, his or her maturity level, and the family's traditions and religious beliefs. To help parents, Margaret Mahler and Ruth Henning wrote a pamphlet called "Children Must Be Told Too" that was made available by the New York State Committee on Mental Hygiene. In the pamphlet, Henning, assistant executive secretary of that organization, and Mahler, an associate in psychiatry at Columbia University, first reminded parents that since death was a fact of life, everybody, including children, should be told about it when it entered their lives. Trying not to do so would be futile anyway, they told readers, the child surely to wonder why his or her daddy had not come home as others had. How should an adult—almost always the mother of the child— deliver the bad news? Grounding the conversation in whatever experience the child previously had with death, such as that of a grandparent or pet, was a good way to begin, Mahler and Henning advised. Once the child had something to relate to, it was probably best to explain that dad had died defending their family and country. "Just as father would rescue [you] should someone bigger and stronger hit [you]," the authors wrote, so did he help save America when it was attacked by a powerful enemy.[31]

With little more to be said, all the mother could now really do was to see how her child reacted, each one to show his or her feelings a little differently. Questions would no doubt follow, sometimes the same ones over and over again, the answers offered understandably not providing the information the child was seeking. Including the child in whatever collective emotions the family as a whole was feeling was important, the two counseled, the sense that he or she was being shut out in some way or that there were secrets being withheld guaranteed to make the situation worse. Also imperative was to make it crystal clear to the child that daddy had not gone away because he did not love him or her. The temptation to tell a boy that he was now "the man of the house" was a mistake, they added, this putting too great a burden on him. Finally, Mahler and Henning advised parents to not be shocked or angry when their child exhibited what might be considered odd behavior after being told their father was dead. Children sometimes wanted to immediately go out and play, this a perfectly natural coping mechanism. Children also were apt to ask the fathers of friends, neighbors, and classmates "Will you be my daddy?," this, too, something not to get upset by. Although they took a psychological approach in their pamphlet, the authors pointed out that grieving families that were religious should by all means use their faith to get through their suffering. There were some general guidelines, in other words, but each family had to find its own, unique way to process the devastating loss and continue to move on in life.[32]

A PRECIOUS MEMORY

Polly McKeethers was one of many war widows to know this firsthand. That the family dog Sleepy also happened to die in the spring of 1943 only adding to their grief. It may have been bright and lovely outside, but darkness filled the inside of their home, the lingering presence of Dad seemingly everywhere. With a ten-year-old boy and fourteen-year-old girl, McKeethers had a fine line to walk in getting the family to move on from the tragedy. Her natural inclination was to "dispel the shadow" hanging over the house, thinking that it would be unhealthy for her children to dwell in the sadness for an extended period of time. This is what she knew her husband would have wanted, and she was certain that the family's memory of its good times would last forever. Living in a small town, however, she had to be careful, the prevailing sentiment there being that widows should spend a full year in solemn, visible mourning.[33]

McKeethers decided to embark on a course that she felt would satisfy everyone, including herself. First, she encouraged her children to fully express their grief, which essentially meant letting them cry their eyes out. Embarrassed to be sobbing, McKeethers's son was comforted by her assurance that "even brave men cry sometimes." ("Even MacArthur?," he asked, to which his mom replied that yes, even the five-star general cried once in a while.) Next, McKeethers had the family write "thank you" notes to everyone who had offered comfort to them, this also something she felt her neighbors would recognize as a proper public display of grief. After that, McKeethers and her kids created a scrapbook of memories of Dad, putting in it all the pictures they could find of him. A newspaper article about his appointment as a judge, membership cards of the various organizations to which he belonged, the masthead of the law school magazine he had edited, and other ephemera went into the book, this the final step before, as McKeethers expressed it, "we turned our face to the light again."[34]

The grieving process officially if not effectively over, it was time for what was perhaps an even more difficult thing to do: take a look at their budget in order to decide how to rearrange and redecorate the house now that things were different. McKeethers did not have a lot of money, meaning changes to the house "so memory wouldn't haunt it" would have to be minor. McKeethers decided to make what had been her husband's office into her son's bedroom, repainting it and its furniture in more kidlike colors. The only other alteration was to buy a green rug for the living room, this for her newly organized "radio listening group" to sit on. Now all McKeethers could do was to wait to see if her two children would, as the experts advised, accept or deny "the fact that a door in our life had quietly closed." McKeethers got her answer one morning when her kids asked that a boy who occasionally stayed with them move in for a full year and be a part of the family. Even though they recognized that their allowances would have to be cut to afford this, the children felt it was worth it to have another male presence in the house. McKeethers took this as a good thing, that they were finding a way to leave the past behind in order to move forward. "A precious memory abides with us always, but I believe courage and common sense have dispelled the shadow," she wrote in *Parents' Magazine*, feeling she did the best job she could have in what were extremely challenging circumstances.[35]

Others took a different route to process the loss of their loved ones during the war. In May 1943, Ralph E. Shannon, an Iowa newspaperman, received a telegram in a little yellow envelope from the War Department with this message:

> The Secretary of War desires that I assure you of his deep sympathy in the loss of your son, Captain Robert H. Shannon. Report just received states that he died May 3, 1943, in European area as result of an airplane accident. Letter follows. Ulio, the Adjutant General.[36]

The following night, Shannon wrote a letter to his son, Bob, as he had done every Thursday for the past two years. "Dear Bob," his letter began, "I am writing you tonight in the full knowledge that you will not be home." Shannon "told" his son how he and his wife believed the telegram would contain the good news that he had arrived in the United States, his tour of duty nearly over. The letter to his dead son continued, informing him how he delivered the news to his wife and how friends and neighbors came over to their house to express their sympathy. "Writing this letter to you now seems to help," he penned, the act itself more important than that the words would never be read. Shannon continued his weekly letter-writing campaign for months, telling his son everything from how they and the small town were managing his loss (the YMCA's Men's Club named its community room in his honor) to the trivial (it was "mushroom time" in Iowa).[37]

Dee Ruekert of Staten Island, New York, twenty-three-years-old and already with two children, received a similar "two-star" telegram a year after Shannon received his. (Telegrams with two stars at the top were sent by the Adjutant General to notify next of kin of the death of their child, spouse, or sibling. After receiving one, wives often replaced the blue star hanging in their window indicating a family member's service in the military with a gold one indicating his or her death.)[38] Like many wives, mothers, and sweethearts, Ruekert had tried to adopt the feeling of imperviousness that their sons, husbands, or boyfriends often had in going off to war. She, like most others, was less than successful, however, the fear that their loved one would not return always lurking in the back of their minds. Ruekert's fear was realized with the report of her husband, Bill's, death (hers beginning with the dreaded four words "The War Department regrets"), her life now consumed by bitterness, rage, and depression. Not sleeping or eating, both the family doctor and Ruekert's mother had to intervene to prevent her from a total collapse.[39]

Thankfully, Ruekert's mom seemed to instinctively recognize what and what not to do with someone in such misery. First, do not try to make them talk about it, she knew, with no words more helpful than those included in the telegram: "It should console you that your husband gave his life in the service of his country." Second, allow them to cry but, after the tension was released, try to get them to stop to prevent it from becoming routine. Third, encourage them to be as busy as possible, ideally with activities outside the home. "Under intense sorrow, what we need most is work and plenty of it," advised Lieutenant Commander Leslie B. Hohman, an associate in psychiatry at Johns Hopkins University serving in the U.S. Naval Reserve. (Ruekert took a job, finding it not only therapeutic but also financially necessary given her limited monthly income of a $78 widow's pension and $55 in life insurance.) Finally, keep the spirit of the departed alive, Ruekert's mother instructed her daughter, this the greatest expression of respect for her husband.[40]

For devout Christians, it was critical that the spirit of the departed be kept alive. Leaders of both the Protestant and Catholic churches feared that in the creation of a new world order after the war people would come to believe that those killed had died for a lost cause. New tensions and conflicts would almost certainly arise as countries jockeyed for power, this line of thinking went, meaning that those who had given their lives for world peace and international brotherhood had done so in vain. "The undeserved suffering and death of these young people unites them with Christ and gives them a part with him in saving the world," John Wright Buckham made clear in *Christian Century* in August 1945, the Allied dead following in the footsteps of Jesus by sacrificing their lives in the pursuit of redemption. Killing and wounding others was indeed an odd way to serve Christ, Buckham admitted, but in this they bore no responsibility. "Take heart, then, you who have given your sons," he told mourning parents, the defeat of evil as noble a cause as any.[41]

THE URGE TO LIVE

The war notwithstanding, Americans for the most part continued to struggle with the idea and practice of death. There was precious little evidence that Americans had accepted death as "one of the great natural facts," despite the recent loss of hundreds of thousands of fellow citizens. Still often shielded from the fundamental truths of death, children were determined to find some answers on their own. One did not have to be a psychologist to know that many children not only thought about death but also were downright fasci-nated by it. Kids were particularly intrigued by the formality and ritual of funerals, not to mention the fact that there was an actual dead person present who would soon be put in the ground. After seeing or just hearing about one, children would sometimes act out mock funerals, a dead bird or old doll standing in as the dearly departed guest of honor. Roles might be assigned, with a clergyperson offering a brief service and mourners (veiled, of course) walking in pairs down an imaginary church aisle. Shoebox caskets adorned with freshly picked daisies were solemnly buried while the kids sang any song they happened to know ("My Country, 'Tis of Thee" was appropriately respectful). By acting out funerals, children were attempting to understand death, something that perhaps could be said for adults attending the real thing. Trips to actual cemeteries, whether accompanied by adults or not (graveyards made an especially exciting field trip for those brave enough to jump over the fence), could be very helpful for kids to learn about death. Seeing familiar names on headstones demonstrated the continuity between life and death, the knowledge that this is where bodies went after they did not work anymore a valuable piece to the puzzle.[42]

It was important for parents to recognize that a child's interpretation of death did not have to match that of adults, wartime experts advised, this part of the prevailing view that kids were not miniature grown-ups. Indeed, it was unlikely for children and parents to have the same understanding of any subject, especially one as complex and enigmatic as death. Hundreds of years ago, it was common for adults to try to instill in children their view of death—that it could happen any time. ("Now I lay me down to sleep, I pray the Lord my soul to keep; if I die before I wake, I pray for God my soul to take," went the popular eighteenth-century New England prayer, making early Americans literally well versed in the unpredictability and cruelty of death.) By the 1940s, however, such an approach to childraising was quite out of date, with psychologists warning parents and teachers about causing any and all kinds of psychic trauma to young peoples' minds. Current psychological thinking was that children could not even conceive of their own demise, making such bedtime chants completely inappropriate. "The urge to live and to live abundantly is too deep-rooted and strong for most children to harbor for any length of time a thought of the possibility of their own near death," Fahs wrote in *Parents' Magazine*, the message for parents being that they should not tamper with that natural self-protection mechanism.[43]

Some teachers seized the rare opportunity to help young students learn about death. Adopting some kind of class pet could do the trick, the fish, turtle, gerbil, or some other small critter likely to meet its maker over the course of a school year. Mary McBurney Green, for example, saw her chance to discuss death with her nursery school class when their pet salamander died. The class thoroughly enjoyed caring for "Sally," but that ended one day when Green found the lizard out of her bowl, thoroughly dead. Green quickly called the students over to observe the stiff, shriveled corpse. The four-year-olds instantly surmised that Sally was no longer alive and posed theories about what had happened. "She got stepped on. A car ran over her," offered Jane, then suggesting that they put Sally in water to try to revive her. When this did not work, the class decided to bury the lizard in the school playground, some students knowing that anything "dead" should be covered up by dirt. That task completed, Katy offered her idea of where Sally now was to the rest of the class. The amphibian was in "Springfield," Katy had decided, apparently remembering that that is where Abraham Lincoln went after he died.[44]

Once in a while, however, death struck close to home, meaning parents had to confront the subject more directly with their children. Very little research had been done in this area to date, leaving it up to parents to mostly improvise in a tough situation. Again, children who lost one parent or a sibling were apt not to worry about their own deaths but would feel that something had been taken from their lives, a completely fair assessment. Experts felt that after such an experience a child would react one of two ways: the death of a family member could either accelerate the child's emotional growth or, conversely, set him or her back years. In the case of a parent dying, again two opposing scenarios could develop. The child could become more emotionally reliant on the remaining parent or else go the reverse direction by realizing that he or she now needed to become more independent. Remaining family members often felt guilt (for surviving) after one of their loved ones died, as well as regret for the acts of unkindness they had showed to him or her. Unable to verbally express these feelings, children acted them out in various ways, none of them productive. Professionals advised mourning families to not be afraid to talk about their dead loved ones, and even to make mention of their faults as well as their virtues.[45]

Having lost their eight-year-old daughter, Winnifred Ariel Weir and her husband knew much of this well. With another daughter one year younger, the Weirs recognized the importance of keeping the memory of their other girl alive, even though it was at first very difficult. "If you do not speak in the first few weeks of the loved one who is gone, you may never be able to do so naturally again," Weir wrote, the process made even harder by the strange looks nonfamily members would give them when talking about their recently dead daughter. Focusing on just her good qualities, Weir and her husband quickly realized that their other child might get jealous of her dead sister, and they purposely mentioned the problems and difficulties the latter had had. Social gatherings proved to be the most challenging situations, they found, their friends meaning well but obviously uncomfortable in acknowledging the family's loss. The next problem the Weirs faced was the growing dependence of their daughter upon them, the fact that they were spending most of their time together making her grow up too fast. Winnifred came to the conclusion that the best solution would be for her and her husband to have another child, not at all an easy decision. While knowing it was impossible to replace one child with another, Weir believed this was the best way for them to become a happy family again, something that proved to be so.[46]

Another common feature in the case of a family member dying was for siblings or the surviving parent to blame and perhaps hate the party considered responsible for causing the death. God was quite often appointed as that party, especially in homes where emotions tended to run high. In short, well-adjusted families adjusted well to the death of one of their own while poorly adjusted families adjusted poorly, experts logically concluded. That a good number of children had problems when a family member died was not surprising given that there was no education process to prepare for a loved one's death (or one's own, it could be said). Psychologists offered lots of advice for how parents should handle children's question of where babies came from—that is, how life began—but precious little on questions relating to how life ended. That job belonged to religious leaders, they felt, the differences in views about the afterlife making them recuse themselves from that responsibility. Religious leaders were, however, more familiar with Bible verses about death than the emotions that typically came along with it, and they also leaned toward metaphors and moralities versus honest, direct conversation. This left a big gap in children's knowledge about death and how to deal with it when it did take place, something probably as true today as seventy years ago.[47]

That many if not most Americans, both children and adults, had serious issues when it came to death had much to do with our deep fear of it. In fact, there was no greater fear, it could safely be said, the urge to keep alive the most primal of our basic instincts. Although scientists had not yet located a biological component for it, one could theorize that the fear of death is genetically based, something inherent to the species (and maybe all species) to encourage survival. Intentionally increasing the chances that one would die, as in times of war, was thus quite a feat for anyone to do, that person inclined to believe that there were more important causes than one's own life. Psychologists advised the spouses and children of those enlisting in the fight that fearing the death of their loved one was perfectly natural and that they should not pretend to feel calm when they did not.[48]

Besides the evolutionary explanation to fear death, there was of course a deep philosophical well going back centuries from which to draw. That it spared no one was a rude reminder that we were not as unique as we would sometimes like to believe, many had observed, all of us in the same boat when it came to the fickle whims of the Grim Reaper. Death was the great equalizer, all the wealth in the world not doing an ounce of good should the pale rider arrive at one's door. Likewise, we were not as powerful as we thought, a captain of industry or even king just another human life and, sooner or later, death. Our grand ambitions and material desires did not stand a ghost of a chance against death, so to speak, its utter apathy reducing our big egos to silly flights of fancy. More concretely, death permanently separated us from everyone else, at least in this life, making it the ultimate form of loneliness. Whether or not it led to the greatest reward or greatest penalty, if one chose to believe in heaven and hell, death remained the end of life as we knew it. For all but the deeply devout, the unknown future of eternity was a scary proposition, that there was no going back equally unnerving. For the clearly nondevout, death was just an empty room, its nothingness certainly not something to look forward to. That death could turn out to be the greatest adventure of all kept many going in this life, however, the prospects of what may come having a direct effect on what to do on this mortal coil. War magnified all these thoughts, the scope of this one still believed to perhaps have a profound and perhaps permanent impact on Americans' attitudes toward death.[49]

YOU DO FEAR DEATH

Much of the prevailing sentiment about death in the 1940s, and specifically the fear of it, was rooted in Freudian theory. With psychoanalytic theory not just dominating psychological and psychiatric practice in the United States but shaping everyday life in America, Freud's ideas about death gained greater currency during the war. "Whether you admit it or not, or even realize it consciously, you do fear death," wrote Robert D. Potter, science editor of *The American Weekly*, in 1943, clearly borrowing a page from the father of psychoanalysis. The fear of death was not only universal but also a defining trait of what it meant to be human, most American psychiatrists had come to think, this belief taking on a special resonance during wartime. (Freud forged the theory during the last world war, fittingly.) However, rather than increase in wartime, as one would expect because of the presumably greater chance of getting killed, the fear of death decreased, the counterintuitive theory went. Gregory Zilboorg, one of the country's leading shrinks, made that clear to his colleagues at the American Psychiatric Association annual meeting in 1943. In fact, the closer to the fighting one was, the lesser the fear of death would be, he explained (a proposition that some serving on the front lines might have challenged). The Russians and the British thus feared death the least (no mention was made of the Germans or the Japanese), and Americans the most because they were furthest from the actual fighting. Should the fighting reach the (continental) United States, Americans' fear of death would drop dramatically, Zilboorg continued, that primal feeling subordinated by tremendous anger and hate.[50]

Zilboorg's Freudian-based theory, which was broadly accepted by the psychiatric community, was backed up by hard evidence, he claimed. The last thing most pilots, bombardiers, and tailgunners thought of while in action was death, he proposed, those soldiers at the business end of a machine gun also too occupied to worry about getting killed. It was only normal people in normal situations who could afford the luxury of fearing death, Zilboorg suggested, the corollary being that crazy people (or at least those in crazy situations like war) suspended or submerged their fear to more immediate matters of survival.[51]

Zilboorg was hardly through parsing psychoanalytic theory for his fellow psychiatrists. The fear of death, or more precisely ways to lessen it, could be found across everyday life in America. Sports, especially more violent ones like football and boxing, served as cathartic releases for our common fear of dying, that athletes survived their "battle" proof that death was not always the victor. News reports of death, especially those of a calamitous nature like train wrecks, airplane crashes, fires, floods, and murder, also served to alleviate our own fears of dying, that we were left untouched a sign of immortality. Even religion was, psychologically speaking, a device to help us manage our driving fear of death, that God and his followers were immortal, a comforting reminder that our souls would continue to exist after our bodies expired. The mere act of thinking long term was in effect a means to sublimate our fear of death, he added. "We marshal all the forces which will still the voice reminding us that our own end must come some day and we are suffused with the feeling that our lives will go on forever," Zilboorg stated, this the only way we could remain sane.[52]

Although it was hard to believe that those with a Focke-Wulf fighter on their tail were not afraid of getting shot down and killed, the fact was that soldiers often acted flippantly when death was all around them. Covering the war for *The New Yorker*, for example, Sam Boal noticed on his trip to France in 1944 GIs' tendency to casually and jokingly talk about how they'd like to die. "Soldiers talk a lot about dying and how they would prefer to die, but it is not morbid the way they do it," Boal wrote, their mock choice of death a way to not have to think about a more likely one. "I want to be hit by a ten-ton bomb when I'm with a blonde . . . or two blondes," one soldier told Boal, another saying that "I want to die dead drunk on bourbon in Atlanta." In addition to making light of death, many soldiers were perfectly capable of ignoring entirely real events that might very well cause it. Some were not disturbed in the least by enemy shelling and strafing, others not even bothering to look up at German planes whose bombs were aimed directly at them.[53]

Few people seemed as comfortable around death in both wartime and peacetime than Captain Eddie Rickenbacker. "In a life crowded with drama and adventure, he has looked on death perhaps more often than any other living man," wrote the editor of *The American Magazine* in 1943 as an introduction to Rickenbacker's article, "When a Man Faces Death." A top auto racer before World War I and an ace pilot in that war, Rickenbacker certainly had looked death in the eye on numerous occasions. Now the president of Eastern Airlines, Rickenbacker reflected on his many close calls with death and ruminated on how they affected his life. His first brush with mortality occurred when he was just three years old when he was hit by a streetcar in his hometown of Columbus, Ohio. Rickenbacker was tossed into the gutter but was completely unscathed, this narrow escape setting the tone for the next few decades of his life. At seven, Rickenbacker fell thirty feet out of a tree, again no worse for the wear, and around the same time successfully ran back into a burning schoolhouse to retrieve his cap and coat. He also fell under a train that fortuitously stopped before running him over, this making him think that "something is taking care of me," as he recalled many years later.[54]

Oddly, it was none of these events but a much safer one that prompted Rickenbacker to fear death. Helping his father build a fence when he was nine years old, Rickenbacker was suddenly struck by the realization that one day he would die and thus would not live to see "the world's progress." Deeply upset by this sad prospect, he cried for a couple of days until his father demanded to know what was wrong. When told, Rickenbacker's father got angry and beat him, believing his son had no business thinking such things. Rickenbacker could not stop thinking about the world moving forward without him, however, coming to the conclusion that he was destined to be a part of the future. This revelation, quite an amazing one for a nine-year-old, would prove to serve him well as he faced death over and over in the years ahead. Racecar wrecks, plane crashes, or being adrift for twenty-one days on a rubber raft in the South Pacific could not stop Rickenbacker from believing that he was "a dynamic part of progress and life" and that a higher power was looking out for him. Rickenbacker did not understand people who could not do things because they once had come close to getting killed while doing it. "One's cumulative escapes should be proof of his invulnerability, of his being kept alive for some purpose, some fulfillment," he felt, his own survival despite the odds literal living proof of this.[55]

NEW FORMS OF FLYING DEATH

As the war drew to a close, it became clear that many Americans intended to be a part of the future by starting families. America's population soared during the war, this despite statisticians' belief that just the opposite would happen. The nation's home front death rate was up (as a result of a relatively older population because of the millions of young men overseas), but the birthrate was very much up.[56] Moving around the country for work in war plants, not to mention the absence of a good many potential fathers, seemed to be having little effect on the propensity to reproduce. For each battle death, in fact, there were twelve births, something that caught government officials and corporate numbers men by surprise. Over nine million children were born in the United States between early 1942 and 1945, a figure reflecting a 30 percent higher birthrate than prewar levels. In short, busy Americans were somehow finding a way and the time to breed like rabbits. (Birthrates were up in Europe as well, even more surprisingly.)[57] Was this a result of good economic times after a decade of the Depression or a natural human urge to reproduce when threatened? The data suggested that women were getting pregnant before their husbands shipped out, perhaps a conscious effort to leave a legacy should one not come back from the war.[58]

Another reason to explain the higher birthrate was the simple fact that more babies (and mothers) were surviving childbirth than in the past. Infant deaths (as well as maternal deaths) reached record lows in the United States during the war, despite shortages of both medical supplies and personnel.[59] Lower death rates for both mothers and babies was also the result of the still increasing likelihood of births taking place in a hospital. Some 70 percent of births in 1945 occurred in hospitals, while a decade earlier it was just 40 percent.[60] That was not good enough for Martha M. Eliot, associate chief of the Labor Children's Bureau, a government agency. Maternal deaths "must be reduced to half of their present annual rate of 7,000 in this country," she told a group at a November 1945 meeting sponsored by *Baby Talk* magazine, believing that the number of mothers (and infants) dying during childbirth was still much too high.[61] Eliot's comments signaled a growing "unacceptance" of death as the United States transitioned from war to peace. Just a few months after the end of World War II, the beginnings of what would become a full-out war against death in the postwar years could be detected.

Promoting the idea of birth went hand in hand with this emerging attack on death. As soon as the war was over, the push for Americans to settle down and start a family began in earnest. Restoring "normalcy" was predicated on establishing a strong domestic presence, the realization of such believed to encourage both national security and economic well-being. That married people lived longer than those single was perfect fodder for those in some kind of official capacity to suggest that all eligible Americans get hitched, the sooner the better. "Get Married and Live Longer!," declared a November 1945 headline of *Hygeia*, the article making a statistically compelling case to say "I do." "There is not the slightest doubt that Father Time favors the married when he swings his scythe," Halbert L. Dunn wrote in the magazine (which was soon renamed *Today's Health*), with Census Bureau data speaking for itself. Some 141 single men died for every one hundred married men twenty years old or older, and 117 single women for every one hundred married women. Even the widowed and divorced lived slightly longer than "the bachelor or the old maid," as Dunn put it, nipping that argument to avoid marriage in the bud. Being single was hazardous to one's health, it appeared, especially for men.[62] Dunn suggested that women looking for a husband take full advantage of the situation:

> What an unusual argument this offers for a member of the gentler sex to catch her man in the coming post-war era of "women without men"! With her head snuggled on his shoulder, she can murmur her promise to him: "Marry me, darling, and you'll live longer than you will if you stay a bachelor." Or perhaps, "Let's get married. We'll be happier and live a longer life together than we would apart." . . . Who knows, perhaps some time in the future the family doctor will prescribe marriage as she now prescribes golf in Florida for the failing heart.[63]

Few people were more keenly aware of the battle that was about to be waged between life and death than David Sarnoff. Sarnoff, president of RCA and a brigadier general during the war, wrote an essay titled "Science for Life or Death" just a few weeks before the formal surrender of Japan. Now that the atomic bomb was a reality, he argued, it was already time to think about the stakes of a third world war. Advancements in science had changed the rules for both better and worse, "The General" believed, the possibility of whole cities if not the entire world being destroyed in an instant something we now needed to take very seriously. "A third world war a generation hence would be so horrible in its power of destruction as to constitute a threat to our national security and to civilization itself!," he wrote for the *New York Times* in August 1945, the scenario of a preemptive strike ending a war before it really got started. "We must have similar projectiles, or rays, that we can instantly release to seek and to destroy these new forms of flying death before they reach their targets," Sarnoff urged, the missile race with an unknown enemy already in the making.[64]

Soviet scientists were already actively exploring the boundaries between life and death. Those attending a film shown in New York a couple of years earlier at the National Council of American-Soviet Friendship were amazed to see what appeared to be dogs coming back to life after being dead as a doornail. In the first demonstration of the bizarre film (narrated by J. B. S. Haldane, a distinguished British physiologist), all the blood of a dog was drained out of its body, this naturally resulting in death. But after an "autojector" pumped the dog's blood back into its body and oxygen was added to the mix, the animal was apparently revived. A few days later the reborn dog was seen as frisky as ever, its brush with death just a bad memory. The second demonstration in the film, in which a dog's head was totally severed from its body, was even odder. Connected to the autojector, the dog's head seemingly lived on, its eyes able to see, ears to hear, and tongue to taste. Had the Soviets figured out a way to bring animals back to life, American scientists seriously wondered after seeing the film? Could people killed by accidents be similarly resuscitated? "The method . . . offers the possibility of reviving such persons, provided their vital organs are still intact," thought *Science Digest*, our wartime alliance with the Soviet Union to perhaps pay off big dividends.[65]

As absurd as that might sound, that possibility came close to reality less than a year later, according to Soviet scientists. Soviet doctors working on the front successfully restored life to twelve "dead" soldiers, *Pravda* (and then the *New York Times*) reported, the men revived by this new, miraculous method of autojection. (The case of one particular soldier "snatched from death," as Albert Deutsch of *PM* described it, was published in the *American Review of Soviet Medicine*.) As with the experiments with dogs, both blood and oxygen were pumped into the bodies of the seemingly dead soldiers, their heart and lungs no longer working. The process, under the direction of Dr. Vladimir Negovski of the All-Union Institute of Experimental Medicine, allegedly worked on another thirty-nine soldiers, but they "died again," as Deutsch put it. Still, the feat was no less than astounding if true, and at the very least lent additional support to the growing belief that the definition of death should be reconsidered. The cessation of respiration and blood circulation did not necessarily mean the end of life, these strange experiments suggested, something that would drastically reshape the culture of death in America for the next half century.[66]

A NATIONAL DISGRACE

Until the day in which the dead could be brought back to life, however, the familiar causes of death remained worrisome. Now that many had returned from overseas and the gasoline and tire rationing had been lifted, the country's roads were again turning into somewhat of a demolition derby. Deaths from automobile crashes were up about 20 percent in 1945 over 1944, with twenty-nine thousand killed (and over a million injured) that year. "The drivers and pedestrians who behave in suicidal fashion apparently haven't learned much from the tragic experience of those who have gone before them," said Ned H. Dearborn, president of the National Safety Council, the problem especially bad in rural areas.[67] The number went up to thirty-four thousand in 1946, the carnage on the nation's highways showing no signs of slowing down.[68] The figures were about the same in 1947, leading President Truman to call the nation's accident record "a national disgrace." Truman even organized a White House conference on highway safety to address the issue, the deaths, injuries, and destruction of property "a drain upon the nation's resources which we cannot possibly allow to continue." Somebody in America was killed in a traffic accident every fifteen minutes, with aggressive driving, drinking, dangerous roads, and mechanically faulty cars blamed for most. Cars were getting faster and, while more safety features were gradually being incorporated (e.g., safety glass, four-wheel brakes, defrosters, and better lights), consumers were more interested in how cars performed and looked. Night driving was a particular problem; two-thirds of accidents occurred in the evening even though two-thirds of traffic volume was during the day. As the call for "urban renewal" became louder in the late 1940s, some politicians pointed out the need to make cities not just more modern but more car—and pedestrian—friendly.[69]

The chorus to end all kinds of deaths considered avoidable got louder and louder after the war. Accidental deaths of children became a primary concern of health professionals, not too surprising given the boom in childbirths. Martha Eliot, now associate chief of the U.S. Children's Bureau, urged other governmental agencies to do everything they could to prevent children from dying from accidents. Parents and educators also each had a responsibility to stop "the tragic loss of life among children" from accidents, she said in 1947, especially when it came to safety in the home.[70] Some seventeen thousand Americans died as a result of industrial accidents that year, this another thorn in President Truman's side. The president was in the process of launching an "Operations Safety" program to reduce deaths and injuries on the job, which numbered more than those from auto accidents (and perhaps even war, given that two million Americans got hurt in industrial mishaps in 1947). One American worker was killed or permanently crippled in industry every four minutes, the wasted "man-days" and resulting loss in production deemed as problematic as the human suffering involved.[71] An even bigger problem, however, were the many more Americans dying from infectious diseases that were entirely preventable. The failure to apply known methods to control such diseases was resulting in the deaths of one hundred thousand people every year, according to Leonard A. Scheele, U.S. Surgeon General in 1948, this another area health professionals needed to address.[72]

Interestingly, it was against the backdrop of this campaign to stop unnecessary deaths that a movement to allow "mercy killing" began in New York State. In late 1947, a petition urging that voluntary euthanasia be made legal was sent to all members of that state legislature. One thousand physicians signed the document, all of them members of the "Committee of 1776 Physicians for Legalization of Voluntary Euthanasia in New York State." The Euthanasia Society of America was also involved in the petition, its members no doubt hoping this would be the beginning of a national trend. With people living longer, the number of people suffering from painful, chronic, and degenerative diseases was sharply on the rise, the petition stated; that the cancer death rate had reached a new high was another reason that euthanasia should be allowed. "Many incurable sufferers, facing months of agony, attempt crude, violent methods of suicide, while in other cases distraught relatives of hopeless incurables who plead for merciful release secretly put them out of their misery and thereby render themselves liable to prosecution as murderers," argued the petition, a "mercy death" the much more humane thing in such cases. Why not bring out into the open something that was already being done surreptitiously?, the committee asked legislatures, the legalization of euthanasia to make the practice safer by conforming to a set of agreed-upon standards and regulations.[73] Over the next decade, the issue of "mercy killing" would become a central concern in America, the lines between life and death fuzzier than ever.

Chapter Three

Why Can't We Live Forever?

"Death is an imposition on the human race."
—Alan Harrington, *The Immortalist*, 1969

John Steinbeck had death on his mind in the late 1950s. Both retirement and life insurance could hasten the process of dying, the fifty-six-year-old author of such classics as *Of Mice and Men* and *The Grapes of Wrath* was thinking, each of these literally dangerous to one's health. Steinbeck had recently read about a research study showing that American businessmen tended to die soon after they retired, an occurrence he believed had more to do with idleness than being terminated from their job. "It seems to me that when survival ceases to have a purpose, some great part of life force disappears," the American icon wrote in the *Saturday Review* in 1958, concluding that your typical retiree was more prone to acquiring a fatal disease when he saw no valid reason to remain alive.[1]

But it was life insurance with which Steinbeck had the bigger problem. Deluged by magazine, radio, and television advertising to purchase life insurance (which he consistently resisted), the author had come to believe there were "serious implications in relation to the survival quotient of the American male." How so? For men like him who had little money in the bank, it was essential that one not just stay alive but remain productive in order to support their families' lifestyles. Steinbeck felt that such men could not afford to die, their will to live directly linked to the need to continue to produce income. Because he and his fellow breadwinners were "irreplaceable," Steinbeck theorized, they were resistant to illnesses that otherwise were likely to prove fatal. Having a large insurance policy that ensured the financial security of their dependents made them entirely replaceable, however, this destroying their immunity to disease. Knowing that one was worth more dead than alive was a dangerous thing, Steinbeck concluded, truly believing that life insurance could turn out to be a death sentence.[2]

Steinbeck's interesting theory about how to stay alive (he would die ten years later, presumably still without life insurance) reflected Americans' rather peculiar attitudes toward death in the postwar era. Death was perceived as a sinister threat to domestic family life, with much debate over how to handle the loss of a grandparent, parent, or child. Science declared war on death and dying in the 1950s and 1960s, some of the best minds of the day dedicated to extending the human life span yet further. Why couldn't there be another quantum leap in longevity, many were wondering, or the possibility that we could abolish death altogether? Such lofty aims would, however, prove to be a classic case of "be careful what you wish for." As advances in medical technology enabled new ways of living, it became increasingly clear that there would be new ways of dying as well. Tough decisions about who should die and when had to be made, the very definition of death in flux as science and technology sped forward. That America was experiencing somewhat of an existential crisis was not helping matters, the superficial tranquility of the times making many ask not just the big questions of life but of death. The better we got at avoiding death, the more we seemed to fear it, this tension one of the main undercurrents of midcentury America.

THE HARDEST QUESTION OF ALL

A still-lingering tension was dealing with the death of soldiers killed in World War II. Into the early 1950s, wives and parents of men killed in the war frequently had to answer what one of them called "the hardest question of all." The question was "Where is my daddy?," asked by a young child whose father had not come home. Most other children had daddies, after all, many of whom had returned safely from the war, and picture books often depicted fathers in all kinds of family settings. For the former, however, daddy was just a photograph, something understandably confusing and troubling. Adults who knew that one day they would likely have to answer the question armed themselves with advice from the many "experts" who retained a special kind of status in the postwar years. Handling the situation badly could make children have an unnatural fear of death or cause major psychological trauma, it was believed in these Freud-obsessed times, good reasons to be ready when "the hardest question of all" popped up.[3]

"Your daddy is dead," mothers and grandparents typically told their children, following specialists' recommendation that honesty was the best policy. Using a normal voice was critical, how one delivered the news considered as important as the words themselves. Children were then likely to ask, "What is dead?," a frequent (but not advised) answer to that tough one "It's like being asleep." Days could then go by before the matter came up again, the child having more detailed questions after having some time to think about it. "Why is daddy dead?," "Is daddy happy?," and "Will daddy come home?" were the most common follow-ups, the last requiring particular sensitivity. Informing children that his or her father would not be coming home while making it clear that he would if he could was imperative. Having the child continue to love his father even though he was dead was considered the ideal scenario, the knowledge that he also continued to love him or her equally important. More questions would usually arise later, however, the mystery that was death unable to be solved through such pithy responses.[4]

If and what to tell children about death went beyond those who had lost their daddies in the war. "Do the children have to know?," asked *Woman's Home Companion* in 1951, that question addressing the tricky subject of whether or not to discuss death and dying with little ones. The topic was difficult if not impossible to ignore given that the news was filled with reports of death, sometimes on a massive scale. Children often picked up on their parents' discomfort regarding death, this making them only more curious and concerned what it was all about.[5] Much attention was paid to help children understand "the facts of life" but surprising little about "the facts of death," it could safely be said. That death was a fact of life was almost completely ignored, even the dreaded "birds and the bees" talk easier to broach with children than trying to explain that all of us would someday no longer exist. Recognizing that parents could use some help in this arena, the Child Study Association issued a pamphlet in 1958 called "Helping Your Child to Understand Death." Religious or philosophic explanations did not work very well, nor did metaphors likening death to a long journey or eternal sleep, according to the pamphlet, its author advising parents to stick to the basic facts as best they could.[6]

Another question involving children and death in the family-oriented 1950s was whether they should go to funerals, usually that of a grandparent. Parents often drew upon their own experience as children in the 1920s and 1930s, with those who grew up in rural areas more likely to have attended funerals than those who had been raised in cities. Many parents were nervous about the effect a funeral might have on a young child, a reflection of the pervasive fear and paranoia surrounding psychological maladjustment in the postwar years. Those in favor of children going to funerals argued that it was the perfect way to learn about death, seeing them more as celebrations of life than grisly, macabre affairs. Being exposed to death at an early age made it easier to accept later in life, these adults argued, being shielded from it more potentially damaging in the long term. If nothing else, children were undoubtedly curious and perhaps concerned about funerals and death in general, so why not have their questions answered by seeing the real thing? Those parents against it believed a funeral could very well make a child depressed or upset, however, the knowledge that death came to those we loved a sad piece of news for the young.[7]

In search of the right answer to the funeral question, parents often consulted with their minister. Because they were intimately familiar with death (and believed in an afterlife), however, ministers were almost certain to be profuneral, frequently bringing their own children to those of church members. (Norman Vincent Peale, a pastor when he was not writing best-selling self-help books, felt that protecting children from death was actually more likely to lead to "abnormalities.") Another way to get advice on the subject was to get a copy of Arnold Gesell and Francis L. Ilg's *The Child from Five to Ten*, which had a section on children's attitudes toward death. While children were known to react differently according to their age, the authors pointed out, none were likely to be permanently scarred by attending a funeral, even that of someone close to them in age like a cousin or friend. In fact, a five-year-old was probably more interested in where the flowers came from or who was singing than existential issues about life and death, Gesell and Ilg made clear, with older children more apt to be understanding than alarmed. Especially sensitive children might need special preparation, but there was not much to worry about "average" children going to funerals, most experts agreed, only the parents' own fear of death likely to lead to problems down the road.[8]

The death of a grandparent remained a challenge for many parents of young children, however, especially when he or she lived with the family. Advice in handling the situation was often again sought from ministers who themselves were likely to have consulted with child psychologists. Reactions differed significantly according to the age of the child. A four-year-old, for example, did not have much understanding of death beyond that which took place in cartoons or shoot-'em-ups, meaning any kind of emotional outburst was unlikely. (Some kids, informed that their grandfather had died, were known to ask, "Who shot him?").[9] By six, however, children recognized that death was not just something that happened on television or to old people. Real, not-so-old people could be killed or die from sicknesses, he or she probably now knew, and that hospitals were often involved. Six-year-olds in fact typically had a keen interest in coffins, funerals, and cemeteries, the mystery surrounding them no doubt part of the appeal. A child at that age typically did not worry that he or she might die but was quite concerned that his mother could. By eight, a child usually understood that all people would eventually die, with his or her attention turned to what might come after death. For all children, it was advised that parents themselves break the news and avoid vague and misleading language like "Granddad's gone away." It was important for parents to strike a balance between keeping their emotions under control while not hiding their grief and sense of loss. Answering the series of questions that could follow ("Will he come back?" "Will you die, too?" "Where did you take him?" "What makes people die?" "How old do they have to be?" "Will we get another Granddad?") simply and honestly was best, postwar experts recommended, the things adults did not talk about considered more troubling to children.[10]

Special care had to be taken when a young classmate died. Elementary and nursery school teachers knew they had better be prepared for such a rare but very sad occasion. Telling children why a member of their class was missing was not easy, as was trying to tell them why he or she died. The child had a sickness that few ever get and the doctor was not able to make him or her better went the typical explanation. Convincing classmates that they would not get this sickness was paramount, experts advised. As with sons and daughters who continued to want more information about their fathers' deaths, however, schoolchildren often asked teachers for more specifics or else created alternative scenarios with which they were more familiar. Having seen many cowboys, Indians, soldiers, and bad guys get killed in movies or on television—the most visible depiction of death in America—some children presumed this might have been the way their classmate had actually died. Other children reasonably compared the situation to what had happened to their dog, cat, or turtle. Once what had taken place fully registered, children realized death was a possibility for their siblings, this requiring a reminder that they were in good health. Telling their parents that one of their friends had died was another component to how children came to grips with death. Some excitedly yelled it as soon as they got home, while more nervous ones waited for weeks to whisper the news into their mother's or father's ears. Teachers welcomed this whole discovery and rationalization process, knowing that it was young people's own way to make sense out of what understandably was to them a strange and foreign experience.[11]

Far more difficult was deciding what to do or say when the child himself or herself was dying. The first impulse for parents was to make whatever amount of time the child had as pleasurable and fun as possible. On second thought, however, parents would try to have things be thoroughly normal given that the child's having a terminal disease was not at all normal. Sharing their child with siblings and friends was the hardest part of all, their natural inclination to spend every minute with him or her. It was not unusual for families in such trying situations to become more religious than they had been, finding church services and Bible services of considerable comfort. Psalm 23 ("The Lord is my shepherd . . .") was especially helpful, not too surprisingly, as was Romans 8:35 ("Who shall separate us from the love of Jesus Christ? . . .") and Psalm 121 ("I will lift up mine eyes unto the hills . . ."). More than anything else, parents viewed every day they spent with their dying child as a gift, thankful for the precious time they had remaining.[12]

THE LESSONS OF SORROW

Could anything good come out of losing a child, an event that was generally viewed as the most difficult thing in life? Joe E. Brown, the famous entertainer, thought so, telling his story ten years after he lost his son in 1942. A pilot in the war, Captain Don Brown crashed his plane in the California desert during a test flight, the tragedy the basis for what his father would come to call "the lessons of sorrow." Brown thought his experience could be helpful for parents who were losing sons in the Korean War or, for that matter, from disease or accidents. "I feel that the experience of losing someone you love dearly can be a force for good, *must* be a force for good," Brown wrote in *Better Homes and Gardens* in 1952, convinced it was up to individuals to decide if their loss would be constructive or destructive in their own lives.[13]

Upon hearing the news, Brown (who was playing in a show in Detroit) went through the initial disbelief and disavowal stages of grief, not believing it was true and then not understanding how it could happen if there was a God. After one day of this, however, Brown found a divinely inspired metaphor to make some sense of the situation:

> If every day were full of sunshine, warm and with a gentle wind, we would soon become accustomed to perfection, bored by it. Instead, we have the seasons, and we have days of mist and rain. We have something to judge the good days by, and thus we know their worth when they come.[14]

The death of his son also led Brown to change his orientation to life by being more appreciative of what he had and had achieved. Like many others who had gone through some kind of traumatic event, Brown believed that God had put him on a "new path," committed now to help others who were less fortunate than he. Rather than seek out sympathy, which he considered selfish (black clothing and arm bands were "a conscious effort to tell the world how much you have suffered," he thought), Brown had thrown himself into the war effort by doing what he did best—make people happy. His faith tested but unbroken, Brown continued to have confidence in what he called "the ultimate wisdom of God." "Our responsibility to the dead is very real," he made clear, part of the job of the living to carry on the work the departed had been doing. That was better than any kind of physical monument to their memory, he concluded, even little actions speaking louder than a bronze statue in a park.[15]

Marguerite Higgins, a Pulitzer Prize–winning foreign correspondent, received her lessons of sorrow upon losing her five-day-old child to jaundice. Higgins believed she was well acquainted with death after having visited Buchenwald soon after the concentration camp was liberated and by covering the war in Korea. At Buchenwald, the dying had whispered unintelligible messages in her ear, and she saw prisoners shoot Nazi guards in revenge; in Korea, she witnessed American soldiers get torn apart by machine gun fire. But nothing, it turned out, had prepared Higgins for the death of her own baby. "I made the discovery that I had seen death and yet I had not known it," she wrote in *Good Housekeeping* in 1954, certainly sorry for all the dead and dying people she had observed but having no real emotional attachment to them or the experience itself. "I had not known how the death of another could be the death of a part of yourself," Higgins added, only this event allowing her to understand the meaning of compassion. Unlike Brown, however, Higgins was not so sure she was glad to have gained this knowledge, her loss making her question whether there was a plan or purpose to life.[16]

Brown's and Higgins's stories illustrated the growth, willing or otherwise, that individuals could experience when someone close to them died. While each bereavement was somehow different, reflecting the unique relationship between two people, there were common elements. The death of a loved one often felt first as a special kind of punishment no one else had to endure, a pain so great that it made the griever question whether life was worth living. But soon grievers developed empathy for those who experienced similar losses, this frequently leading to a new awareness of the value of life. Many felt a kinship with humanity for the very first time, a deep desire to be closer to family, friends, and even strangers. Losing someone could also make one have a greater appreciation of time, especially that shared with other people. That all this could take place was all the more remarkable given how unprepared people were for the death of a loved one and how little the subject was discussed in postwar America. Separating mourners from others through special treatment and assigned behavior probably did more harm than good, turning death into a peculiar occasion distinct from the rest of life. The social pressure to quickly move on from the unfortunate experience also contributed to segregate death from life, something from which to recover and perhaps forget. Containing and repressing death only made it more challenging when it did take place, however, a problematic pattern of behavior for midcentury Americans.[17]

Some of those who knew they were soon going to die were able to break that pattern by refusing to focus on themselves. Upon receiving the bad news, usually inadvertently, terminal patients typically went through the mental anguish of knowing that their time was short. Realizing this was not doing anybody any good, however, their thoughts often turned to what they might leave behind or bestow to others. Bequeathing money or property was great if one had them, but what if one didn't? By the early 1950s, significant progress was being made in organ transplantation, the perfect opportunity for the less well-to-do to make some sort of contribution. Eye banks had already been established, and similar repositories for bones, muscles, and veins were being set up. Mary Alson, a woman given six months to live in 1953, for example, wrote a letter to Dr. Alan Moritz, head of the Institute of Pathology at Western Reserve University and one of the leaders in the nascent field, to learn what her options were. Dr. Moritz provided Alson with a list of doctors who could help grant her wish to donate her organs, adding that allowing her body to be autopsied was another way she could advance "modern medicine." Alson wrote a note to her family making her intentions clear, finding great comfort that she was "leaving her body to science," as the expression went. "Mine is no magical formula that makes death anything less than a dreadful inevitability," she made clear in an essay for *McCall's*, but the knowledge that she would "keep on working" after she died was a tremendous morale booster. Her decision had not only brought a measure of tranquility to her life but also had restored her faith in God, a classic case of what she astutely called "successful dying."[18]

Alson's decision to authorize an autopsy was indeed considered a valuable contribution to medicine in the science- and research-oriented postwar years. As the postmortem examination of a body to determine the cause of death, autopsies allowed doctors to confirm their bedside (or clinical) diagnosis. Autopsies would also tell doctors if their diagnosis had been wrong, something that could benefit future patients by increasing physicians' knowledge of a particular disease. Determining the cause of a disease could eventually lead to a cure, health professionals believed, this the ultimate reason hospital officials asked next of kin for permission to do an autopsy (at no cost to relatives).[19]

Doctors pointed out, however, that it was also in the family's own best interests to have an autopsy done on their newly dead relative. Knowing definitively why their relative died was a good thing for a number of reasons. First, the family would find comfort that it was indeed a disease that caused death, assuming this was so, rather than, say, a medical error. Some insurance policies in fact required proof of the cause of death, with an autopsy the highest legal standard. Families would also learn if a hereditary disease played a role in their relative's death, information that could perhaps help prevent it from killing them. Such reasons were justification for the next of kin to allow the hospital to proceed with an autopsy even though it was typically a highly emotional decision made at an especially emotional time.[20]

The strong feelings attached to autopsies had much to do with the idea that the bodies of their loved ones would in the process be mutilated or desecrated. "He has suffered enough" was a not uncommon response to a hospital's request to do one, an illogical but sincere sentiment. Because autopsies were, like death itself, something not to be talked about, many did not realize that little "damage" would usually be done to the corpse during the procedure. Pathologists took the same care and applied the same precision as surgeons did in operations on live bodies, with just tiny bits of tissue (versus whole organs) typically removed. All attempts would be made to leave blood vessels intact to allow for embalming. It was not unusual for undertakers to try to talk relatives out of giving the go-ahead for an autopsy, however, their work made somewhat more difficult because of the incisions made to the body. Telling relatives that they would not be able to hold a (more expensive) open casket funeral was, for some undertakers, business as usual.[21]

Given the other kinds of objections next of kin could have regarding an autopsy, undertakers frequently got their way. "She died of old age" was one, the relative not understanding that people did not really die of old age and that knowledge about chronic illnesses was actually more valuable than that of sudden death. "You already know why he died" was another, the relative not appreciating the full range of issues involved (e.g., contributing factors to death, how life could possibly have been prolonged, and if suffering could have been lessened). "This was a usual case" was yet another, the relative not realizing that more knowledge about the most usual cases could possibly save the most number of lives. Thinking one's faith did not permit autopsies was also quite common, although the truth was that no major religion in the United States officially objected to them. Verbal or, better yet, written permission had to be obtained for an autopsy to be performed, however, with instructions for such ideally specified in an individual's will. Exceptions were made in the case of "indigents," who had no say in the matter, and when a coroner ordered an autopsy due to an accident, an act (or suspicion) of violence, or when death occurred unexpectedly.[22]

A NEW WAY OF DYING

Hospital staffs' concerted interest in performing autopsies was one sign of the war being waged on death in the 1950s. Much more attention was being paid to cause of death as millions of research dollars were poured into the effort to eradicate diseases. The causes of death in America had shifted dramatically over the past few decades. Before World War I, an American was most likely to die from heart disease, pneumonia, influenza, and tuberculosis (the latter sometimes called the "Captain of Death" because of its high mortality rate). Sulfa drugs introduced in the 1930s, followed by antibiotics, had knocked pneumonia and influenza out of the top killer list, but other diseases had taken their place. Heart disease remained number one, but now cancer and cerebral hemorrhage (i.e., stroke) were taking the lives of most Americans.[23]

Breaking down the cause of death by age and gender was an important part of researchers' massive effort directed against diseases in the 1950s. Slightly more baby boys were born than baby girls, nature's way of accounting for males' higher attrition rate throughout life. In 1945, the number of American females had surpassed that of males (partly as a result of fewer immigrants coming into the country than before the war), a trend that showed no signs of reversing because of improved health care during pregnancy and childbirth. Until one was in his or her sixties (sixty-four for men and sixty-seven for women), an American was most likely to die in the first year of life than any other. (The mortality rate for babies less than one year old equaled that for the next thirty-five years of life combined.) Accidents were the leading cause of death for young adults, cancer for the middle-aged, and heart disease for the elderly. Although cancer, stroke, and accidents had surged over the course of the first half of the twentieth century (the latter due much in part to the invention of the automobile), Americans' average life span continued to climb. An American baby born at the turn of the century had about a 40 percent chance of reaching his or her sixtieth birthday, but by the early 1950s it was roughly 70 percent.[24]

While living decades longer was considered miraculous, increased longevity carried a heavy price. The seeds of what would be called the "right to die" and "death with dignity" movement could be clearly seen sprouting in the late 1950s. Medical technology had by then advanced far enough in which a terminal patient could be kept alive for weeks or months longer than if there was no intervention. Both the law and the Hippocratic oath required physicians to do everything possible to sustain life, a policy that was proving to be problematic as the options at doctors' disposal progressed and multiplied. One widow anonymously told her painful story in *The Atlantic* in January 1957, an early indicator of much bigger things to come.[25]

"There is a new way of dying today," she began, the process a much different thing than in the not-so-distant past because of modern medicine. Instead of dying at home surrounded by family and minimally medicated, most Americans were now likely to spend their final days heavily drugged in an impersonal metropolitan hospital. Having witnessed her husband's prolonged death in such a setting, this woman could not help but feel that this new way of dying was "a ghastly imposition against God's will." The widow-to-be viewed the way in which most Americans now died as a battle between spirit and medicine, with the former ultimately to win. But medicine fought spirit with everything it had, a merciless, agonizing process for the patient and family members. "Every new formula, all the latest wonder drugs, the tricks and artificial wizardry, are now prescribed and brought to bear," she wrote, the spirit ready to depart but repeatedly dragged back to this world. Eventually her husband's spirit won out, even modern medicine unable to keep it and his body alive. Did this new way of dying represent progress, one had to wonder, or was the old way more peaceful and humane?[26]

The vengeance with which American doctors fought death belied the fact that humans, like all animals, could be said to be in a constant state of dying. The death of cells was an important way we remained alive, each one somehow knowing the precise moment to expire when its work in the body was done. If cells did not die off, there would be an excess for which there was no room, with death an eventual certainty. (Some diseases such as cancer and leukemia were the direct result of the failure of cells to die when they normally should have.) Having taken a few courses in biology, doctors knew that millions of cells died in the human body every day, this perfectly natural event one of the most basic (yet mysterious) keys to life. Why then did they resist the death of the entire human organism when it decided it was time to die, determined to delay the process when they knew it was almost certainly a futile effort? Humans were, after all, essentially a collection of cells, each of us somehow programmed to live and die as nature dictated.[27]

Some in the American medical community, however, felt strongly that delaying the arrival of death through advanced technologies and drugs was not nearly enough. "Why can't we live forever?," asked Joseph W. Still, an MD and author of *Science and Education at the Crossroads: A View from the Laboratory* in 1958. Writing in, rather oddly, *Better Homes and Gardens*, Still challenged the "assumption" that death was the inevitable end result of living despite the fact that no one in history had provided evidence to the contrary. Still, who specialized in the "disease of aging" (the mere idea that he and many other postwar medical scientists viewed aging as a disease spoke volumes), approached the issue of life and death from the opposite point of view. "The only factor which prevents our living forever is death," he argued, a statement that was perhaps circular logic but actually difficult to challenge. One could certainly not dispute that, since the late nineteenth century, "science" had prevented some diseases from causing death, this largely accounting for the thirty or so years' gain in longevity.[28]

For Still and other midcentury men and women of science, however, this was just the beginning. Life spans could be extended much further, he was convinced, with no reason to believe that most humans could not live to 150 years of age or more. Now that science had dealt a serious blow to infectious diseases—the leading cause of death until the relatively recent development of antibiotics and vaccines—it was time to conquer degenerative diseases with an equivalent effort. Victory on this battlefield would help pave the way to take on the ultimate enemy, Still foresaw, the pesky problem of aging now in our sights. "Aging may prove no more fatal or inevitable than germs," he mused, seeing no biological barrier for humans to one day achieve the eternal dream of living as long as one would like.[29]

How would arguably the greatest scientific feat in the history of mankind be achieved? The solution resided in first determining why people aged and, then, the much trickier business of preventing it from taking place. There were three general theories about why humans aged and, as a result, died (assuming a disease, act of violence, or childbirth caused death prematurely). The first was the "biological-clock" theory, which simply stated that people had a defined and limited amount of time to live and, when the sand in one's hourglass ran out, death occurred. The second was the "cumulative-poison" theory that posited that our cells gradually acquired toxins (either from the environment or metabolically) that caused aging and for the human organism to eventually expire. The last was the "loss-of-control" theory, which made the case that our physiology and body chemistry "gum up" over time, this leading to aging and death. Joseph Still favored this last theory, and thus believed this was the area that researchers like him should focus their efforts. "Medical experience has taught us that when we fully understand a chemical event, we are able to manipulate and alter or modify it," he explained, aging potentially as curable as previous messengers of death such as smallpox, polio, pneumonia, or tuberculosis.[30]

Other scientists believed that the key to living forever, or at least a lot longer than seventy years, might reside in enzymes. In his essay in *Horizons in Biochemistry*, a 1963 textbook, for example, D. E. Koshland Jr. of the Brookhaven National Laboratory made the case that hormones, a kind of enzyme, could explain why people aged and ultimately died. Koshland speculated there was a "death hormone," an enzyme that was designed specifically to cause destruction to the human body. Why would God or evolution embed such a thing in a living organism? "Death has value to the species as a whole even if it is unpleasant for the individual," he wrote in perfect seriousness, that value being natural selection. Death encouraged humans to advance biologically over time, this theory went, the going off into the good night "nature's way of correcting errors and developing new and more efficient living systems." The death of individuals also allowed the human species to adapt to environmental changes, Koshland argued, clearly trading on Darwin's concept of the "survival of the fittest." (The steadily increasing human life span could be seen as evidence of these theories.) If this was all true, "an enzyme or drug designed to counteract that hormone would be of considerable interest," Koshland added, quite an understatement given the reception an antidote to aging and death would receive.[31]

Other American scientists were exploring ways to defeat death or, if that were impossible, make its victory more difficult. The old saying "everybody worries about dying but nobody does anything about it" was no longer true as men and women in white jackets strove to turn postwar Americans into modern-day Methuselahs. Robert C. W. Ettinger was one of the leaders of the emerging field of cryobiology (or cryonics), which involved freezing a body and storing it until science had learned how to cure its cause of death. Cryobiologists (incorrectly) viewed dying as a disease, the fact that many people had been "brought back to life" from drowning, asphyxiation, electrocution, and heart attacks taken as evidence that death was not necessarily fatal. Cryobiologists were correct in their view that the boundary between life and death was not as sharp as once believed, this the premise that they felt justified their unusual research. Rather than being absolute, the definition of death was directly related to the state of medicine, they held, allowing Ettinger to make claims such as "today's cadaver [will] be tomorrow's patient."[32]

How did cryobiologists intend to make death less certain than taxes? Freezing the body immediately after clinical death was important, as was storing it at a temperature of liquid nitrogen (-196 degrees Celsius). There would, they admitted, be some freezing damage, but not as much as skeptics (likening bodies to decades-old Birds Eye vegetables) claimed. Ettinger's book *The Prospect of Immortality* laid out the process of cryobiology in considerable detail, a possibility that Jean Rostand of the French Academy had first posed in 1946. "To those who choose not to be frozen, all I can say is rot in good health," Ettinger warned in *Esquire* in 1965, convinced that over time more people would recognize that "the freezer is more attractive than the grave."[33]

Americans were not the only ones in the postwar years seriously considering that death might be unnecessary. The Soviets, too, were pioneering the field of "death reversal," an area of research that posed major implications during the Cold War. What the Russians were actually up to was unclear until the 1962 publication of *Resuscitation and Artificial Hypothermia*, a book written by V. A. Negovskii, a member of the USSR's Academy of Medical Sciences. "Death reversal" was based in the discovery that cooling the body could delay clinical death that occurred when the brain was deprived of oxygen for more than five to eight minutes. When refrigerated or put on ice, experimental animals survived for as long as an hour, the Soviets had found, this the breakthrough that could possibly lead to stopping death in its tracks. "We may prophecy that perhaps at the end of the twentieth or the beginning of the twenty-first centuries active and successful treatment will be given in any case of sudden death," Negovskii wrote in the book, the Grim Reaper sent back to where he, she, or it came from.[34]

A NEW REALISM IN OUR THINKING

Less ambitious but more personal efforts related to death were pervasive in the postwar years. Death and dying memoirs emerged as a distinct literary genre, a sign of Americans' interest in writing and reading about the loss of a loved one. "Privately printed and distributed memorials to distinguished men are not new, but the intimate description of death, put forth as a commercially published book, seems to be appearing in increasing numbers," the *Saturday Review* observed in 1957, with four notable books in this genre published in just the last few months. All documented the death of a family member. John Gunther's *Death Be Not Proud* was a tribute to his young son who died of a brain tumor; Catherine Gabrielson's *The Story of Gabrielle* described the death of the author's ten-year-old daughter from liver cancer; Lael Tucker Wertenbaker's *Death of a Man* was a detailed account of her husband's death from cancer; and Betsey Barton's *As Love Is Deep* was about her mother's lengthy bout with cancer and her own spiritual crisis. Was this flurry of books about personal experiences with death symbolic of some kind of psychological shift taking place in American culture, or merely a coincidence? The *Saturday Review* was not sure, but there was no doubt that more attention was being paid to the complex emotions involved in the grieving process.[35]

More books about death were published over the next few years as postwar intellectuals mused over the meaning of life and what might come next. (The belief that God may be dead was of course an important part of philosophical thought in the 1950s and 1960s.) No less than twenty-one experts from a wide variety of disciplines contributed essays to the 1959 book *The Meaning of Death*, a surprisingly optimistic work. The book's big idea was that a better understanding and acceptance of death was good for mental health, with attempts to avoid acknowledging it often leading to psychological problems. "Attitudes concerning [death], and its meaning for the individual, can serve as an important organizing principle in determining how he conducts himself in life," wrote the book's editor, Herman Feifel, a professor of psychiatry at the University of Southern California, a point many Americans seemed to be missing. In fact, if denying the fact that one would no longer exist was indeed a factor in mental illness, could the United States be considered collectively crazy given how much its people stuck their head in the sand when it came to death?[36]

The plethora of books about death in the late 1950s and early 1960s suggested, however, that Americans' attitudes may have been changing. Writing for *Saturday Review* in 1961, Harry C. Meserve ventured that "a new realism in our thinking" could be behind the publishing trend, foreshadowing the explosion of "death culture" that was about a decade away. Besides Jaroslav Pelikan's revelation-oriented *The Shape of Death* and S. Ralph Harlow's paranormal-themed *Life after Death*, there was Cyrus Sulzberger's existential *My Brother, Death*, an exploration of how humans have confronted the end of life and attempted to find meaning in it. Meserve was encouraged by this new kind of honesty regarding death, thinking it was a step in the right direction. "So much of our society is involved in the conspiracy of silence on the subject of death, and the apparent effort to pretend that if we do not look at it death will go away," he wrote, that some had the courage to treat it as a fact of life a rare and good thing.[37]

"The new realism in our thinking" about death in the early 1960s could be detected in other ways. Some physicians were, rather remarkably, telling terminal patients they were dying, a clear break from standard medical practice. Sixteen women in the Boston area with incurable cancer were informed by their doctors that they would not live much longer, for example, something so unusual it became the subject of a study by two Harvard psychiatrists. After reviewing the case histories, Drs. Thomas Hackett and Avery Weisman concluded that dying patients should be told the truth despite the prevailing opinion holding otherwise. The patients were relieved to not have to continue pretending to be optimistic about their prognosis, suspecting it was hopeless even though they had not been told so. "Well, I've finally broken the sound barrier," said one of the women who learned the truth, happy that someone confirmed what she had been feeling all along. Critics argued that breaking the "conspiracy of silence" would make terminal patients die faster, leading Dr. Hackett to respond, "Why not?" More traditional doctors remained unconvinced that honesty was the best policy, however, thinking that even the terminally ill should not be completely deprived of hope. Doing so was akin to what those on death row experienced, one such critic suggested, the misery of knowing when one was going to die is worse than the experience of death itself.[38]

Critics' concerns about the dying confronting their own deaths were grounded in psychological theory that went back at least a half century. In 1915, Freud had famously argued that the unconscious mind was incapable of imagining its possessor's own demise except perhaps as an abstract intellectual exercise. (Freud also likened fears of death to those of castration.) In his own research into the psychology of dying in the 1930s, Felix Deutsch made the interesting case that our fear of death was rooted in the helplessness we felt as infants. More recently, Avery Weisman had also argued that it was the weakness and physical decline of dying that was most upsetting, another reason perhaps to not tell patients that death was fast approaching. In his 1955 book *The Psychiatrist and the Dying Patient*, Kurt Eissler showed the extent to which people would go to deny the reality they would soon be dead, part of our larger cultural taboo surrounding death. Whatever the theory, it appeared that humans had some kind of built-in mechanism to protect themselves from the certainty that they would one day no longer be alive, something with which it might be best not to tinker.[39]

Even with this mechanism or perhaps because of it, however, there was no doubt that most people feared death to some degree. While understanding this was perfectly natural, inspirational leaders of the postwar era urged individuals to not let it get in the way of the business of living. It was not surprising that the author of such books as *The Power of Positive Thinking*,

Stay Alive All Your Life, and *The Tough-Minded Optimist* instructed Americans to rise above the fear of death. "We have allowed ourselves to think of it as a dark door," Norman Vincent Peale wrote in *Reader's Digest* in 1963, he thinking of death more as "a rainbow bridge." Death had gotten a bum rap, the pastor thought, especially since it was more likely to be seen as friend than foe when it arrived. That a better world awaited after death was all the more reason to not fear it, he and other devout Christians explained, with a lot of "scientific" evidence to suggest that one's soul survived one's body. "Believe me, death is only a momentary rim of shadow," he evangelized, "the radiance of eternal life" waiting beyond.[40]

Despite such ministering, it is safe to say that the fear of death in twentieth-century America was quite a different thing than in other times and places. For centuries, many people, especially Christians, specifically feared God's judgment when they died, not quite sure how and where they'd spend eternity. In a more secular, self-oriented culture, however, the Dante-esque concepts of heaven, hell, purgatory, and limbo had a lot less currency, accounting in part for a shift in the fear of death. Now it was more likely to be the snatching away of what one felt entitled to that was so upsetting, the end of this life more disturbing than the possibilities of an afterlife. "Though the hope of immortality persists, the traditional Christian view of death as a transformation into a fuller life remains at best a minority opinion," noted *Newsweek* in 1966, viewing religious mythology now as "too primitive and plainly unattractive, even to those who still believe in a Christian afterlife."[41]

While the remaining faithful took comfort in their belief of an afterlife, there were entirely rational reasons to fear and dread death. First, dying (if not death itself) could be painful, making anyone not want to look forward to that experience. Second, leaving the joys of this world, especially the people one loved, was an unhappy prospect, a certain loss even if there might be some kind of gain. Last, what if anything would come after death was entirely unknown, the human mind especially good at conceiving the most unpleasant kinds of scenarios. On the other hand, as philosophers throughout history had observed, the knowledge that death would one day arrive could be said to make life all the sweeter. Death, arguably more than anything else, helped us to fully appreciate life, this simple bit of wisdom something to which everyone could relate.[42]

LIFE'S MOST APPALLING CIRCUMSTANCE

Knowing that death was inevitable may have made life sweeter, but that did not deter experts in the postwar years from trying to figure out how to put it off as long as possible. How Americans died or were likely to were major areas of study among both government and corporate scientists within the booming "military-industrial complex" of the 1950s and 1960s. (A longer-lived, healthier population was no doubt seen as a kind of weapon during the Cold War.) After *Reader's Digest* published its "Cancer by the Carton" article in 1952, for example, health professionals began taking a closer look at the potential dangers of smoking. By the much-anticipated release of the report to the Surgeon General on smoking and health in January 1964, there was substantial evidence that cigarettes were directly linked to various diseases. Deaths from emphysema and other respiratory diseases were on the rise, with smoking strongly suspected of being the primary culprit. Cigarettes also appeared to contribute to the leading cause of death in the United States—heart disease coupled with strokes—although there was not yet definite proof of such. Interestingly, lung cancer, which was widely believed to be connected to smoking, was in the early 1960s a relatively small killer of Americans. Just one-sixth of all cancer cases leading to death were lung related, this making the Surgeon General hesitate to name cigarettes as a literal smoking gun.[43]

All kinds of causes of death were being closely examined in the hope of extinguishing them once and for all. Although it was relatively rare, sudden infant death justifiably terrified new parents in the postwar years, reason enough for a research program solely dedicated to it. Infants who died from the mysterious syndrome often had never been sick, this one thing that was so frightening about it. Pregnancies had also typically been normal, with no indication of the tragedy that would strike when the child was less than a year old. There also appeared to be no real correlation to class, geography, ethnicity, race, or gender, and it certainly was not strictly a modern phenomenon. (Hippocrates himself noted that infants were prone to die at forty days.) Despite having done nothing wrong, mothers usually felt tremendous guilt about their child's death. Doctors knew little about the syndrome in the mid-1960s but, because it came without warning, they considered it the cruelest of causes of death. About twenty-five thousand infants in the United States died annually in such a way at the time, enough to make new mothers and fathers check their baby obsessively to make sure he or she was still breathing. Death was believed to take place while infants were sleeping, this keeping many parents up until the wee hours of the morning. Suffocation had long been assumed to be the cause of sudden infant death, but this just was not so. Other possibilities—an enlarged thymus gland, an allergic reaction to cow's milk or the lack of breast milk, and a viral infection—were considered, but no one knew for sure. "The best we can do is alert parents to the disease—if it is a disease—and collect as much systematic data about it as possible," fretted M. Renate Dische, MD, in *Ladies Home Journal* in 1965, offering little comfort to young mothers and mothers-to-be.[44]

Americans had quite a lot less fear that they might die from an accident in the home, although it was just as common as sudden infant death syndrome. Accidents ranked fourth as a cause of death in the United States in 1965, with those occurring just in the home (twenty-seven thousand) greater than the number of deaths from tuberculosis, diphtheria, polio, syphilis, rheumatic fever, appendicitis, and murder combined. Dying from some diseases had fallen dramatically since 1950, but that was not the case with accidents, a matter of considerable concern for health professionals. Danger seemed to lurk everywhere in the home, especially with lots of children likely to be running around. Accidental death could result from falls, fire, home heating systems, electricity, poisoning (including that from automotive gas), cuts, firearms, mowers and lawn tractors, and even gardening, the American dream house a virtual war zone. "The sooner we start believing that accidents can happen to us in our own cozy homes," *Today's Health* warned parents, "the quicker we can make our home a safer—and happier—place in which to live."[45]

Regardless of the cause of death, some were taking notice that dying as a whole was not what it used to be. "Once upon a time man knew how to die," thought William Kitay, the deathbed vigil among family and friends at home a thing largely of the past. Now many died alone in hospitals, their minds clouded by drugs and bodies tethered to machines. "It seems that dying has become something to be ashamed of," said Kitay, writing in *Today's Health* in 1966, "a sign of weakness and defeat." Extending the process of dying not only created additional suffering but also was degrading, he and a growing number of people thought, an affront to what it meant to be human.[46]

Who or what had caused this cultural shift in how Americans died and, consequently, viewed death? Some felt that associations or societies dedicated to eradicating a particular disease were largely to blame, their fund-raising campaigns instilling the idea that death was something that could be conquered or "solved." Others, notably Jessica Mitford in her *The American Way of Death*, believed the funeral industry was largely at fault by making corpses as lifelike and beautiful as possible, an illusion that cloaked the reality of death. Physicians, too, were doing a disservice, it could be said, by preserving life at any cost and virtually ignoring the business of death and dying. It was true that medical schools in the mid-1960s did not offer courses in the care of the dying, choosing to focus exclusively on recovery. In short, a cured patient represented success while a dying patient signaled failure, a strange point of view given the inevitability and normalcy of death.[47]

Physicians' reluctance to inform patients they were dying was another important factor contributing to the denial of death in America. Relatives of the dying were complicit in this process, it need be said, their desire to protect loved ones only making the situation worse. There were moral, ethical, and practical reasons why the dying should be told they would not live much longer, those on the leading edge of an emerging "death with dignity" movement pointed out. Everyone had the right to "put their house in order," it could be argued, that house being both financial and spiritual. The knowledge that one would soon be dead was an impetus to review wills and trust funds as well as provide final direction to business partners, lawyers, accountants, and secretaries. Many spouses and children had to spend years and large sums of money untangling Byzantine estates simply because the dying person was not told of his or her dire condition. Knowing that one's days were numbered also encouraged the dying to find closure with their life and, perhaps, better prepare themselves for death. That the final stage of many people's lives was not only wasted but also experienced under false pretenses was simply wrong, more people were starting to think, the tide of death in America beginning to turn.[48]

Simone de Beauvoir's *A Very Easy Death* of 1966 vividly illustrated how little dignity there was in doctors' attempts to keep alive a body that was obviously dying. Witnessing the end of a loved one's life was never easy, de Beauvoir made clear in the memoir of her mother's death from cancer, but modern medicine had seemed to make the experience even more difficult. More than that, however, de Beauvoir blamed society as a whole for turning death into such an agonizing event for all parties involved.[49] In his review of the ironically titled book, Malcolm Muggeridge of *Esquire* suggested that it was our collective denial of death that was the bigger problem:

> Death is . . ., from the mid-twentieth century point of view, life's most appalling circumstance. We hide it away, pretend there's no such thing; persuade ourselves that "science" will soon ensure that it doesn't happen; deck up our corpses to look as though they are still alive, scent them and curl them and dress them as for a date or a ball.[50]

So committed to its way of life, where had Americans gone wrong when it came to its way of death?

DEATH WATCH

In answering that question, all roads seemed to lead to the principal location of death in America: a city or county hospital. While the dying were often not told of their condition, they ironically did receive special treatment in hospitals. If a patient was determined to be terminally ill, his or her name was often posted on what hospitals called the "critical patients' list." Patients on this list were allowed to receive visitors at any time rather than just during the designated hours. Being posted on the list also alerted hospital staff that death was likely to come soon, allowing them to make the appropriate preparations. Hospital morgues typically made a preliminary schedule for the upcoming week, using the list to plan workloads and to estimate the number of potential autopsies. Morgue attendants frequently consulted the list in order to know what body parts might soon be made available to doctors. Attendants were known to chat up nurses in this regard, knowing it was they who were most familiar with the patient's wishes and those of his or her family. Physicians were not shy in making their search efforts known, however, putting up signs like "Dr. X needs eyes" or "Dr. Y needs kidneys" everywhere from the admission nurse's desk to the doctors' lounge. Some doctors were also not above discussing patients' upcoming autopsies with colleagues before they were dead, hoping that their body parts would prove useful.[51]

There was, in fact, an incentive for hospitals to perform autopsies beyond learning more about the causes of death. In order to offer internships and residencies, a hospital had to have an autopsy rate of at least 25 percent of its deceased patients. (Autopsies were performed on about one-sixth of the 1.8 million Americans who died in the mid-1960s.) Prospective residents often asked administrators what its autopsy rate was, with doctors-to-be giving preference to those hospitals with the highest percentage. (Some teaching institutions such as Massachusetts General had a whopping 70 percent rate.)[52] Over time, doctors developed keen skills in knowing which relatives of dying patients were likely to grant permission for an autopsy and which were not. Interestingly, both uneducated and sophisticated people were considered the toughest nuts to crack, the more "average" the better when it came to allowing hospitals to do a postmortem examination of their next of kin.[53]

Sometimes, however, the dying never made it to the "critical patients' list." Those admitted in the evening to B-list (usually county versus metropolitan) hospitals in a near-death state—very low blood pressure, wildly erratic heartbeats, and a barely detectable pulse—were often left on stretchers and put in the lab or even a supply room. Because death was a virtual certainty, nurses were reluctant to assign these patients a bed, which would soon have to be stripped and remade. As well, the room in which the patient died would have to be scrubbed down and disinfected, too much of a bother given that he or she was on death's door. Once in a while, however, such patients would survive the night, in which case nurses scurried to assign them beds before doctors and relatives arrived.[54]

Still, nurses were generally better than doctors at predicting which patients would die on a particular day, as David Sudnow found in his extensive tour of American hospitals in the 1960s. Extra special treatment was given to patients determined to be on what doctors and nurses sometimes called a "death watch." These patients, in the final stage of dying, were viewed to be in a transitory state somewhere between life and death (not unlike that of a coma). As their condition swung more toward the death side of the seesaw, patients were treated more as bodies than people. Less attention was given to trying to save the patient or even making them comfortable and keeping their room clean, more attention to their clinical signs of life. Medication was frequently no longer administered despite doctors' standing orders, the patient still biologically alive but discussed, treated, and moved around more as an object than a human being.[55]

Worse, perhaps, relatives were more often than not present when their family member died. This was actually preferred by staff members at some hospitals who felt that relatives should not be the first to discover that a patient had died. Not having a relative present also freed up physicians to attend to other, healthier patients, something they would much rather do. Physicians treated dying and death matter-of-factly, their job understandably requiring they distance themselves emotionally from patients and the process as a whole. (Nurses, too, treated death routinely, except in the case of children when they were known to break down in tears.) The word *dying* was not even in most doctors' vocabulary, at least that used with family members, because of its vagueness, unpredictability, and negative associations. Transferring the dying patient's fate from the domain of medicine to that of "God" was a tricky business, requiring a keen sense of timing and tact. Prematurely telling a family member that their relative would die could very well overextend the predeath bereavement period, while waiting too long would not allow sufficient preparation time.[56]

When they did show up after their relative died, next of kin were sometimes asked if they wanted to view the body, an offer usually declined. Should one of them accept, the body was completely wrapped except for the head, which was neatly placed on a pillow. Nurses' aides beautified the head as best they could, a preview of the steps a mortician would take to make the body look as attractive and peaceful as possible. Physicians rarely if ever handled dead bodies except to pronounce death and in autopsies. (Senior physicians made more junior doctors turn bodies over if they happened to be present during an examination.) Nurses also considered moving bodies dirty work, leaving the job to aides and orderlies. Wrapping a body in a "morgue sheet" was done exclusively by orderlies working in teams, the vast majority of which were African American. This job, too, was disliked, however; no one seemingly wanted to have anything to do with death, even in the place where it occurred most often.[57]

Some hospital physicians' desire to snag body parts before the newly dead even cooled down added a new dimension to the cultural dynamics of death in America in the late 1960s. The first heart transplants in December 1967 made many fear that organs would become an even hotter commodity, adding fuel to the already contentious issue of the definition of death. Plainly put, it was not clear when a body was dead enough for its organs to be removed, and recently developed resuscitation techniques further complicated the matter. "As the state of the transplant art progresses, the moral and theological questions are certain to become more complex," *Newsweek* noted soon after the two heart transplants, with some scenarios right out of science fiction. Were human brain transplants next, for example, and, if so, would recipients still be themselves or would they now be, for all practical purposes, their respective donor? With the brain the repository of an individual's memory, intelligence, emotions, and personality, the answer was not at all clear.[58]

More practical and urgent questions related to medical transplants were swirling, the most important one being, "Who should live and who should die?" By June 1968, about 1,200 people around the world were alive after receiving a kidney transplant, with others getting a new lease on life after receiving a new pancreas or liver. With coronary disease the leading killer of Americans (and six hundred thousand citizens having a bum ticker), the possibility of heart transplants raised the stakes dramatically, increasing the "value" of dead people. Already there were many more people in need of a kidney than organs available, the beginning of what could be a booming postmortem transplant business. (A close, living relative could donate a kidney if there was a good match.) Those with nonfunctioning or failing kidneys were in a race against time, with access to dialysis limited and very expensive. Fifteen states still forbade any kind of organ donation, this adding to the preciousness of a healthy kidney that its recently dead owner no longer needed.[59]

Hospital staffs were thus faced with the extremely difficult decision of who should receive a scarce cadaver kidney, explaining doctors' not-so-subtle search to find one. Preferential treatment for the relatives of staff members appeared to be a factor in some hospitals' decision-making process, with political connections and social status other criteria entering the equation. Race, religion, and gender could also be a basis for discrimination, some worried, not to mention subjective measures like "value to society." Most hospitals were forming committees to try to establish objective, medical-based selection standards, hardly an easy task. Older patients and those with life-threatening conditions other than their bad kidneys were unlikely to be one of the lucky recipients. Traffic accident fatalities were the primary source of organs (sixty thousand occurred each year), with other kinds of accidents, sudden deaths, murders, and homicides accounting for most of the rest. Interestingly, despite the dearth of organs to be had, those of prisoners and suicides were turned down, the concern that pressure would be put on the former to be donors and that the latter were of "unsound mind and body." One day there would a "bank" of organs, those with foresight envisioned, and perhaps a card that those who wanted to donate their organs would carry to facilitate the current inefficient transplant logistics. Hope was also reserved for both animal-to-human transplants and artificial organs, each of these offering a potentially unlimited supply of much-needed replacement body parts.[60]

THE IMMORTALIST

Need it be said, the tremendous interest in organ transplants made it all the more important to know if and when a person was dead. The parallel development of mechanical means to sustain breathing and heartbeat made that moment more difficult for physicians to pinpoint, however. At the 1968 AMA annual meeting, one anesthesiologist proposed the rather novel idea of using a point-based "scorecard for death" to determine when artificial resuscitation could be stopped and the patient declared dead. Life (or death) was based on five physical functions: heartbeat, pulse, brain activity, reflexes, and breathing. Two points were earned for a function being normal, one if extraordinary measures were required to get a response, and none if no response could be generated. A total of zero points meant the patient was dead by any measure, at which point life support could and should be discontinued. If the patient was a donor, organs could then be removed and transplanted to someone in need, all parties content with the knowledge that no unsavory actions had been taken to procure the valuable parts.[61]

A committee of distinguished Harvard faculty members had a similar idea, using four criteria to determine brain (versus heart) death. Total unresponsiveness to all stimuli, the inability to move or breathe on one's own, no sign of reflexes, and no brain activity as measured by EEG equaled death, the Ad Hoc Committee of the Harvard Medical School to Examine the Definition of Brain Death concluded. Before the advent of respirators and heart pumps, vital body systems would collapse like dominos if one failed, with death taking place in a matter of minutes as the brain was deprived of oxygen. That all changed with the development of such devices in the late 1950s and 1960s, the burden now being placed on patients, families, and hospitals and the need for "fresh" organs demanding that death be, in a word, "updated." Although the committee suggested using four criteria to declare someone dead, it was clear they viewed a flat EEG (indicating no brain activity) as the most important measure (and heartbeat the least).[62] Their opinion, which was published in the AMA's journal, carried no legal weight but, given its source, was likely to be adopted by hospitals around the country. Meanwhile, at its 1968 meeting in Sydney, the World Medical Assembly established a policy stating that two physicians had to determine a patient was dead before he or she could be used as a source for organ transplanting. Again, however, the decision was not legally binding, used only as a moral guide for the world's doctors.[63]

All these tough issues would nicely go away if we could just abolish death, as Alan Harrington proposed we do in his 1969 *The Immortalist*. Given how much of life was really about death, he argued, we as a society should seriously begin to consider the possibility of immortality. Since most of us acted as if we would live forever, in other words, why not try to make it true? While his thesis might have been a stretch, Harrington made a compelling case that many of our pursuits, institutions, and philosophies were at their root ways we "competed" with death. Everything from art to war represented an attempt to cheat death, he suggested, our fear of aging and what followed driving both thought and action. "Death alone, all by itself, may be what is at the core of the human neurosis," Harrington posited, clearly borrowing ideas from everyone from Freud to Dostoevsky. Even religion was merely an excuse for not killing ourselves, he thought, and the late 1960s counterculture was less about peace and love than "an attempt to achieve immortality now." Criminals were not trying to get rich quick but doing their best to leave their mark on society. Likewise, the real aspirations of businesspeople and politicians were to be remembered after they were dead, this quest for immortality something we all shared. It was incumbent upon us to do everything we could to make this deep desire for eternal life more than an illusion, Harrington concluded, recent developments in medical science such as organ transplants, cyronics, and genetic research precisely the kind of efforts that should be stepped up to make immortality a reality.[64]

While he did not go nearly as far as Harrington, Howard Luck Gossage agreed that Americans were mighty neurotic when it came to death. Gossage, an advertising executive writing in *The Atlantic* in late 1969, thought "our society views dying as being in questionable taste despite the fact that ten out of ten still do it." How could something so universal be so unpalatable? Our bias toward youth over maturity explained a lot of it, he believed, our extended life spans favoring the front end while virtually ignoring the back end. Our language reflected this denial of death and the things that caused it. In fact, the word *death* was hardly used except in the legal arena, with surrogates like *passed on* much preferred. Similarly, people were now more likely to be "taken by" a disease rather than "died" from it, Gossage noted, this euphemism another way we repressed the uncouth idea and practice of death. Even the zodiac sign Cancer had become in some newspaper horoscopes "Moon Children," suggesting that just mentioning the "C word" in any context was something to be avoided. "This refusal to recognize a threatening phenomenon, or even to utter its name lest it gain power over you, is magical thinking of a primitive order," Gossage wrote, finding Americans to be a highly superstitious people when it came to death and dying.[65]

Rather than being just a silly superstition, however, Gossage believed there was a heavy cost to our denial of death. The refusal or inability to confront dying took the joy out of living, he was convinced, a direct correlation between accepting death and enjoying life. "When life stretches out indefinitely, world without end, there is no yardstick for momentary pleasures," he suggested, "and passing pains are blown up out of all proportion." Evading the subject had made life in America essentially a random series of events, with no real personal or social narrative for individuals to follow.

Gossage knew of which he spoke, having recently contracted leukemia that doctors believed would prove fatal in six months. The disease went into remission but soon reappeared; Gossage died just a few days after he finished his article for *The Atlantic*.[66]

As one of the most tumultuous decades in the nation's history wound down, social critics reflected on what they saw as the generally sorry state of death and dying in America. Death had somehow become disconnected from life, a tacked-on epilogue rather than the final and perhaps climactic chapter. "Instead of incorporating his mortality into his total view of what he is and how he should, instead of confronting his finitude with all the resources of myth and hope and wonderment that are his heritage, modern man seems to be doing his best to dismiss death as an unfortunate incident," *Time* magazine observed. Some of the top psychologists of the day warned that by abandoning the traditional view of death, "modern man" had, ironically, made life less meaningful. Carl Jung viewed death as "the fulfillment of life's meaning and its goal in the truest sense, instead of a mere meaningless cessation," while Rollo May believed that our repression of death had made modern life "banal, empty and vapid." Now that death from childbirth and among infants was relatively rare, the average American family often did not encounter the death of someone close to them for decades, an anomaly from a historic sense.[67] This was about to change, however, as death and dying entered a new orbit in its unpredictable trajectory.

Chapter Four

Living Your Dying

"Life is a terminal illness."
—Harvard Medical School student Jerry Avorn, 1971

A few days after Christmas 1970, members of the newly formed Institute of Society, Ethics, and the Life Sciences met in Chicago for a symposium called "Problems in the Meaning of Death." The organizer of the symposium, Leon Kass of the National Research Council, invited an all-star cast of experts in death and dying to try to answer such weighty questions as "What is death?," "What dies?," and "Is death a natural process or a disease?" Scholars from Indiana University, Cornell, and Harvard presented papers, as did a woman named Elisabeth Kübler-Ross, who was currently getting a lot of attention with her unusual views on terminal illness. "The meaning of death is an abiding human problem," noted Kass in his opening remarks, he and his colleagues in agreement that the issues surrounding the end of life were becoming more complex than ever.[1]

The members of the Institute had good reason to believe a closer examination of death and its "problems" was a worthwhile endeavor. Social and technological changes had already dramatically reshaped the culture of death in America, and the ever-growing powers of medicine were continuing to challenge some of our basic beliefs and values. The 1970s would prove to be arguably the most "problematic" period in American history when it came to the matter of death, however, as a number of events pushed the subject to the forefront of the national conversation. Like other taboos that had been pushed aside by the forces of modernism and the counterculture, death was ready to come "out of the closet," as one critic observed at the time. The process would not be an easy one, however, Americans' resistance to accepting death as a natural part of life a powerful thing to overcome.

AN ENGINEERING PROBLEM

One did not have to be a scholar to recognize that death in America remained a troublesome topic as the 1970s began. Although the fear of death was commonplace around the world, Americans seemed to have a particular dread that life would inevitably wind down like a clock or, worse, come to a screeching halt. Non-Americans perhaps knew this better than ourselves, able to see Yanks' trepidation of the Grim Reaper from an outsider's perspective. English essayist J. B. Priestley would often bring the subject up at dinner parties in this country, for example, gleefully watching as previously festive people began to squirm uncomfortably in their seats. British historian Arnold Toynbee was more direct. "Death is un-American," he flatly said, a violation of our constitutional rights to "life, liberty and the pursuit of happiness" and contradictory to the notion of the United States being an earthly paradise.[2] For American author William Saroyan, our entire capitalist system was a response to our terror of death. "Aspiration, accumulation, wealth, success, achievement . . . are fantasies of defense [to dying]," he suggested in *The Nation* in 1973, our busy lives and acquisitional pursuits just a futile attempt to put off the inevitable.[3]

Death had even apparently done the once unthinkable: leapfrog over what had traditionally been the country's most taboo topic. According to David Belgum, a professor of religion and medicine at the University of Iowa, death had surpassed sex as America's "most forbidden topic," the former a subject few now felt comfortable discussing. "Dying used to be openly discussed in our society but sex was obscene," he told a group of ministers in 1971, but recently the tables had been turned. The problem with this was not a moral one but that the dying were having trouble finding anyone to listen to them talk about their impending death and the effect it would have on their families. With death not permitted in polite conversation, Belgum implied, religious leaders should be particularly receptive if and when church members had the courage to bring up the tough subject with them.[4]

For a major social taboo, however, death was certainly making the rounds. More scholars were writing about death than ever before, for one thing, and three universities (Stanford, Oregon, and Chicago) were offering courses on the subject. Wayne State University even had a Center for Psychological Studies of Dying, Death and Lethal Behavior, with a similar research lab at the University of Minnesota. Death was also a hot topic in pop culture, as filmmakers, musicians, and novelists used it as a lens through which to tell their stories. Critics weighed in on why there was so much interest in death as the new decade began. In an increasingly individualistic society, confronting one's own mortality had taken on a special resonance, some argued, the fullest measure of someone determined by how he or she faced death. Secularism and, in particular, doubts regarding the existence of an immortal soul, were also making many Americans think long and hard about the sheer finality of death. The atomic bomb was another factor in the expansion of death in the American psyche, critics suggested, the possibility of millions or billions of people being exterminated in an instant still a relatively new and terrifying scenario. Less alarming but certainly of concern was the widespread belief that we were slowly destroying the ecology of the planet; this, too, ultimately spelling doom for its human inhabitants. (The first Earth Day was held in April 1970.) "Death is the most important question of our time," believed Yale psychiatrist Robert Jay Lifton, thinking that this "question" had led the United States to a critical juncture in its "psychohistory."[5]

Of course, Americans shared a direct connection with death through the Vietnam War and, in some parts of the country, urban violence. The unpopularity of the war, especially among the nation's youth, had much to do with the prevailing negative attitudes toward death, psychiatrists like Lifton argued. Lacking a noble purpose and seemingly not winnable, the Vietnam War had exposed our vulnerability and, by default, our mortality, shrinks suggested. One recent study of Americans' attitudes toward death also showed that there was a sharp divide between the rich and the poor. The disadvantaged typically viewed death as a personal calamity, filled with suffering, while the well-off reportedly worried more about how their demise would affect their loved ones. (Having life insurance partly relieved that concern, much to the delight of the insurance company that sponsored the study.) For most Americans, the expectation to live a long life had encouraged putting off thinking about death, something that proved troublesome when it did come calling. That cemeteries were usually located outside of cities was another reason most Americans treated death like a stranger, social critics hypothesized. It was true that city folk frequently asked the physicians of dying loved ones to preserve life at any cost, while those in rural communities, presumably more familiar with the natural cycle of life, did not. Would moving cemeteries closer to town, as they had been long ago, solve America's death problem?[6]

Unlikely, given the larger containment of dying and death to designated, out-of-the-way locations. "Old folks' homes" and terminal wings of hospitals (the latter sometimes referred to as "Death Valleys") were the primary launching pads for the nation's mechanistic approach to body disposal that would follow. After relatives were notified and organs removed if the newly dead was a donor, bodies were whisked to a mortuary for processing and presentation. "Cosmeticized and clothed as if he were a guest at his own wedding," as Kenneth L. Woodward wrote in *Newsweek* in 1970, bodies typically lay in coffins for a couple of days in the "slumber rooms" of funeral homes. Burial or cremation would follow after a thirty-minute or more service, the entire sequence of events handled with "cool, efficient dispatch," as Woodward described it. "Death in America is no longer a metaphysical mystery or a summons from the divine" but rather "an engineering problem," he observed, the situation still very much as Mitford described it in *The American Way of Dying* seven years earlier.[7]

THE DYING HOUR

Psychological and sociological reasons to explain America's death problem were all well and good, but the simple fact was that one of the principal players in the process—physicians—just did not think too much about the subject. Preserving the life of a patient was doctors' focus and, when that proved impossible, interest in the case soon faded. Historically, one of the very few responsibilities of physicians when it came to death was determining if a patient was no longer alive. This was not so clear before the twentieth century, when people were occasionally buried alive. (Some stipulated in their wills that their bodies must begin to smell before being put in the ground.) The only other major decision doctors had to make regarding death was whether or not to tell the patient he or she was dying. Medical technology and embalming had put the buried-alive matter to rest, so to speak, but this other issue remained essentially the sole commitment physicians had to make to death in the late twentieth century.[8]

Indeed, not much had changed in the medical community in the arena of death and dying since 1912 when Roswell Park, a Boston doctor, proposed in an article in the *Journal of the American Medical Association* that the topic warranted serious study. His call to create the field of "thanatology" (from the Greek word *thanatos*, or "death") was ignored, however, with little literature produced on the subject in the six decades that followed. There was Hereward Carrington's *Death: Its Causes and Phenomena*, also published in 1912, but chapters such as "Photographing and Weighing the Soul" suggested that Western medicine had a long way to go to make thanatology a legitimate discipline. For American physicians before World War II, death and dying were a consequence of disease, pure and simple, with little need to think beyond that clearly limited perspective.[9]

In the mid-1960s, however, death did begin to get noticed by the medical community, perhaps in part as a result of Mitford's groundbreaking book. Elisabeth Kübler-Ross's study of dying patients at the University of Chicago's Billings Memorial Hospital led doctors at other institutions around the country to believe that their concern with death had to be more than checking to see if there was a pulse. In 1967, a group of New York City physicians created the Foundation of Thanatology to promote the study of death and dying (while carefully avoiding the "D" word to lessen the chance of scaring away potential philanthropists). Despite the organization's wordsmithing, few angels were interested in providing support, something independent researchers in the area had also found. Whatever its name, death and dying remained largely off limits in Western medicine and American culture as a whole, the fear and discomfort surrounding them still very much in play.[10]

Much of this had to do with the basic physiology of death. As it had been for millennia, doctors' knowledge of death in the 1970s was almost entirely after the fact. Autopsies typically revealed the cause of death, now most often defined as when the brain stopped functioning. No electromagnetic activity indicated by the flatline of an EEG spelled brain death, something very rarely reversed. (Many doctors, following a set of standards proposed by a group at Harvard University in 1968, waited twenty-four hours and did another EEG test before determining brain death.)[11] The underlying cause of brain death was the lack of oxygen, this in turn generally a result of heart or lung failure. The number of ways this could happen were, however, many, this the area where Western medicine was largely in the dark. Physicians were experts in how a body stopped working, in other words, but why it did was a completely different matter. In a fair number of cases, in fact, doctors admitted they had little or no idea why someone died, quite amazing given how far medicine had come since the days of Hippocrates.[12]

The nonphysiological dimensions of death were even more mysterious, it could safely be said. The difficulty of most healthy people to think of their own death was almost certainly some kind of protective mechanism, something hardwired in humans (and probably all animals) to somehow help us survive.[13] Not just patients but doctors and nurses did not like to talk or think about death, as did the people in a position to fund research in the field. What people specifically feared about death was hard to say, but it was the loss of self or "me-ness" that seemed to be at the heart of it all. The instinctual fear of the dark and the unknown was also part of it, no doubt, this explaining how difficult it was to be comfortable with the prospect of one's demise. That doctors were reluctant to tell patients they were dying probably made the situation worse rather than better. Four out of five patients wanted to know the truth, studies showed, even if it was quite literally a death sentence.[14]

Why not give patients the bad news? Death was a defeat for practitioners trained to be "winners," firstly, the profession's notoriously healthy egos another contributing factor. (Some thought their healing powers were God-like or magical, so much so that they prescribed less medication than they should have to dying patients.)[15] In addition, doctors believed patients would find the truth too upsetting and thus weaken their fight for life. That any diagnosis was not 100 percent certain was another reason to avoid the conversation, doctors argued, convinced that patients really did not want to know. Given doctors' and nurses' tight lips, patients frequently had to piece together the real story, a complex process (sometimes involving the setting of verbal traps) described by Barney G. Glaser and Anselm L. Strauss in their book *Awareness of Dying*. "Our hospitals are admirably arranged, both by accident and design, to hide medical information from patients," they wrote in their book, something that both shaped and reflected Americans' death phobia.[16] Ironically, both nurses and physicians believed that most of their patients knew the hard truth anyway despite their silence (or outright lies), this only magnifying the "unmentionability" of death in terminal situations.[17] The staff's behavior and visitors' "distancing" were often tip-offs, with patients using these nonverbal clues as confirmation of what they intuitively believed.[18]

Herman Feifel, the editor of *The Meaning of Death*, thought there were other reasons that doctors were reluctant to tell their patients they were dying. Physicians had "significantly stronger death fears than do most other persons," he proposed, thinking that desperate measures to save lives were sometimes more for their own benefit rather than their patients'. Whatever the reason, most doctors just did not want to bring up the subject of death with patients who were likely to die. Surveys done by *Medical World News* showed that as many as 90 percent of American physicians were "opposed to telling the patient his illness is probably terminal," with a variety of strategies used to conceal the truth. Doctors' standard modus operandi was to not lie but not reveal anything more that what the patient specifically asked. For especially inquisitive patients, however, more drastic measures were required. Using medical jargon was always good, as was the constant ordering of more tests to put off a negative prognosis. If those didn't do the trick, simply keeping a stethoscope in one's ears and sticking a thermometer in the patient's mouth usually did.[19]

With such practices business as usual in the medical community, it could easily be seen how valuable a course being offered at Billings Memorial Hospital could be. Hundreds of nurses, interns, social workers, and chaplains-in-training had attended the "The Dynamics of Death and Dying" weekly seminar since it was first offered in 1964, perhaps the most unusual thing about it being that it was "taught" by dying patients. By listening to the terminally ill tell their stories and describe how they felt, "death professionals" were better equipped to deal with the emotional needs of the many others in similar situations they would encounter in their careers. Before "D. & D.," as it was commonly known, it was often the hospital's cleaning ladies who provided the most emotional support for dying patients, strangely enough; these women were the easiest to talk to and not afraid to broach the subject of death. Even the hospital's physicians had seemingly absorbed the essence of the seminar, these men and women of science more willing to be frank with their patients about their not-very-optimistic condition.[20]

There was, in fact, already a program designed specifically for physicians to be more conversant about death. In 1970, the National Cancer Institute (NCI) had launched a seminar teaching doctors how to overcome their own fears of death and how to be more supportive to dying patients. Once a week over the course of five months, a handful of physicians planning to specialize in the care of cancer patients got together in sessions that closely resembled group therapy. By 1975, fifty physicians had completed the seminar, all of whom were now caring for the terminally ill. Interestingly, one graduate acknowledged there was a direct link between death and medicine, the fear of the former acting as a sort of magnet to the latter. "I think it is the innate fear of one's own death that draws a person into medicine because he feels that it is as close as he can come to conquering it," said Joel Schwartz, a rare admission for a physician. Only when doctors experienced their own "existential anxiety" could they be of real help to dying patients, the leaders of the seminar argued, one of them, not surprisingly, a psychiatrist. Changing physicians' fundamental orientation from saving lives to, in the case of a dying one, easing his or her death was another objective of the NCI program. A seminar modeled after the one at NCI had been started at Grady Memorial Hospital in Atlanta, and elective courses in dealing with dying were being offered at Harvard, Tufts, and a few other medical schools. While the American medical community remained chronically death averse, progress was clearly being made.[21]

A similar course for the relatives of dying patients would have been a good idea. (Lemuel Shattuck in Boston was one of the first hospitals to offer therapy for families of dying patients.) If they knew the truth and believed the patient did not, family members also often did not reveal it or lied about the diagnosis in order to keep his or her hopes up. Deliberately lying about the condition could also be a form of denial for relatives, both that their loved one would die and that they would eventually die themselves. Patients would typically get suspicious, however; this attempt to protect a dying person rarely worked. In fact, the situation would frequently get worse, with the patient's anxiety growing as he or she picked up clues about the truth. The terms *dying* and *death* were particularly hard for relatives to say, as if their simple utterance would accelerate the process. Asking a family member if he or she was feeling better or how they slept were ways to avoid the more important conversation, with talk about an upcoming event such as a previously planned vacation another tactic to deny the reality. Ironically, once the jig was up (patients sometimes learned the truth by overhearing doctors consulting with each other), the family usually enjoyed the time they did have remaining by taking, as the expression went, one day at a time.[22]

Although most patients claimed to want to know the truth about their dire condition, some denied it when it was obvious they were dying. Even the arrival of a sibling one had not seen in years, sometimes coming from thousands of miles away, would not convince the patient that death was near. Such patients insisted they would recover from their fatal disease or they turned it into something much milder, like a particularly bad case of the flu. In his 1972 *On Dying and Denying*, Avery Weisman focused on this aspect of death, finding many forms of denial among the 350 terminal patients he studied. "My doctor wants to be sure I don't have anything serious," was one typical comment among the gravely ill in denial. Some would voice concern about who would care for them went they went home, something that was not going to happen. Others went so far as to go on a diet to rationalize their weight loss, Weisman, a psychiatrist at Harvard, found, the natural fear of death magnified by our "conspiracy of silence."[23] The inverse was when patients were sure they would die, which sometimes proved accurate and sometimes not so. ("I'm going to die tonight" was a fairly common prediction among the terminally ill.) Persuading those who believed they would die otherwise was not easy for doctors and nurses, especially among patients who had observed them purposely tell dying patients they would live.[24]

When it was clear a patient was going to die, everyone involved—doctors, nurses, family members, and close friends—often retreated, treating the individual almost as if he or she were already dead. This detachment was a kind of "pre-grieving" for the patient, psychologists suggested, a way of preparing for the inevitable. Not wanting to be around death also seemed to be part of this process, rooted perhaps in superstitions of the past. The unpredictability of how long it took for someone to die further complicated matters. Some went surprisingly quickly; others lingered for months when by all measures they should have expired in days. In either case, there was almost always some kind of a "fight" for life, the degree to which determined how long a patient would live. Doctors were reluctant to predict how long a dying patient would live precisely because of this unknown variable, often as surprised as everyone else by what followed. Acceptance of death typically brought with it a sense of peacefulness and even bliss, this final period of life sometimes referred to in centuries past as "the dying hour." The struggle over, patients began to distance themselves from life, preparing for whatever might come next.[25]

Fittingly, then, it was the final moments of life that were the most incomprehensible for anyone who had not experienced them. Case after case suggested the dying were ready to depart, an ironic twist given the dread most of us have toward death throughout our lives. That the dying did not find it difficult to die remained one of the great mysteries of life, and evidence for those inclined to believe in God or another supernatural force. Even doctors found this sense of surrender puzzling and enigmatic, hesitant to use the word *soul* or *spirit* but able to admit something divine appeared to be at work. "We are begging the issue by trying to define death when we can't even define life," said Austin Kutscher, one of the cofounders of the Foundation of Thanatology, as good an answer as any why the "problem" of death was not going to be solved anytime soon.[26]

AN INCREASINGLY FICTIONAL EXISTENCE

In fact, "thanatologists" could not even agree whether death was a "process" or an "event." Dying was generally considered the former and death the latter, but experts in the field had different points of view on the issue. A passionate debate on the death-as-process versus death-as-event quandary took place in the early 1970s between Robert S. Morison, professor of science and society at Cornell, and Kass of the National Research Council. Their papers were presented at the 1970 "Problems in the Meaning of Death" conference in Chicago and subsequently published in *Science* magazine. Morison thought that the traditional view, solidly entrenched in literature, the arts, and the legal system, was not just wrong but harmful to society. Borrowing A. N. Whitehead's theory of the "fallacy of misplaced concreteness," Morison argued that death (or life, for that matter) was not a thing and thus should not be considered or referred to as a discrete event. Something could indeed be dead but death itself was an abstract concept (like time or gravity), this distinction more than just semantics. Reifying and sometimes personifying death (into "Death") was the basis for the kind of medical intervention being done to sustain what Morison called "an increasingly fictional existence." Through technology, in other words, corpses were being kept alive because "death" (as a noun) was determined to not yet have occurred. For Morison, however, death was not "a single, clearly delimited, momentary phenomenon" with "no magic moment at which 'everything' disappears." Morison had some biology to back up his case; some parts of the body continued to "live" moments after the brain stopped functioning, and some cells could potentially exist indefinitely.[27]

While Kass agreed with Morison that prolonging life at virtually any cost was a serious problem, he disagreed with everything else his colleague had to say. There was a big difference between living and dying, Kass felt, and any attempt to blur the distinction between life and death was a bad idea. "Death is the transition from the state of being alive to the state of being dead," he simply explained, holding firm to the traditional view. Life and death were not part of a continuum, as Morison held, but separate entities with very different characteristics. The question of whether someone was alive or dead was thus not just a social or moral issue but a scientific one, Kass argued, with clearly defined boundaries between these two states both natural and necessary.[28]

Although they could not agree on what death exactly was, Morison and Kass each objected strongly to delaying its arrival through extraordinary means. Many felt similarly in the 1970s, with the debate over "death with dignity" increasing in intensity. It was becoming clearer that prolonging life was also prolonging dying, and that in many cases the former did not justify the latter. The reality that terminally ill patients were having to undergo unnecessary suffering (such as by force-feeding) caught the attention of the U.S. Senate, which formed a Special Committee on Aging in 1972 to investigate the issue. Legislators in a number of states had already introduced bills to make "death with dignity" legal, the passage of which would allow patients to die "naturally"; that is, without special intervention. ("Natural" death could be seen as analogous to the early 1970s interest in "natural" childbirth.) Those who testified were careful to distinguish "death with dignity" from euthanasia or mercy killing, which used proactive measures to end a life. As many as three-fourths of American doctors were already practicing "death with dignity," according to supporters, but making it law would ensure that virtually all did. By signing a document called a "living will," the bills proposed, individuals would be allowed to die in certain situations, with a relative or designated members of a hospital staff permitted to make the decision if no such document existed. Some objected to the legalization of living wills, believing that through them possibly fatal outcomes would be made certain. As well, the phrase *death with dignity* was vague, critics pointed out, insisting that doctors knew what was best for their patients.[29]

Propelled by the time's focus on the self, the "right to die" movement sailed ahead despite critics' warnings. In December 1973, the AMA passed a "death with dignity" resolution, allowing the terminally ill to be removed from life-sustaining machines if they had signed a statement saying as much. (Letting doctors administer heavy pain-killing drugs was another part of the resolution.) Even most church members had approved of the proposed resolution, the AMA had found, accepting the fact that death would likely be hastened because of these actions. The AMA flirted with a "brain death" resolution, but some members were not quite ready to urge that the legal definition of death be changed from the currently accepted criteria. Still, the AMA resolution represented a major milestone in the history of American medicine, arguably the first time doctors had directly confronted the moral and legal consequences of artificially prolonging life.[30]

Some felt, however, that "death with dignity" did not go far enough. "Our society's whole attitude toward suicide is profoundly wrong," wrote John Fischer in *Harper's* in 1973, challenging the widespread belief that taking one's own life was an immoral act. In certain situations, in fact, suicide (or "termination," as Fischer preferred to call it) was not just moral but sensible and even praiseworthy. When a human body became a burden, both to oneself and to others, and recovery was impossible, the decision to end one's life was logical and ethical, he argued. A more rational society would understand this, Fischer felt, hoping that we would come to our senses and allow this kind of termination to be practiced openly.[31]

Others, particularly those in the clergy and medical profession, did not share Fischer's view, not surprisingly. Despite what supporters of "death with dignity" claimed, it was the rare physician who believed in the early 1970s that a person had the right to die at the time of his or her own choosing. Some assuredly allowed dying patients to "slip away" without intervening, while others, fewer certainly, "helped along" the process through direct action. The majority, however, held fast to the imperative to keep a patient alive as long as possible by whatever means possible, something prescribed by Western medicine and implied by the Judeo-Christian ethic. But now that the average life expectancy of Americans was about double what it had been a century earlier, Fischer pointed out, it was time for the stigma of suicide to be removed. Nursing homes were full of octogenarians in pain and misery, he explained, with no recourse for them except to hope the end would come soon. Only a "change in the public consensus" could remedy the situation, he believed, calling for ordinary Americans to start talking about the important issue with others and with their doctors.[32]

A LEVEL OF TRANSCENDING AWARENESS

Given what a typical cancer patient had to endure as he or she gradually died, any proposal to add some dignity to the process sounded like a good idea. Progressive pain, not only from the disease but also often multiple operations, could not be fully eased by narcotics and sedatives of the day. One by one, organ systems would fail, part of the nasty downward spiral of a degenerative disease like cancer. Tubes connected to various parts of the body made the experience that much more unpleasant, all of this making one understand how a quick killer like pneumonia had become known as "the old man's friend." The psychological dimensions of such a process were arguably as bad. Terminal patients were typically isolated, with doctors and nurses prepared to talk about particular aspects of the illness or treatment but not the fact that the person was dying. In such a scenario, taking place in hundreds of hospitals across the country everyday, it is easy to see how the arrival of a nurse with a shot of morphine was the highlight of a dying patient's day.[33]

Needless to say, working in the terminal ward of a hospital was tough work. Although it was for a number of reasons one of the least desirable places to be assigned, nurses were almost invariably cheerful for the patients' presumed benefit. Many of them wore yellow plastic buttons with the ubiquitous smiley face, another attempt to make the ward less depressing. Terminal patients often did not want relatives and friends to visit, not wanting to be seen in what they felt was such a sorry state and demeaning position. It was also a chore for patients, typically feeling terrible from treatment, drugs, and the disease itself to be polite toward visitors. Not being able to do much besides watch television all day did not improve matters. While not wanting to die, many did not want *not* to die, their weariness and knowledge they would never really enjoy life like they once did creating a strong feeling of indifference to the whole sad affair. Although possibly saving patients or prolonging their lives was the official mission of hospitals, the actual, unstated purpose was to save the lives of future patients by learning from the dying ones. In teaching hospitals, it was especially obvious that terminal patients were in some respects "guinea pigs," there for the benefit of others down the road.[34]

Especially when viewed against the backdrop of the fading counterculture, one could expect more creative individuals to come up with some different ideas to help terminally ill patients. One of the more interesting was the use of LSD, a drug that had previously been given to mental patients and alcoholics as part of their therapy. A good number of these patients reportedly described the (positive) feelings of "dying" and "being reborn" while under the influence of LSD, leading some psychiatrists to believe the drug could be useful for the terminally ill. Proponents of LSD believed the drug should be used not just for therapeutic purposes but could perhaps revolutionize the way we thought about death. Once located within the provinces of philosophy and theology, death had over the past couple of hundred years migrated to the realm of medicine, a costly trade-off for Western civilization, some argued. "Somehow in the process, we have made death another mass-produced, impersonal commodity controlled by expert providers," thought Jerry Avorn, writing for *Harper's* in 1973. Avorn was not a shaman but a fourth-year student at Harvard Medical School, one of a growing number of health professionals who believed psychedelic drugs could possibly ease the transition from life.[35]

The epicenter of the LSD-as-therapy phenomenon was the Maryland Psychiatric Research Center in Catonsville, Maryland, right outside Baltimore. By 1973, psychiatrists at the center had been exploring the use of LSD for the dying for a few years without much public attention. Terminal patients' psychic anguish was as important as their physical pain, director Albert Kurland and his colleagues at the center believed. Their drug of choice was used in conjunction with counseling to help them achieve, as Avorn put it, "a transcendent level of awareness from which it may be possible for them to deal more easily with impending death." The intersection between dying and LSD went back to the early 1960s, when Eric Kast, a physician at the University of Chicago Medical School, found that the largely unknown drug had powerful pain-relieving properties. Kast administered the drug to terminal patients purely as an analgesic, thinking it was superior in some ways to opiates.[36] Kast noted a distinct side effect of LSD, however, as he mentioned in an article published in 1964:

> In addition to pain relief, these patients displayed a particular disregard for the gravity of their situations, and talked freely about their impending death with an affect considered inappropriate in our western civilization but most beneficial to their own psychic states. This approach to their disease was noted usually for longer periods than the analgesic action lasted.[37]

Just a year later, a staff member at Catonsville, diagnosed with untreatable cancer, volunteered to become the first terminal LSD subject. The group considered the results positive and, over the next decade, cooked up quite an eclectic therapy with psychedelics as the main ingredient. Psychoanalysis, music, neuropharmacology, Buddhist cosmology, existential philosophy, and Western medicine all went into the therapeutic mix, with the results designed to, per Avorn, "guide the dying patient through his suffering and, ideally, into a level of transcending awareness."[38]

Drug sessions at Catonsville (which followed conventional psychotherapy to help patients confront their mortality) were a lot more structured than those of recreational LSD users. In the morning, the therapist assigned to the case, along with a specially trained nurse, arrived in the terminal patient's room with a portable stereo, headphones, eyeshades, fresh roses, and a dose of LSD that was three or four times stronger than what was available on the street. As the drug took effect, the therapist encouraged the patient to pursue whatever "trip" the LSD led him or her on. Therapeutically, "bad trips" were considered as important as good ones, with any psychic journey, regardless of how disturbing, significant in some way. Absolute trust for the therapist was thus critical for the patient to not just face any demons that might appear but to let go of, in psychiatric terms, his or her ego structure. That achieved, the patient could "achieve a sense of unity with all creation so strong that the decomposition of his earthly body will seem infinitely less important," as Avorn described the experience.[39]

As suggested by the presence of the stereo and headphones, music was a vital part of the therapy. Therapists selected music based on "where" they thought the patient "was," with posture, gestures, and comments used as cues. That all Catonsville therapists had themselves underwent at least one such session also helped them know which musical direction to go. Wagner was considered very good for battle scenes, for example, while Debussy was deemed ideal for serene imagery. Just a few, specific selections were judged worthy for the much desired "peak" experiences in which transcendence was said to occur, however: the climax of Wagner's *Tristan and Isolde*, the "Transfiguration" portion of Strauss's *Death and Transfiguration*, and Gounod's *St. Cecilia Mass*.[40]

The highly unusual kind of therapy being used at Catonsville (the federal government had in the late 1960s squashed all other LSD research except there and a facility in Topeka, Kansas) had roots in humanistic psychology and religious mysticism. There was much anecdotal evidence to suggest that great joy could be realized by those who somehow suddenly gained a fuller understanding of the meaning of life. LSD appeared to augment what was sometimes referred to as the "death-rebirth-ecstasy" experience that typically left a psychedelic "afterglow." Long after the drug left the body, people retained a profound sense of clarity, this the state the researchers at Catonsville believed would prove therapeutic to the terminally ill. In some cases, patients were given DPT, a drug whose effects lasted three to four hours rather than the eight to twelve hours of medicinal LSD.[41]

How and why did the psychedelic experience lessen the psychological anguish of dying? Rather than be seen as the loss of self or "me-ness" and disappearance into a black void that so many feared, death often became viewed as a transition into a different kind of existence. That consciousness continued after the body died was a wonderful revelation, as was the discovery that one was part of an all-encompassing "cosmic unity." Leaders of the project at Catonsville admitted they did not know if what patients experienced was real or a drug-induced delusion but, given the very real therapeutic benefits, that was almost irrelevant. Interestingly, whether one was religious or not did not seem to matter, the results similar among atheists and the devout. What the terminally ill experienced while on psychedelics paralleled concepts found in Taoism, Hinduism, Christianity, Buddhism, and various forms of mysticism, more reason to believe that the trips they were taking were deeply spiritual journeys.[42]

Although from today's vantage point the use of psychedelics in any kind of medical setting seems odd if not unethical, that was less the case in the freethinking early 1970s. That psychedelics were clearly helping the terminally ill (and reportedly harmed no one physiologically or psychologically) was reason enough to continue the research, project leaders at Catonsville felt. While not everyone achieved cosmic consciousness, many did gain a greater insight into the meaning of death, most importantly his or her own. And as the initial research in the field showed, psychedelics helped the dying tolerate their pain, this alone making them a viable course of treatment. But with small samples and a "success rate" of LSD-assisted death therapy difficult at best to quantify, even the project's leaders had serious doubts that it would gain broad acceptance. Mind-altering drugs and death each remained cultural taboos in mainstream America, after all, making it very unlikely that the established medical community would embrace them when combined. Catonsville's predeath counseling component alone was considered too offbeat by most physicians, although that was about to change as death and dying began to assume a more prominent role in the United States.[43]

LAST RIGHTS

In fact, some research was showing that one did not need a superpowerful hit of acid to experience bliss before dying. Russell Noyes, a University of Iowa psychiatry professor, found that there was a common pattern to almost-fatal incidents with sudden death: resistance, review, and, finally, transcendence. In the "resistance" phase, the victim struggled to remain alive, the losing battle leading to a sensation of profound tranquility. At this point, Noyes discovered, some entered the "review" phase that was much like the proverbial life-passing-before-one's-eyes. Vivid memories flashed through the mind, a sped-up movie of mostly pleasant past experiences. Last was the "transcendence" phase that about one-quarter of the people Noyes studied had reached. Here time did not seem to exist, with flashes of light, visions, and feelings of ecstasy typical (and consistent with many culture's description of dying throughout history). And like the terminal patients on psychedelics, those who had close brushes with sudden death sensed the presence of "an outside force" and, more rarely, that of a fusion with nature. "It was the most perfect state of easeful joy that I ever experienced," said one person who almost drowned, claiming that he or she "understood everything." Someone who almost died by falling off a mountain reported that "a divine calm swept through my soul" and that "everything was transfigured, as though by a heavenly light." Noyes frankly did not know what to make of it all but was understandably intrigued, mostly because subjects told much the same story.[44]

Whether or not bliss was part of the dying process, chemically induced or otherwise, there was growing evidence to conclude that the idea of death was in ascent in America in the early 1970s. That these years represented one of the decidedly low points in the nation's history probably had something to do with it. Political, social, and economic upheaval—especially the seemingly unsolvable problems of overpopulation and pollution—as well as general "malaise" were perhaps making many think of mortality more than they previously had. "Old age, dying and death are coming out of the closet," observed Leonard C. Lewin in *The Nation* in April 1973 after noticing that mass-circulation magazines were now regularly publishing articles about different aspects of the end of life. "The way publishers follow trends," he remarked, "one might think concern with death were something recently 'discovered,' like air pollution or ecology." Lewin thought that Americans' struggle to find closure with Vietnam had a lot to do with the media's interest in dying, the lingering unpopularity of the war fueling a more general sense of disillusionment.[45] Others noticed that attitudes toward death in America had recently been irrevocably altered. "For some reason death is coming into its own," wrote William Hamilton in *The New Republic* in November of that year after observing conferences, medical schools, churches, and community groups "huddling together over it." Hamilton viewed death as the latest American obsession, following in the not-so-proud tradition of other major post–World War II concerns such as anxiety, alienation, and violence.[46]

In addition to the flurry of magazine articles, lots of books were being published on the subject, more proof of death's increasing "popularity." One of them was *Death in American Experience*, a collection of essays on the topic by some top intellectuals. The book asked and tried to answer some very big questions. Did Americans have a unique avoidance of death? Is fear of it a universal experience? Was transcending the fear possible? Through some especially weighty writing ("Death is now understood to be an important mechanism enhancing the adaptive flexibility of the species, through the sacrifice of individuals," began one sentence), the book demonstrated the complexity of Americans' relationship with death and dying.[47] More accessible was David Hendin's *Death as a Fact of Life*, an overview of the "right to die" debate, and Sharon Curtin's *Nobody Ever Died of Old Age*, a passionate appeal for Americans to honor and respect the entire life cycle, including the final part. "Pretending that death doesn't exist, or is somehow in bad taste, robs the old of the chance to complete their life," Curtin wrote in her book, an appeal that would perhaps resonate more today than in the heyday of American youth culture.[48]

Others agreed that the country had, rather suddenly, rediscovered the reality of death. "About two million people die each year in the United States, and the American culture has finally decided to take note of this fact," Daniel C. Maguire wrote in *The Atlantic* a couple of months after Hamilton's article appeared. Death was having its "belated due," Maguire thought, his forthcoming book *Death by Choice* testament to that idea. Unlike some others (such as Toynbee), Maguire thought the boom in thanatology was a good development, something that could take place only within a mature society. Advancements in medicine had forced the issue, specifically the debate over when someone was dead. "Death with dignity," not that long ago somewhat of a fringe idea, was turning into a full-fledged movement. Over fifty thousand Americans had requested copies of "A Living Will" from the New York–based Euthanasia Educational Fund in 1973, with many more than that expected the following year because of the passage of the AMA resolution. More amazingly, a bill for the legalization of euthanasia had recently been proposed in the New York State legislature (led by physicians wanting to avoid malpractice suits), with such a bill pending in Hawaii. And in Montana, a proposal to "allow every citizen to choose the manner in which he dies" had been entered into that state's Constitutional Convention, another sign that Americans across the country wanted to be in control when it came to literal matters of life and death.[49]

One of the more interesting points that Maguire, a Catholic, had to make was that the United States was hardly innocent when it came to intentionally causing death. In at least some parts of the country, no less than four ways of ending human life were perfectly legal: abortion, capital punishment, war, and suicide. "Mercy killing," however, which arguably had better intentions than all of these, was illegal everywhere. Our history, checkered with wars including the one just winding down in Southeast Asia, was an undeniably violent one. "We have overestimated our right to kill in a military setting, and underestimated it in some medical and private settings," he wrote, a claim that would be difficult to dismiss. Things were beginning to change, however, as Americans gradually embraced the notion that ending a life could be an act of compassion. "These are times when the ending of life is the best life offers," Maguire concluded, confident that "moral man will see this."[50]

Another book, appropriately titled *Last Rights*, also made "a case for the good death," as its subtitle went. A new attitude toward death was needed in America, Marya Mannes argued in her book, calling for honesty and confrontation to replace the hypocrisy and evasion surrounding the subject.[51] *Last Rights* was also an unapologetic manifesto for the legalization of euthanasia, however; something some reviewers believed it went way too far. Writing for *Esquire*, for example, Malcolm Muggeridge was highly critical of Mannes's treatise, thinking the realization of state-sponsored euthanasia would lead to nothing less than wholesale "slaughter." Seeing big money to be saved by closing hospitals and homes for the mentally ill and senile, the government would actively push for "mercy killing" any chance it could, Muggeridge believed. "Just a little whiff of euthanasia, and you can get rid of the lot, and on the highest principles of humanity!," he exclaimed, thinking such a scenario would be awfully tempting to bureaucratic wonks eager to cut costs wherever they could. (Remember 1974 was an especially bad recessionary year.) Call it whatever you want, but euthanasia was really eugenics, and not that different from what the Nazis had done thirty years earlier to the rest of the world's horror. Although such a future was horrific, Muggeridge considered it inevitable, a logical step after the country's legalization of contraception and abortion. "The prospect of taking a crushing load off the national budget by liquidating the unproductive and unfit" would prove irresistible, Muggeridge fretted, his admittedly Catholic orientation obviously informing his point of view.[52]

Another book published in 1974, Philippe Aries's *Western Attitudes toward Death*, put the transformation of death and dying in America in the twentieth century in valuable context, showing how the changes that took place were part of a much longer historical process. In the Middle Ages, it was not unusual for Europeans to dance, gamble, and drink in cemeteries, a good example of what Aries referred to as the "promiscuity between the living and the dead." This changed between the thirteenth and seventeenth centuries, Aries argued, as Europeans gradually became uncomfortable with the intimate relationship they once had with death. By the late nineteenth century, death and dying in Western society had become distasteful and grotesque, a perspective that accelerated through the first half of the twentieth century. "Given that life is always happy or should always seem to be so," he wrote, "it is no wonder that men should wish to keep death a secret from one another, and that strong emotions in the face of death should be discountenanced."[53]

The surge in magazine articles about death and dying and a bevy of new books on the subject (others included Stewart Alsop's *Stay of Execution: A Sort of Memoir*, Melvin J. Krant's *Dying and Dignity: The Meaning and Control of a Personal Death*, and John Langone's *Vital Signs: The Way We Die in America*) caused considerable puzzlement to some. "What are we to make of the intensified interest these days in the subject of death and dying?," asked Giles Gunn in *The New Republic*, not sure if Americans were finally getting comfortable with the subject or just wanted to be titillated by it. In their *Living and Dying*, Robert Jay Lifton and Eric Olson argued it was the former, with a cultural shift taking place that posed major implications for American society. The authors argued that it was the rise of "nuclearism" that made death "unthinkable," the extinction of the individual now inexorably linked with that of civilization itself. The thought of it intolerable, death had been individually and collectively repressed, their psychoanalysis-based theory went, making us neurotic when it came to the prospect of life ending. Naturally, as Freud himself might have suggested, the solution was for us to directly confront our psychosis of death, something we thankfully were beginning to do.[54]

Death also on his mind, Michael J. Arlen decided to take an unorthodox approach to figuring out how Americans felt about the subject: watch television. Arlen's uncle had recently died in a way with which he was unfamiliar—calmly and methodically—describing his passing (from a heart attack at age seventy-three) as "a modest, commonplace event." Was there some kind of "invisible community" where mortality was treated as a "mass, ongoing, collective activity," Arlen wondered, an ordinary occurrence? Arlen believed turning to another invisible community, television, might provide some answers, reporting his findings in a 1975 issue of *The New Yorker*. For one week, ten to twelve hours a day, Arlen watched television, recording any reference to death or dying. Fictitious (always violent) death popped up regularly on soap operas, cop shows, westerns, and in movies, and the real variety on the news as a result of airplane, bus, and train crashes, mine disasters, murder, war, starvation, drowning, earthquakes, and fire. Radio and television star Jack Benny happened to die that week, as did Amy Vanderbilt, the etiquette columnist (with suicide suspected of the latter). Finally, a bully appeared to die from a fall in an episode of *Popeye* (conveniently landing in a coffin), as did a few bandits in another episode of the cartoon when they were blown up by dynamite.[55]

Did anybody around the world, besides Jack Benny, die calmly and methodically like his uncle, Arlen had to ask? It was hard to know what his nonscientific survey revealed, but one thing seemed certain: Americans sure liked to see violent and tragic death on television. Ordinary death was almost entirely absent, the narrative presented on television very different from what his uncle and millions of other Americans experienced every year. (Dying in bed from a disease, usually brought on by old age, was how most of us expired.) Americans preferred death stylized, a euphemism for the real thing, if television was a mirror of society, the result of either a violent crime or a tragic event. Privately, Americans undoubtedly experienced grief, but publicly the emotion did not even seem to exist, this as disturbing as our equation of death with violence and tragedy.[56]

Death was not at all like it was on television, Stanley Keleman argued in his book *Living Your Dying*. It was not surprising that death was portrayed horrifically in popular culture, Keleman thought, given Americans' prevailing mind-body orientation. Our "disembodied" culture, in which the mind ruled, had turned death into the ultimate enemy because it threatened to destroy our life support system. However, humans had a built-in genetic program specifically for dying, Keleman believed, a natural device that was beneficial if we only could tune into it. Our fear of death was largely artificial or constructed; in other words, something we could and should unlearn by "living our dying."[57]

With death and dying so pervasive in the American zeitgeist in the mid-1970s, it was almost inevitable that advice regarding how to perform them well was forthcoming. In "The Gentleman's Guide to Death," which ran in *Esquire* in 1975, J. P. Donleavy offered suggestions for going off into that good night properly, with both taste and grace. His tips were many and, while humorous, quite sensible. Choose a final resting place free from dampness. Do not skimp on a mausoleum if you can afford one in the first place. Be neat if opting for suicide, meaning no hanging, shotguns, or poison. Keep final letters brief and unapologetic. With so many self-help guides offering instruction on how to improve one's life in the 1970s, why not one on how to improve one's death?[58]

Not even a guide to death could adequately prepare Americans for *Dying*, however, a documentary that ran on PBS stations the following year. Three terminal cancer patients in the Boston area were featured in the film, with viewers afforded the rare opportunity to enter the lives of those knowing they would soon die. Most impressively, perhaps, the film showed that the ways in which people died varied tremendously. "People die in the way they have lived," its creator, Michael Roemer, put it, believing that "death becomes the expression of everything you are." Sally, forty-six-years-old but looking much older, returns home to die, fearlessly accepting the fact that it was her time to go. It is a much different story for thirty-three-year-old Bill, whose wife, Harriet, blames him for abandoning her and their two sons by dying. "The longer this is dragged out, the worse this is going to be for all of us," she tells him, his final stage of life hardly the wonderful experience Kübler-Ross thought it could and should be. Finally, we see Reverend Bryant, a fifty-six-year-old pastor at peace with his life and death. Surrounded by his family and congregation, Bryant was convinced he was "living some of [his] greatest moments," this despite the fact that he was dying. "I don't think Rockefeller could be as happy a man as I am," he says in the film, a perfect example of "the good death" for which we all hope.[59]

THE FINAL STAGE OF GROWTH

Americans were in fact doing everything they could to increase the odds they, too, could experience a "good death." Already a contentious issue, whether a person had the "right to die," as the "death with dignity" move-ment was also known, reached a boiling point in the mid-1970s. By late 1975, eleven states were considering bills to make "passive euthanasia" le-gal, with another three debating "active euthanasia," in which a lethal drug would be injected at the dying patient's request. No country had yet to legalize this latter form of "mercy killing," a clear violation of the Hippocrat-ic oath, although it no doubt took place.[60] The language and specifics varied from state to state, but the basic idea was the same: allow individuals to decide that extraordinary measures not be taken to keep them alive if they had no brain function. Living wills were becoming increasingly popular but were not legally binding.[61]

While legislators quibbled over the pros and cons of "death with dignity," one particular case made the issue front-page news. A New Jersey judge refused to allow the respirator to be removed from a twenty-one-year-old woman, Karen Ann Quinlan, as her parents had requested in court (after consulting with their priest). Quinlan had went into a coma some seven months earlier after drinking a few gin and tonics and taking a mild tranqui-lizer but, while in a "persistent vegetative state," she was not brain dead. "Humanitarian motives cannot justify the taking of a human life," said Judge Robert Moir Jr. in his ruling, arguing that such a decision was a strictly medical one. Quinlan's physicians had opposed disconnecting the machine, claiming such an act could be considered homicide in that state. The broader significance of the Quinlan case was that the "right to die" would be made on an individual basis, with doctors determining what was best for each patient. But would doctors and families want such machines turned on in the first place if they could not be legally turned off, many reasonably wondered?

Malpractice suits, already a big concern among doctors and hospitals, could also jump as a result of the decision, some feared, with families and the medical community perhaps more likely to disagree about what to do.[62]

"Right to die" and "death with dignity," phrases Americans had been becoming more familiar with for years, were now suddenly the stuff of watercooler talk and cocktail party conversation. The Quinlan case served to both personalize and polarize the issue, the tragic plight of a real, young, and pretty woman making the concept much more than an interesting exercise in ethics and morality. Experts on both sides of the fence immediately weighed in. Christiaan Barnard, the famous heart transplant pioneer, for example, quickly came out on the "doctor" side. Physicians were "the only people qualified to decide" if and when a particular patient should be allowed to die, Barnard felt, with symptoms, complications, and possible procedures all important variables to consider. "You treat each case on its own merits," he flatly stated, a family much too emotionally invested and technically ill qualified to make such a decision. Edmund Pellegrino, a professor of medicine at Yale, had a much different view. Certainly an individual had the right to participate in the decision to let nature take its course when no positive outcome was possible, he told *U.S. News & World Report.* "Give the physician too much power, and it can be abused," Pellegrino added, believing the family should be the advocate for the patient for a case like Quinlan's.[63]

The Quinlan family agreed, of course, and decided to appeal Judge Moir's decision to the Supreme Court of New Jersey. Meanwhile, Wells Fargo guards protected Karen's room from the many people who wanted to see her. Faith healers were coming to St. Clare's Hospital in droves, all of them claiming to be able to offer cures. Considerable numbers of the media were also showing up, hoping to get what would be a very lucrative story or, better yet, a photo. Some photographers arrived disguised as priests in pursuit of the picture *National Enquirer* announced it would pay $10,000 to have. (The Quinlans themselves received an offer of $100,000 for a photo of Karen in the ICU.) In March 1976, four months after the initial ruling, the appellate court unanimously reversed Moir's decision. "Ensuing death would not be homicide but rather expiration from existing natural causes," the court stated in what was the first right-to-die ruling in legal history, much to the joy of the Quinlan family and fellow supporters. A couple of months later, Karen was taken off the respirator and transferred to a private room. A month after that, she was moved from St. Clare's Hospital to a nearby nursing home. Karen was still hooked up to feeding tubes and given antibiotics for her recurring infections, but the Quinlans had gotten their wish.[64]

The trickle-down effect from the Quinlan case was immediate. Hospitals around the country scurried to enact "right to die" policies to protect both themselves and their patients. In November 1976, one year after the lower court's decision in the Quinlan case, California became the first state in the nation to pass a "death with dignity" law by making a living will a legally valid document. With a one-page "Directive to Physicians" (which was made freely available at both doctors' offices and retirement communities), the state's Natural Death Act ensured that physicians and hospitals would not be sued for withholding or withdrawing life-sustaining treatment. In California, at least, the major obstacle to "death with dignity" was thus removed. Within a year, seven states—Arkansas, Idaho, Nevada, New Mexico, North Carolina, Oregon, and Texas—had passed similar legislation.[65] Karen Ann Quinlan had of course never signed a living will, but many others, having heard about her situation, no doubt would.[66] Even the Pope had said that it was morally justified to withhold heroic measures from people who were about to die, a clear sign of how broad-based the "death with dignity" movement now was.[67]

Largely because of the state-by-state legalization of the right to die, Americans were in the mid-1970s talking about death with more candor than ever before. Someone arguably more influential than the Pope when it came to dying was in the process of taking the conversation to an even higher level, however. The meteoric rise of Elisabeth Kübler-Ross began a decade earlier, when she reportedly could not find a dying person to interview in a six-hundred-bed hospital. That no one had a terminal illness in the hospital, as doctors and staff maintained, was absurd, making her realize how taboo a subject death was not only in American society at large but also within the established medical community. Over the next decade, Kübler-Ross built a miniempire devoted to death and dying, her seminars, public talks, and 1969 best seller *On Death and Dying* heavily responsible for changing how Americans felt about the topic. No one had ever presented such a complete theory of the dying process, her five psychological states (denial, anger, bargaining, depression, and acceptance) resonating with both professionals and ordinary people thrust into the orbit of death.[68]

In the mid-1970s, Kübler-Ross, who received her medical degree in Switzerland before becoming a psychiatrist, was focusing on hospice work (especially among children), a practice she and a few others had imported from England. As she argued in her 1975 book *Death: The Final Stage of Growth*, the grief and pain often associated with the dying of loved ones did not have to be a terrible experience, as Americans typically treated it. In fact, as the title of her book suggested, the death of a family member or friend could be one of the richest parts of one's life. Anguish, suffering, and trauma ultimately changed people for the better, she believed after spending thousands of hours in the company of the dying and those close to them, a lot of good eventually coming from the bad. (It often took years for people to appreciate what they gained from the death of an individual, she made clear.) Kübler-Ross's even larger point was that the dying taught others how to live, making us realize how precious life was. Was it surprising that with such a life-affirming message, she was able to help popularize the once unmentionable subject of death?[69]

Kübler-Ross was not the only one "reinventing" death in America, however. In 1975, William Roberts, an ex-public relations executive in Los Angeles, founded Threshold, which supplied "death companions" to the dying. Threshold was a for-profit business, charging lonely, isolated clients $7.50 an hour for some companionship with a complete stranger. Roberts believed this could be just the beginning of something much bigger, however. "I've even thought of making some kind of production out of it—like having the Mormon Tabernacle Choir come sing at your bedside, if you could afford it," he told *Time* magazine, thinking that dying was "spectacular."[70] Up the coast, the terminally ill in the Bay Area could contact the Shanti Project for help and comfort, with nearly one hundred volunteers available for emotional counseling or just running errands. Shanti (Sanskrit for "inner peace") staffers would make visits to people's homes or hospitals, doing whatever they could to make the situation a little better. There was a tremendous lack of support for the dying and their loved ones, the founder of Shanti, Charles Garfield, believed, agreeing with Kübler-Ross that the final stage of life could be a blessing rather than a curse. Many more similar projects had popped up around the country, evidence that more Americans were at least attempting to embrace the notion of death.[71]

A MORE DEATH-ACCEPTING CULTURE

By the end of the 1970s, there was little doubt that death and dying had become an integral and passionate part of the national zeitgeist. "Americans by the millions are taking a new and unflinching look at the reality of death and how to cope with it," observed Stanley N. Wellborn in *U.S. News & World Report* in late 1978, thinking a "death awareness movement" was afoot. Wellborn astutely recognized that the heart of the movement was Americans' desire to regain control of their dying process and, if necessary, that of their loved ones. A confluence of forces had made death and dying— once as simple as could be—a highly complex affair, the Karen Ann Quinlan case an extreme example of what could happen when a family's wishes collided with medical technology and the legal system.[72]

Looking back, it was abundantly clear that death and dying had come a long way since the end of World War I, mirroring the professionalizing of American society (as well as its litigiousness). Prior to the war, doctors were much more forthcoming about a patient's dim prospects to pull through, and neighbors prepared to dig the grave of a member of their community. It was not unusual for young girls of the nineteenth century to mention death in their needlework, illustrating how even children accepted dying as a basic fact of life. ("When I am dead and in my grave and all my bones are rotten look at this and think of me when I am quite forgotten," went part of one New England sample from 1841.)[73] Now a number of powerful institutions claimed to know what was best for the dying and were jockeying for control of an individual's final days. Could Americans recover the ability to be in charge of their own death?[74]

No one could answer that question, of course, or even explain exactly why Americans had rather suddenly become "aware" of death. One theory was that death was simply the final taboo to be conquered, all the others crushed by the triumph of modernism in the twentieth century. Others proposed that death and dying, once something everybody had to be cognizant of, was now primarily the province of "old people," a result of the aging population. Some 80 percent of the 1.9 million deaths in the United States in 1978 were of those sixty-five-years-old or older, making it supposedly easier for younger people to think and talk about it. Relatedly, the rise of youth culture in the 1960s and 1970s could be said to have made death and dying more apparent, a violation of young people's adulation of beauty and physical fitness.[75] One could also make the case that the health craze of the 1970s had brought more attention to death, all the jogging and macrobiotic food in the world unable to help you if a fatal disease or drunk driver came your way.[76]

With no definitive answer, more theories were proposed to explain the death awareness movement of the late 1970s. The "Bomb" had changed everything, one went, the constant threat of nuclear war and annihilation of the human race bringing death into the open. The media explosion of the last couple of decades was another explanation, with television and a new generation of filmmakers each making death more visible and visceral. Julius B. Richmond, the nation's Surgeon General, had a different idea. "After 20 years of social ferment from the civil rights revolution to Watergate, we've entered a quiet period politically," he proposed in 1979, Americans now able to focus more on themselves, including their mortality.[77] Last, the secularization of Western society could be at the root of it all, death increasingly disconnected from Christianity and its assumption of an afterlife. "For better or worse, America now seems on its way to becoming a more death-accepting culture," Wellborn concluded. What that meant for the nation was a question that could only be answered in the future.[78]

Chapter Five

The Other Side

"The life story of every human being is a variation on the theme of loss through death."
—Herbert and Kay Kramer, *Conversations at Midnight* (1993)

In May 1994, Kirkpatrick Sale, a writer for *The Nation*, mused about how to kick-start the flagging American economy. With the collapse of the Soviet Union in the early 1990s, death should be established as our new archenemy, Sale proposed, an action that would be in the nation's best interests. It was the battle against communism that fueled our economy during the boom of the postwar years; after all, the creation of the military-industrial complex was an effort that put lots of money in lots of people's pockets. But now that communism was kaput we needed another villain to spark new technologies, seed new industries, and encourage massive bureaucracy and, with death, we had exactly that. Universally feared and despised and, more important, unbeatable, death was even better than communism in some respects, Sale thought. Unlike some "puny ideology that crumbles after a few decades," he wrote, death was "something we can set our society against four-square . . . and *never* vanquish." While perhaps having a little fun at his readers' expense, Sale seemed to be onto something. For the first time in the nation's history, the government was spending more money on health care ($267 billion) than the military ($261 billion). The emerging "medico-industrial complex" might be the best thing to happen to the United States since the Cold War, economically at least.[1]

An official pronouncement that death was our archenemy was largely unnecessary, however. Over the course of the 1980s and early 1990s, death was elevated to a status it had never achieved in this country, with the medical community waging an active war against it just as many citizens decided to make it a close ally. An unmentionable topic just a generation earlier, death continued to come out of the closet through these years as a wide range of social factors came into play. The aging of baby boomers to middle age was the most important of these, as thirtysomethings and forty-somethings dealt with the aging and death of their parents. Realizing they, too, were mortal (despite all the steps they were taking to slow the aging process), boomers adopted a proactive attitude toward death, seeking ways to manage and control their ultimate demise. Other events, notably the AIDS epidemic, brought death further into the national conversation. Being aware or conscious of one's impending death took on a certain cache, an indicator of a certain kind of enlightenment. Rather suddenly, dying a "good" death, whether naturally or through some kind of intervention, was part of the public discourse, as was a pronounced interest in what might come next. In the early 1990s, death emerged as a bona fide theme in popular and consumer culture, no longer pushed to the margins because of the shame only recently associated with it. Death had become, in a word, mainstream, Americans seemingly ready to acknowledge its presence even if they could not accept its full consequences.

A GOOD DEATH

One sign that death was becoming less of a forbidden topic was simply the growing number of people openly talking or writing about it, in part a by-product of the 1970s self-help movement. The subject came up frequently in "life-study" research, a bit ironically, with psychologists gaining insight into the emotional roller coaster of a loved one's death through extensive inter-views or "portraits." In 1980, for example, Thomas J. Cottle, a lecturer on psychology at Harvard Medical School, spent hours listening to a forty-year-old Bostonian recount his recent experience watching his mother die over a period of several months. Although observing the day-by-day physical dete-rioration of his mom—thinning hair, increasingly transparent skin, and ever blacker-and-bluer arms from the needles—was of course difficult, the man seemed to have an appreciation for being part of the profound experience. Besides providing some sense of closure, the daily bedside vigil in a hospital served to forge memories of his mother that he otherwise would not have had. "I can still see the curve of her head; never had seen it that way before, and I knew her almost 40 years," he told Cottle, just one of many details for which the man felt grateful.[2]

Just as common, however, were feelings of regret among those who did not experience the death of a loved one in a way they later wished they had. Seven years after the death of his father, for example, writer Anthony Brandt described the missed opportunity to tell his dad what was really on his mind while the man lay dying in a hospital's intensive-care unit for four days. "I visited him three times and never said what I wanted to say, so there were no last words and there was no benediction," Brandt wrote in 1982, clearly still upset about it. What did Brandt want to say? Knowing that his father, not a religious man, feared death, the son wanted to tell him to not be afraid, this the most important and meaningful thing he could have said. "If I would have pulled his fear into the open, I tell myself now, got it out there where we would all look at it, perhaps he might have risen to the occasion and exorcised it," Brandt explained, the right last words for his father never spoken.[3]

Simply acknowledging the fear associated with death was an indication of the more open climate surrounding it. The fear of death was more pervasive than popularly believed, many felt, the end of life a topic that often simply could not be dealt with in ordinary conversation. Rather than fear death or sublimate it, however, some argued it was better to think of it often and, ideally, consciously prepare for and even welcome it. Doing so helped immensely to live a good life, these folks, many of them with religious backgrounds, insisted, this perspective likely to encourage acts of honesty, courage, freedom, and community. "The point of everything is to die a good death, so to live accordingly," wrote Michael Novak in the *National Review* in 1980, his Catholic upbringing a wonderful foundation to do just that.[4]

Whether philosophically motivated or otherwise, a surprising number of people near or at midlife appeared to be giving more thought to the subject of death as the end of the century approached. Ironically, having a first child, as many baby boomers were doing, occasionally was the cause to think about death, the beginning of a new life mentally triggering the consequences of one's own life ending. (The first purchase of life insurance was and is often made upon the birth of a child, something the industry has fully exploited for decades.) Losing a parent was another reason to, naturally, as was when a parent of a close friend died. Reaching the age when a parent died also sometimes brought forth thoughts of mortality, the occasion potentially more emotional than the parent's death at the time itself.[5] For the elderly, especially those in institutions or long-term care facilities, death was, of course, a familiar presence. Outliving peers, siblings, and even sometimes children was one of the costs of making it to eighty or ninety years, with bereavement a constant reminder of mortality, including one's own. Some eight hundred thousand new widows and widowers were created in America every year, these folks intimately acquainted with death and its consequences for the surviving spouse.[6]

The greater awareness of and openness toward death during these years raised an interesting question: Was it better to be lied to by doctors when one was almost certainly dying or was it better to be told the truth? The trend was definitely toward the latter, but Philippe Bouvard, writing for *Le Figaro Magazine* in 1990, was of the former persuasion. Since he had been lied to all his life (e.g., "studying hard brings success," "love is forever," "one becomes wise with age"), one last fib was fitting, Bouvard argued, going against the grain of what was sometimes called "conscious dying." "If lies are the best way to numb our fears, then I want to be lied to shamelessly on my death-bed," he wrote, thinking, "maybe the ostrich was right."[7] Bouvard may have been a little less fearful had he known that death often came peacefully and painlessly, not the horrible ordeal many thought it was and would be for them. "Not all older persons should necessarily expect to experience a slow, painful, or lingering period of dying accompanied by disabilities," said Dwight Brock, leader of a 1992 study called "The Last Days of Life" con-ducted by the National Institute of Aging. The study found that more than half of the people in the survey died in their sleep with friends and family nearby, encouraging news for those thinking that death would be not just the last but the worst experience of their lives.[8]

And for the many secular people thinking, and usually fearing, that the afterlife would consist of a never-ending state of "nothingness," Thomas W. Clark had a firm answer. "Rejecting visions of reunions with loved ones or of crossing over into the light, we anticipate the opposite: darkness, silence, and engulfing emptiness," Clark, an associate director of the Institute for Natura-listic Philosophy in Cambridge, Massachusetts, declared, "but we would be wrong." Writing for *The Humanist* in 1994, Clark debunked the popular idea of death being an abyss, void, or black hole, this state of "eternal night" depressing if not terrifying to those skeptical of a soul or afterlife. Such a state of "positive nothingness" made no sense, Clark pointed out, the notion of something that did not exist was contradictory. Many brilliant minds throughout history (including William Shakespeare and Winston Churchill, the latter describing death as "black velvet") had fallen into this existential trap, the substitution of nothingness for a heaven or hell equally misguided. "Nothingness doesn't exist, period," Clark made clear, *nonexistence* a better term for the possible condition in which we end up after dying. Those dread-ing an eternal experience of no experience had nothing to worry about, Clark insisted, the concept of such a thing thankfully philosophically flawed.[9]

OUR NEXT FRONTIER

The accelerated interest in and more confrontational attitude toward death in the 1980s and early 1990s were also a result of researchers examining as-pects of it that were never really looked at before. Barbara Chesser, a sociol-ogist at the University of Nebraska, for example, was doing trailblazing research among accidental killers, a group that had rarely been studied up to that point. Chesser had found ten Nebraskans willing to talk about their experience in accidentally killing someone else, her findings adding to the growing field of what could be called "death studies." The circumstances surrounding the deaths alone were fascinating: a nursing home attendant causing a fire that killed a resident when she forgot to unplug a coffee pot; a woman running over her seven-year-old son's skateboarding friend; a hunter accidentally shooting his best friend; a train engineer hitting a car whose elderly driver had tried to get across the tracks in time; a policeman whose comrade died after following his orders (a scene right out of *Vertigo*). Not surprisingly, the emotions among those at least partly responsible were intense and complex: guilt, pity, and, often, hostility. ("Why did he do such a stupid thing?," asked a college student whose car struck a man standing in the middle of a highway, thinking it was not fair that he had unintentionally killed someone.) While the first year after the accidental killing was typically rough (especially when the law was involved), the participants in the study reported that they soon recovered from the trauma. With about 125,000 accidental deaths per year in the United States, Chesser's work was important, her findings perhaps able to help those in a similar unfortunate situations.[10]

"Near-death" experiences also represented a growing body of research in the 1980s and 1990s. Ronald K. Siegel, a UCLA psychologist, was at the forefront of near-death or "afterlife" experience research, his work in part an attempt to bridge the big divide between scientists and the faithful on the matter. Siegel was, of course, following a long line of great thinkers throughout history who had offered theories about what happened when and after one died. Thomas Edison, for example, proposed that a stream of highly charged energy left one's body upon death, this electrical surge continuing to exist as a new form of life in space. (Ever the tinkerer, Edison thought long and hard about inventing a device that could record the existence of these energy forms.) A generation earlier, Charles Darwin argued that ghosts and spirits were real, a reflection of the prevailing view among biologists that humans were the only species that believed in the possibility of immortality. (This despite the fact that elephants often buried their dead with flowers and food, perhaps preparing them for a voyage to another place.) Freud wrote that "our own death is . . . unimaginable, and whenever we make the attempt to imagine it we can perceive that we really survive as spectators" in the afterlife, and Goethe posited that "the soul is indestructible . . . it's activity will continue through eternity." Not just geniuses but ordinary folks tended to believe in an afterlife of some kind (70 percent of Americans did, according to a recent Gallup poll); the ever-growing amount of popular culture and articles in medical journals dedicated to the subject was more reason to take it seriously.[11]

Siegel did just that, first noting in a 1981 article for *Psychology Today* that Kübler-Ross's au courant butterfly-shedding-its-cocoon metaphor of death was not all that different from the views of the Cro-Magnons and Neanderthals some one hundred thousand years ago. Siegel was especially interested in the commonly reported sensory aspects of near-death experiences—the vision of a long, dark tunnel or bright white light, sound of ringing or buzzing, feeling of peace and quiet, and the classic "seeing one's life pass before one's eyes." (In his 1975 book *Life after Life* and sequel *Reflections on Life after Life* published a few years later, Raymond Moody collected a host of such experiences from people who had had them, the work a veritable encyclopedia of near-death phenomena despite his admittedly unscientific methodology.) Many of these experiences were much like hallucinations, drug-induced or otherwise, Siegel pointed out, this perhaps the answer to the mystery that long surrounded them. A feeling of awe and sacredness, of deep insight, and that one was transcending time and space could all be the result of a particularly active central nervous system, Siegel suggested, the near-death experience, like a hallucination, a purely biological event. The emotional and physical processes involved in dying ("a chemically triggered death experience," in Siegel's words) could be responsible for the extraordinary sensory phenomena; in other words, a lot more hard data supporting this explanation than one making a case for glimpses of the afterlife.[12]

Another emerging area of death studies in the early 1980s revolved around those who "survived" the murder of a loved one. Ann Rae Jonas was one such person, writing a book on the subject based on personal experience. In 1973, Jonas's sister was murdered while hitchhiking, the event quite understandably a life-altering experience. "From that moment, my life was engulfed in grief for the loss of my sister," she wrote in an article for *Psychology Today*, "and in anxiety touched off by the sudden intrusion of violence into my world." Jonas had recently begun to have conversations with other close relatives of homicide victims to compare her feelings with theirs, and she found they had a lot in common. A difficulty to accept the death, as well as a sense of outrage and injustice, were universals, with the murder itself a source of focus if not obsession. Playing back the imagined scene over and over was typical, a mini–silent movie that haunted family members. Going anywhere near the site of the killing was often difficult, and seeing the murderer after he had been released from prison truly traumatic. More than anything else, however, the murder usually became the defining moment in the life of both the victim and his or her family, "as if there was never a before," in Jonas's words. A loss of faith and trust in the world as a safe place and a heightened sense of vulnerability were the natural conse-quences of being the "survivor" of a relative's murder, the current death-is-a-natural-part-of-life point of view not applicable.[13]

Other researchers at the time were looking into the possibility that people could choose a particular time to die, either consciously or unconsciously. Anecdotal accounts certainly suggested there was a chance it could be so, with many stories of people deciding it was time to call it quits and then doing just that. One apparently true one had to do with an eighty-year-old retired bank executive who told his son to "take good care of your mother," transferred ownership of his assets to his family, ate a plate of ravioli (his favorite meal), and then closed his eyes and died. Another well-documented one was about a healthy man in his seventies who gathered his family, said "I don't need anything anymore," and died just after completing his bequests. Not just anecdotal evidence but scholarly research suggested there might be something to it all. The medical journal *The Lancet* reported the case of a forty-year-old woman with chest pains who accurately told nurses and her clergyman that she would die exactly a week later on May 28 (the second anniversary of her mother's death), and the scholarly journal *Omega* published two studies indicating the significantly higher likelihood one would die right before or right after one's birthday. (One study showed that the approach of a birthday prolonged life for a short time among women but hastened death among men, suggesting that birthdays serve as a "lifeline" for the former and a "deadline" for the latter.) The Harvest Moon Festival was another such lifeline for Chinese Americans, another study showed, as was Passover for religious Jews.[14] Then there was the case of Sigmund Freud, who happened to have died on Yom Kippur, the Jewish Day of Atonement. Did the date have something to do with the lifelong guilt he felt about his brother's death at six months of age when he was twenty-three-months old, shrinks and some nonshrinks wondered?[15]

While choosing a time to die may have been possible, the latest research showed that another popular belief—that people could die of a "broken heart"—was not very likely. Premature mortality among widows and widowers resulting from their loss was folklore, medical studies of the 1980s were indicating, with grief not the killer it was commonly believed to be. That the survivor of a couple often died soon after his or her partner was more a matter of having shared a similar lifestyle, for example, poor diet or smoking, than not being able to live without one another.[16] Richard Nixon's death in 1994, which followed his wife, Pat's, by less than a year, revived the discussion of mates quickly following each other to the grave, however. The pair had been married over half a century, bringing to mind other couples that had been together many years and died within a short period of time. Historian Will Durant passed away just thirteen days after his wife and writing partner, Ariel, for example, while Buckminster Fuller and his wife died a mere thirty-six hours apart. Did one spouse often go rapidly downhill after the death of his or her longtime partner? Despite the recent research (which contradicted previous studies), experts in the field now were not sure, with many potential factors—stress, depression, loss of routine, and social network—coming into play.[17]

Loss, too, was a growing area of study for scholars, the subject viewed as a window into the range of human emotions. One of them, Froma Walsh at the University of Chicago, was interested in how the loss of a loved one could be an opportunity to deepen the relationship between two people and gain a sense of resolution. Such times could be the most precious of their entire lives, Walsh's work had shown, this the "right" way to die. Conversely, the "wrong" way to die could have a ripple effect over the course of generations, with cover-ups, secrecy, distortion, or denial some of the factors that might cause things to go awry. Walsh even held "life reviews" with family members when one of them was dying to try to clear up any misunderstandings and go over "old business." Through such sessions, individuals had a final chance for reconciliation, and they were less likely to have regrets and hold grudges after the death. Why were such conversations so difficult? "We have social expectations that inhibit us from saying the 'D' word," Walsh explained, with fear and superstition preventing many of us from mentioning death out loud. That publicly showing grief was discouraged in our culture (particularly for men) compounded the problem, the pressure to be emotionally independent impeding the natural process of loss.[18]

While all these studies were undeniably interesting, the most ambitious research into death toward the end of the century had to be the Death and Dying II Project (DDII). DDII was a cross-cultural research study on people's beliefs, attitudes, and feelings about the "afterdeath," a subject the project's director considered "our next frontier." A debatable proposition, certainly, but there was no doubt that most cultures and religions throughout the history of the world had some kind of postlife system, many of them rich and complex. In the project's first phase, researchers were gathering information on the rituals, myths, writings, oral traditions, art, and maps of a dozen cultures around the world. One of them was the Egun who lived on the Brazilian island of Itaparica; another the Fon of the Republic of Benin in West Africa; and another the Yoruba, Igbo, and Ijaw cultures in Nigeria (the latter building houses near the buried, believing they still dwelt among the living). Future phases of the project would explore the afterdeath in China, Russia, Bali, India, Japan, and, yes, the United States. The range of questions DDII researchers asked Egunites and Yorubans and planned to ask Americans was truly astounding. How long and far is the journey, if there is one? Is there time and space? Are there ethics? Good and evil? Animals? Is there a return to this life? Project organizers envisioned the answers to such questions would eventually be used by hospice workers, doctors, the clergy, psychologists, and educators to help people with their own big question: "What becomes of me after I die?"[19]

IT'S BEEN A DELIGHTFUL DANCE

The greater openness toward death and the flurry of research studies exploring various dimensions of it had much to do with the efforts of one woman: Elisabeth Kübler-Ross. The death-and-dying (or "death awareness") movement was still chugging along in the early 1980s, with Kübler-Ross maintaining her unofficial title as the nation's "Queen of Death." With her handful of books (*On Death and Dying, Living with Death and Dying, Questions and Answers on Death and Dying,* and *Death: The Final Stage of Growth*) and the Death-and-Dying Center in Escondido, California, Kübler-Ross was a one-woman empire of what she often referred to as "the other side." Her ideas were used in tens of thousands of colleges, seminaries, medical schools, hospitals, and other institutions, evidence that the movement had crossed over from the fringe to the mainstream. Not just "death professionals"—hospital and hospice workers, the clergy, and psychiatrists—but ordinary Americans looked to Kübler-Ross for inspiration regarding how to depart this world, her contribution to what was increasingly called thanatology (or dolorology) difficult to overestimate.[20]

Not everyone believed Kübler-Ross's work centered around the "five stages of dying" (denial, anger, bargaining, depression, acceptance) was a godsend, however. Based on a good idea—the British hospice movement—the American death-and-dying movement had spiraled out of control, some argued. A nationwide network of death-and-dying centers called Shanti Nilaya had sprung up (with Kübler-Ross's involvement), for one thing, and a London-based organization called the Exit Society had recently published a do-it-yourself Home Suicide Guide that was circulating in the States. A little pamphlet called "It's Been a Delightful Dance" was also making the rounds, a story of a cancer patient who received "cancering" therapy from a California-based organization called Life Force. More alarmingly, a video artist, Jo Roman, had not that long ago killed herself on television (calling it "artistic" and "creative" suicide), this another sign that what Ron Rosenbaum called a "prodeath movement" was sweeping the country. "Is this multifaceted flirtation with death and suicide . . . some self-regulating, population-control mechanism surfacing as the baby-boom generation gets older, the better to thin its ranks before its numbers begin to strain nursing-home and terminal-ward facilities?," he asked in *Harper's* in 1982, convinced something was rotten in the state of death in America. Having an alternative to the interventionist, life-prolonging medical establishment was one thing, Rosenbaum thought, but celebrating and worshiping death as a "beautiful" event was quite another. It was this romancing of death, that it was perhaps better than life, that so irked critics like Rosenbaum. That Kübler-Ross actually believed there was no such thing as death, preferring to refer to the dead as "afterlife entities," was all the more proof that she and her movement had gotten too weird despite its success and popularity.[21]

The flourishing of suicide manuals in the early 1980s was especially concerning to some. Author Arthur Koestler and his wife, Cynthia, had used *A Guide to Self-Deliverance* to help end their lives in 1983, the suicide manual (whose preface was written by Koestler) distributed to the eight thousand members of the British Voluntary Euthanasia Society. Eighteen similar groups were operating around the world, making many question whether all this "self-deliverance" was a good thing. ("The prospect of falling peacefully, blissfully asleep is not only soothing but can make it positively desirable to quit this pain-racked mortal frame," Koestler wrote in his preface.) Such how-to manuals were intended to be used only by the terminally ill in order to reduce unsuccessful attempts, with suicide presented as a last resort for those in great pain. At least one of the several suicides attributed to the British manual was of a young, physically healthy person, however, leading the Attorney General of England and Wales to try to outlaw it. Helping would-be suicides was illegal there, as in the United States, but our First Amendment made the publication of such booklets perfectly legitimate. The Los Angeles–based Hemlock Society's *Let Me Die before I Wake* was sold openly in bookstores; in fact, this manual, like others, showed which drugs and how much dosage should be used to get the job done. (The name of the organization and guide were each inspired by the potion Socrates took to end his life.) Would such publications lead to hordes of depressed, momentarily suicidal people to take the plunge? There were an estimated fifty to one hundred suicide attempts in the United States for every successful one (about twenty-eight thousand in 1981), making the social acceptance of killing oneself (in order to say, relieve society or one's family of a burden) a potential nightmare.[22]

Very much in the spirit, so to speak, of the death-and-dying movement was Stephen and Ondrea Levine's telephone consultation service, the Dying Project. If you were one of the hundreds of people who called the Levines' "hotline" in 1982, you would likely hear this message:

> Hello. This is the Dying Project consultation phone for the terminally ill and those sharing in the death of another . . . In the heart lies the deathless. Have a good day.[23]

The Levines, based in Taos, would call back when they had time to talk with the grieving, the dying, or those caring for them. Recent callers included the father of an eight-year-old girl who had been struck and killed by a car; a woman dying of cancer who had stopped all treatment; a young man still regretting his decision to tell his dying brother to "hold on"; and a suicidal woman holding in her hand the poison she was considering taking.[24]

What could the Levines possibly say to people in such distress? Accept whatever feelings arise as a natural part of death and dying, such advice consistent with their look-the-Grim-Reaper-right-in-the-face attitude? Counseling the mourning, dying, and those close to them was nothing new, of course, but the Levines' (free) consultation service did seem like something different to both participants and observers. The couple also gave dozens of lectures and workshops each year, and Stephen and Ondrea Levine's book *Who Dies?* was being used as a training manual for hospice workers and in college courses. Stephen Levine had worked with Kübler-Ross for a couple of years in the late 1970s but went out on his own after the Queen of Death became involved with an occult group. "There's no one right way to go through this," Levine told a young woman who had just been diagnosed with leukemia, his Buddhist background informing his holistic approach toward "conscious dying." Some of the people calling the hotline were familiar with but perplexed about Kübler-Ross's "five stages," in fact, with the Levines distancing themselves from their ex-mentor. "We often get calls from nurses or therapists who are confused because their patients don't seem to be dying in the orderly way her books say they should," explained Ondrea Levine, that some loved ones were not succumbing as Kübler-Ross advised being a source of considerable frustration.[25]

Over the next decade, principles of "conscious dying" gained further acceptance as the death-and-dying movement moved beyond its New Age origins. Writer Mary Catherine Bateson believed that death had, in her words, a "proper place in life," her focus on making a graceful exit when it was time to go. Should we not finish our life's masterpiece with the same kind of dedication that musicians gave to the final note in a composition or artists gave to the last brushstroke of a painting, she asked? A new "affirmation of death" was needed, Bateson felt, our right to "elective closure" ready to be claimed. Derek Humphry's new book, *Final Exit*, had caused a sensation as a practical guide for assisted suicide, but something larger was needed to spark a real cultural shift in our approach to death, she maintained. The immense resources devoted toward heroic intervention for the dying were of special concern, a drain unfair to younger generations who could make better use of them for health care, education, and jobs. (About 30 percent of all health care costs in the United States were incurred in the last six months of life, far more than in other countries.)[26] "Death is not the goal," she wrote for *Omni* in 1992, "but neither is death always the enemy, the intruder."[27]

Making a truce with the enemy of enemies was also the theme of Herbert and Kay Kramer's 1993 *Conversations at Midnight*, a deeply philosophical examination on, as the book's subtitle went, "coming to terms with death and dying." The married couple was in a unique position to write such a book; Kay was a teacher and therapist in "death studies," while Herb was dying (of bone cancer). Much of the book consisted of literal conversations held in the

wee hours, the two ruminating on death and dying from their different per-
spectives. Although their chats covered a lot of ground, the recurring theme
was the coming to terms with death in order to, as they wrote, "call it out of
the shadows and make its acquaintance." Death "ask[s] nothing more of us
than to recognize it as a part of our lives and to claim it as our own," they
proposed, this the best approach to take since there was no escaping it.
Pushing it away, to deny or avoid it, was not just futile but went against what
Kay believed was a natural process. Getting in harmony with the natural
experience of dying when the time came was the best and only real way to
achieve a peaceful death, a skill that most people in Western society did not
possess. Like those in the "death awareness" movement, Kay believed dying
was not an end but a transition from one state of being to another, something
that those experiencing the process knew way better than the rest of us. "We
are protected by a knowledge that comes across the boundary separating this
dimension of experience from what comes after," she told her dying husband
in one of their late-night conversations, the acceptance of death the path
toward gaining that knowledge. Americans had particular trouble getting on
this path, Kay felt, the denial of death in this country "part of our mythology,
our sense of youthfulness, energy, and individualism." While some cultures
recognized that death was central to life, here it was "un-American," contrary
to our "philosophy of optimism, of progress," this undeniably true. Had
Americans' attitudes toward death and dying really changed, one had to
wonder, or was "the other side" still hostile territory?[28]

A FOREIGN COUNTRY

A solid case could be made either way, but everyone would agree that the
AIDS epidemic was leaving a deep imprint on the landscape of death. The
first cases of AIDS were reported in June 1981 and, by 1987, about seventeen thousand Americans were reported to have died from the disease. In the
1980s, it was difficult to get exact statistics on the number of people who
died from AIDS as the disease was sometimes not mentioned on death certificates as it legally should have been. The Centers for Disease Control in
Atlanta estimated it was able to document 90 percent of all AIDS deaths in
the country to date, although as many as 20 percent of cases in California
were believed to go unreported. Shame or embarrassment was part of the
reason families of AIDS victims pressured physicians to omit the disease
from death certificates, the fear and paranoia surrounding it at the time another factor. As example, Liberace had in fact not died from degenerative
brain disease, as his doctor reported on the fabulous entertainer's certificate,
but of pneumonia caused by AIDS, the county coroner made clear in a much
publicized news conference in 1987. "How many deaths are being covered

up?," asked *Newsweek* in its report of the story, concerned that many more people may have been dying of AIDS than believed.[29]

As with the other approximately 2,127,000 deaths that occurred in the country in that year, Liberace's doctor used the U.S. Standard Certificate of Death, a form that had been around since 1900. Prior to that, deaths were counted by burials, making church officials and cemetery caretakers responsible for the tallying. But with the rise of professional medicine in the nineteenth century, a more scientific method was deemed needed, turning the job over to licensed physicians. Besides recording the time and place of death, the certificate also required physicians to list both the "immediate cause" and the "conditions if any which gave rise to immediate cause," which is where it could get interesting. Reconstructing the sequence of events leading to death is subject to judgment and thus error, brining social norms and morality into the equation. As a case in point, the narrow definition of AIDS in the 1980s allowed doctors to underreport it on death certificates, something that had implications far beyond a particular situation like Liberace's. Data compiled from the certificates were and are used to calculate national death rates for diseases as well as to rank the causes of death, a big factor in how health funds are allocated. Underreporting a disease as cause of death meant less money would be designated toward eradicating it; in other words, bad news for those suffering from a stigmatized condition such as AIDS.[30]

Harold Brodkey's 1993 revelation that he had AIDS did a lot to give a face to and dispel many of the myths that remained about the disease. Brodkey, a sixty-two-year-old novelist with a wife, children, and grandchildren, told his story in an issue of *The New Yorker*, quite a public platform for such a confession. Although he had not been exposed since the 1970s, Brodkey had recently learned he had the disease and thus was convinced he had been given a death sentence. Interestingly, the prospect of dying did not bother Brodkey very much, having felt he was in the presence of death most of his life. Getting and dying from AIDS would also free him from other, perhaps worse afflictions that plagued his ancestors, things such as cancer, stroke, and heart disease, he explained, a quick death better than a protracted one. This, in addition to viewing death as "a relief, a privilege, a lucky and graceful and symmetrical silence to be grateful for," made Brodkey's confession all the more uncharacteristic for an American. "It's my turn to die," he made clear, a remarkably simple but rare observation for anyone in his shoes to make.[31]

Brodkey's essay (titled "To My Readers") was not well received by everyone, however. "There is a pornography of self-disclosure here that, in the present instance, crosses the line of what is to be silently endured," complained Richard Howard in *The New Republic* a few weeks after the article appeared, considering it "entirely a matter of manipulative hucksterism of mendacious self-propaganda and cruel assertion of artistic privilege."[32] Brodkey was not done, however, especially because he had nothing to lose in telling his story. In his "Dying: An Update" published eight months after his first essay in *The New Yorker*, Brodkey told readers about his further struggle with AIDS and the fight for his life.[33] Brodkey would live almost two years longer, dying in January 1996.

The rise of AIDS as well as the increase in youth suicides (the rate for the latter had tripled over the last thirty years, and a number of teenage death pacts in the 1980s had shaken the country) led to a new trend in public schools: "death education." Given these two crises, educators believed the subject of death was timely and, possibly, life saving. Virtually everyone would experience the loss of someone close to them over the course of their lifetime; this, too, made the subject a good use of students' time. Some educators, however, felt that it was the removal of death from everyday life that represented the most important reason to teach the subject. "It used to be that everyone saw people grow old and die in front of them," said Robert Stevenson, who taught a class in death and dying at a New Jersey high school, "but since the 1930s we have moved death out of the home and into funeral homes and hospitals." Because many kids did not see death, Stevenson felt, they could deny the existence of it, something that could lead to devastating consequences.[34]

The introduction of death to K–12 curricula was another sign that the social stigma attached to it was eroding. Before the 1980s, death could perhaps be discussed as part of a literature class, but now it was being taught as a legitimate subject in thousands of public schools across the country. Death education classes could run a full semester or just a few days, with topics ranging from its physical process, students' feelings about it and grieving, the social rituals surrounding it, suicide, euthanasia, the cost of funerals, the right to die, and what to do with the body. Like sex, death was felt to be "relevant," a trend in American education since the early 1970s. Some high school students who had taken death education classes reported they were much better equipped to help their parents deal with the death of their parent or help friends expressing thoughts of suicide. One girl whose mother, boyfriend, and friend died within a few months was very grateful she had taken a course in the subject, familiar at least in theory with the emotional dynamics of losing a loved one.[35]

As with sex, however, the conservative right was not happy about the death education trend, believing the subject should be dealt with at home and in church. Because the subject was so emotionally charged, it could hardly be argued that it was a difficult one to teach and, probably, to learn. Teachers took full advantage of the interactive possibilities. Students were commonly asked to write their own obituaries and wills, and, occasionally, mock suicide notes. Some students reportedly were asked to sit in coffins, an exercise that would purportedly help them confront the fear of death. Others visited funeral homes and crematoria, while one class was shown an embalming and was allowed to touch a corpse. One death education class in Colorado Springs was held in a cemetery, this considered the ideal atmosphere to discuss bereavement. One particularly creative exercise assigned to high school students in suburban Maryland was to write a note to the next of kin of a suicide.[36] One went as follows:

> Dear Mr. and Mrs. Cory:
> I wrote this letter to inform you about your son Richard. Richard had been acting different the past few days. Yesterday I came home from work and found him laying [*sic*] on the floor face down. I checked his pulse but there wasn't any. I went in to the bathroom and I found the sleeping pills open and half gone. I'm very sorry to say your son has past [*sic*] away.[37]

With such exercises (and no special training required of teachers), was "death ed" doing more harm than good?

Perhaps, but there was no doubt that American kids were sheltered from actual death. Adults, both here and in Europe, also rarely invited death to their door despite the greater openness to talk about it. England, in fact, appeared as death phobic as the United States, with a pervasive out-of-sight, out-of-mind attitude. "Death has become a foreign country where we don't know how to behave," said Dr. Richard Lansdown, a hospital psychiatrist, in 1989, thinking the sight of death and the process of dealing with it had become alien to the current generation. The fact that more than 70 percent of Brits died in a hospital (versus 5 percent a century past) had a lot to do with it, death no longer a familiar domestic presence as it was when the dying were cared for at home. As well, the relatives of the few who did die at home typically wanted the body out of the house as soon as possible; this, too, was quite different from ways of the past. Even the elderly were shunning death, a bit surprisingly. One seventy-year-old woman whose husband was dying at home from a brain tumor wanted him admitted to a hospital even though he probably was not going to live for more than twenty-four hours, for example, her never having seen a corpse.[38]

There were other signs that death was not a welcome guest for most Brits in the late 1980s. Children were often not allowed to attend Grandma's or Grandpa's funeral, the experience deemed too traumatic, and fewer and fewer people wanted to view the bodies of their dead relatives in funeral homes. One undertaker reported that half of the married people whose funerals he had managed had never told their spouses how they wanted their body to be disposed of, and only one in three Brits had made a will. Some 75 percent of Brits chose cremation (versus 9 percent in 1945), most of these not including a religious ceremony, and the same undertaker told the London *Sunday Telegraph* that he typically overheard those attending one wishing it would end as soon as possible. There also appeared to be a lot less weeping at funerals (tears openly flowed at many Victorian and Edwardian burials), and popular folk songs were gradually replacing mournful dirges at gravesites. Finally, few people seemed to know what to say to the relatives of the recently dead, this complemented by an expectation for mourners to get over their loss quickly. "The more we have sought to keep death at arm's length, the more perfunctory its rituals have become," wrote Graham Turner for that newspaper, thinking that dying had become a "lost art."[39]

Of course, significantly longer life spans in the West played a large role in the shifting attitudes toward death. In 1900 in the United Kingdom, 143,000 babies died before they were a year old, but now just six thousand did, despite the increase in population. The death rate for those under seventy was also dramatically lower, making the end of life not the exclusive province of the aged but pretty close to it, relatively speaking. "When the Grim Reaper struck at random and took a baby, a nursing mother, or a breadwinner, it left great rifts in the social fabric, and rites of passage were designed to help heal them," wrote Turner, but the expectation to live a long life had changed all that. Interestingly, not all Brits had lost the art of dying. Jews, especially more orthodox ones, had held on to their traditional way of mourning (divided into three distinct periods and lasting eleven months). The initial seven-day period, shiva, was especially intense, with family and friends gathering at the home of the primary mourner to comfort the bereaved. Muslims also had retained their formal periods of mourning, and they eagerly offered the traditional greeting to the bereaved ("My God accept him [or her] in His mercy, give you the strength to endure the loss, and compensate you for it."). It was Westerners' materialism and lack of true faith that accounted for this waning interest in death, some thought, something that was bad for both individuals and society as a whole. "We should think about death far more because it sharpens one's priorities as very few other stimuli can," said John Baker, the bishop of Salisbury, the reminder that life would end an ideal way to make it what it was meant to be.[40]

HOW WE DIE

While the average life span for Americans was still increasing through the 1980s (up to 71.8 years for a man, 78 years for a woman in 1988), better odds of living longer did little to stop many from thinking some sudden, tragic event might intervene. Heart disease and cancer remained by far the leading killers, but that did not stop us from worrying that we would meet our maker through some other, much more interesting way. Americans were what one expert in such things called "risk illiterate," undervaluing the likely ways we could die and overvaluing the unlikely ways. Lots of people were fearful of dying in an airplane crash, for example, but the chances of that happening was just one in one hundred thousand. (One was more likely to be kicked to death by a donkey.) Fear of being murdered was also quite high, yet one was eight times as likely to be killed playing a sport than shot by a stranger. Dying on the operating table was another big concern, yet the chances of that happening (one in forty thousand) were just one-tenth those of getting killed in a car crash. Staying home seemed like the best way to avoid an accidental death, but in fact, it was the worst. More than fifteen thousand Americans suffered fatal accidents at home each year, most of these from falling down stairs. Stairs were literally a deathtrap, in fact, causing more fatalities than those from electrocution, gas poisoning, lightning, floods, tornadoes, polio, meningitis, and fireworks combined.[41]

Ordinary Americans may have been clueless when it came to matters of risk, but insurance companies were downright geniuses. Actuaries armed with statistical tables knew that in the following twelve months very close to 750,000 people in the United States would die from heart disease, 50,000 from pneumonia, 2,500 by accidentally shooting themselves, 2,000 from tuberculosis, 200 in floods, 100 from lightning, another 100 from tornadoes, and 50 from snakebites and bee stings. They knew that being 30 percent overweight took an average 3.5 years off one's life expectancy, that being poor reduced it by two years, and that being a single male lopped off nearly a decade from one's likely life span. Despite all the technological advances and increased safety standards made through the twentieth century, mortality rates for violent and accidental deaths had remained remarkably consistent, this allowing the insurance industry to be a very profitable one.[42]

The U.S. Census Bureau also knew a lot about how and when Americans were likely to die. The Bureau actually had a mathematical model called "loss of life expectancy" (LLE) based on national mortality rates, using it to calculate risks of all kinds. The model, in which days were deducted from one's life expectancy for a particular risk, was chock-full with interesting information related to the likelihood of dying from that risk. Again, heart disease and cancer were far and away the leading killers, but accidents finished ahead of all other individual diseases as the cause of death. Over half of all accidental deaths were automobile related, with half of them involving alcohol. Automobiles were about twenty times more dangerous than jets, trains, and buses per mile traveled, but they were less risky than small planes. After car accidents, mishaps involving falls, suffocation, drowning, poison, and fires posed the greatest risk. As far as occupation, the more timid would probably want to avoid construction demolition and log felling, each of these ten times as dangerous as race car driving and high-wire performing, rather surprisingly. The most hazardous job was, however, having no job at all. A 1 percent increase in unemployment resulted in an incremental thirty thousand deaths per year, in fact; bad news for anyone receiving a pink slip.[43]

Ironically, the precision in predicting how Americans would die was matched by the uncertainty regarding when death actually occurred. The debate over the definition of death was still raging in the late 1980s, with ever-changing medical technology suggesting the issue might never be fully resolved. For centuries, being alive consisted of meeting two criteria—breathing and heartbeat—but that changed with the advent of artificial respiration and other medical technologies in the late 1950s. Over the next decade, neurological criteria (for example, brain activity), replaced cardiorespiratory criteria as the measure of life and, by default, death.[44] One person involved in the original debate, either a physician or lawyer, suggested using the term *biomort* (*bio*, or "life," and *mort*, or "death") to describe someone with irreversible brain damage.[45] Now about twenty years old, the concept of "brain death" was up for grabs as bioethicists and some in the medical community reconsidered what it meant to be dead. Not just those who had no brain functions but those who had no consciousness—were in a persistent vegetative state—should be considered dead, more experts were now arguing. These "cognitive dead" (or, sometimes, "cerebral dead," "cortical dead," or "neomorts") were capable of breathing, sleeping, and digesting food on their own but, like the brain dead, were incapable of thought and were unaware of the world around them. (Sunny von Bülow was probably the most well-known case, having been in an irreversible coma since 1982.) Karen Ann Quinlan had famously been in such a state, her family's lawsuit in the mid-1970s an attempt to have her removed from the life-support system helping to keep her breathing. (Quinlan would keep breathing on her own for nine years, still hooked up to a nutrition-hydration tube, until she died from infection.) The trial (especially Dr. Julius Korein's expert testimony) did a lot to make the distinction between brain death and cognitive death, leading to the 1981 Uniform Determination of Death Act. The act (which read "an individual who has sustained either (1) irreversible cessation of circulatory and respiratory functions or (2) irreversible cessation of all functions of the brain, including brain stem, is dead") was law in thirty-nine states and pending in others in 1987.[46]

By 1990, however, the act was being questioned, its language not applicable to the ten thousand Americans "living" in a vegetative state. Care for these "lost souls" (or "biological tenacious," as Surgeon General C. Everett Koop called them) ran $200,000 or more a year, the psychic pain for families another heavy burden to bear. The sufferer would not want to be in such a state if he or she could do anything about it, preferring to be allowed to "die with dignity," as the growing movement expressed it. Although the AMA had declared it ethical for physicians to cease treatment for such patients, the issue remained a mess in hospitals, nursing homes, and most important, the legal system. A new definition of death was needed, supporters of the movement insisted, one that equated the loss of thinking, consciousness, and "personhood" with the end of life as we know it. A persistent vegetative state (PVS) implied that a body had outlived its owner, advocates of cognitive death argued, a mindless organism no longer really human. Not surprisingly, however, opposition to revising the act to include cognitive death was strong. Could it be possible that people in PVS (such as Nancy Cruzan, the most well-known case besides von Bulow) experience some form of consciousness, even happiness, that could not be detected?[47] Would organs be harvested from the vegetative dead, some wondered (as in the movie *Coma*), or females used as surrogate mothers? Extreme situations, but what to do with a still-breathing vegetative? Taking them off life support was tantamount to killing them, something most doctors, including Korein, were not willing to do. "Withdrawing support from the vegetative is a social decision, not a medical one," wrote Kathleen Stein for *Omni*, agreeing with Korein that physicians should not be placed in a position where they would have to play God.[48]

The gradual transition among states from the heart-lung definition of death to brain death made for some curious scenarios. In 1982, for example, a cognitive dead patient being transferred from a Boston hospital to one in Washington would be considered alive in Massachusetts, dead in Connecticut, alive in New York and New Jersey, and dead again in D.C. A decade later, the issue remained complicated despite most states having adopted the "whole brain" concept of death. Many doctors and nurses understandably had trouble applying the definition of brain death to patients whose hearts still beat and whose lungs still breathed just like those of patients considered alive. (Their bodies were also warm to the touch, pink in color, and had normal blood pressure and body temperature.) And, in certain states, there were exceptions to the rule. In New York and New Jersey, for example, a brain-dead Catholic or Orthodox Jew could be judged alive, these religions hanging on to the beating-heart standard of life. Just as the beginning of life was a source of contention in the abortion debate, so was the end of life in the death debate, with all kinds of factors influencing one's point of view. Organ transplants had compounded the issue, as hearts, livers, and lungs could be used in other people only if they were removed from patients whose veins still coursed with oxygenated blood. Those who might live were dying because a small part of the brain of a cognitive dead person was still active, in other words, this making the matter even more emotionally charged.[49]

Although the legal definition of death continued to remain in flux, most Americans appeared to know it when they saw it. More than half of hospital deaths followed a decision to limit or withhold life-sustaining treatment, anecdotal evidence suggested (there were no national statistics), an indication that many Americans were choosing death over dying for themselves or loved ones. More doctors and hospital staff recognized high-technology medicine created a slippery slope, and they considered death as viable an option as intervention in the direst cases. If the patient or his or her family had not made their preference crystal clear, however, the Hippocratic oath required physicians to err on the side of intervention. Living wills (in which the signer declared his or her dying life should not be artificially prolonged) were helpful but not airtight as they did not address the complex medical situations in which patients could find themselves. Doctors and nurses half-joked they wanted "DNR" (Do Not Resuscitate) etched on an individual's chest, but even this would not provide all the information to make the right call. The best solution was a health proxy who, knowing the patient's preferences, was charged with making medical decisions when he or she could not.[50]

Even if the definition of death could be resolved once and for all, physicians' and many ordinary Americans' wishes to extend the lives of the terminally ill remained a contentious issue. "Our determination to prolong life has distorted the mission of American medicine," wrote Daniel Callahan, author of *The Troubled Dream of Life: Living with Mortality*, the pervasive effort to control mortality wreaking havoc with the nation's health care system. In other industrial countries, it was acceptable to decide that the cost of continued treatment was too burdensome to both patient and society, something almost anathema in the United States. As well, old age was commonly treated as a disease by doctors rather than as a natural part of life and a prelude to death. Death was also often viewed as a medical accident, a mistake or failure that could and should have been averted. Our cultural phobia surrounding death was reflected in health care spending. The two biggest killers, heart disease and cancer, received the largest share of NIH funding while quality of life conditions such as arthritis and mental health received relatively little. In short, it was time to shift our priorities from rescue medicine to preventive medicine, a lot of people were saying in the early 1990s, with the proposed overhaul of the nation's health care system an ideal opportunity to do it.[51]

For a whole generation now, death had experienced a wild ride in the United States, but nothing quite prepared Americans for Sherwin Nuland's *How We Die: Reflections on Life's Final Chapter*. The 1994 book described the physical end of life in blunt, clinical terms, detailing what happens to the human body when a heart attack, cancer, AIDS, Alzheimer's, and old age brought death. Nuland, a surgeon and professor at Yale, was on a much different mission than that of "Dr. Deaths" such Derek Humphry and Jack Kevorkian with their prescriptions for assisted suicide. About six thousand Americans died everyday, but most people viewed death as an unnatural act that intruded on the normalcy of life, Nuland argued, the aura around it still repressive. If death was anything, however, it was normal, his book showed, something we had largely forgotten. Before the early twentieth century, death was considered a "member of the family," he pointed out, so much so that doors on houses were built to accommodate coffins and parlors designed to hold mourners. That changed as science became very good at prolonging life, our additional years coming at a heavy cost, both ethically and financially. How could death once again be viewed as part of life rather than some kind of alien entity? Both patients and doctors learning when to let go would be a good start, Nuland suggested, a lot to be said for going gently into the night when death came calling.[52]

The fundamental message in *How We Die*—death had been for millennia nature's way to allow younger generations to take over, but modern medicine had changed this both for the better (longer, healthier lives) and the worse (prolonged dying)—struck a chord among many Americans. "Life is dappled with periods of pain, but in dying there often is only the affliction," wrote George Will in his praise for the book, seeing big trouble ahead as baby boomers approached their senior years. The doubling of life expectancy over the past century in the Western world has been a decidedly mixed blessing, Will believed, that we were likely reaching the upper end of our species' limit a good thing. "An obsession with longevity distracts us from our duty to live well," he wisely stated, hoping lots of doctors were reading Nuland's book.[53]

No one would have agreed with that more than Anne Ricks Sumers, a New Jersey ophthalmologist, who along with her family made sure her dying brother Rick would not die in a hospital. "A hospital is no place to die," she wrote for *Newsweek* in 1994, with Rick making the same decision when it was clear he was at death's door. Only forty years old, Rick had just learned that he had inoperable brain cancer and would die very soon. "I want to go home," he told his doctors and family, and home he went for the little time he had remaining. That night, friends and family gathered to say good-bye while Rick, enjoying snacks and a glass of red wine, did the same. "It was like a Thanksgiving—good food, lots of conversation, but the guest of honor would be dead in a few days, or hours," Sumers recalled, an expectation that turned out to be precisely right. Rick was in a deep coma by morning and died later that day, again surrounded by friends and family. "Let patients go home," she urged other doctors if there was nothing more they could do, her brother's death an ideal one if it had to happen.[54] Other patients and families were making the same decision because of the impersonal nature of hospital care and its outrageous cost. "More and more, people want to die in their homes," said Dr. Andrea Sankar, a medical anthropologist from the University of Michigan and author of *Dying at Home: A Family Guide for Caregiving.* Although caring for a terminally ill patient at home was daunting and difficult, it also helped families transcend the sorrow and tragedy of losing a loved one, Sankar had found.[55] The winds of death appeared to be shifting, with Americans ready, willing, and able to change its terms if Western medicine would not.

AN AGE OF LOSS

The switch that seemingly was flipped on in the early 1990s was actually three decades in the making. A good case could be made that the "outing" of death in the United States began in 1963 with Mitford's classic, *The American Way of Death*. The main theme of the book was Americans' denial of death and obsession with immortality in the postwar years, something of which Mitford was highly critical. Death was somehow shameful to Americans, an event that should be gotten over with as quickly as possible. The ringleader in all this was the funeral director, a uniquely American profession in charge of briefly presenting and then rapidly disposing of the corpse. Aries's *Western Attitudes toward Death* put Mitford's argument in broader context, showing how it was urban industrialization in the early twentieth century that paved the way for what followed over the next few decades. With the rise of the modern self, death became separated from the traditional, religious view predicated on it being a normal part of life. The helplessness and dependence associated with dying was contrary to our cultural regard for autonomy, Aries also believed. If Mitford looked to the funeral industry as primarily responsible for bringing shame and embarrassment to death, however, Aries blamed the modern hospital. Efficient, orderly (literally), and professional, the hospital of the late twentieth century depersonalized death by repressing its less attractive aspects, Aries convincingly argued. This was a long way from how death was treated during the Renaissance, Aries pointed out, when trade took place freely in graveyards and relatives and friends routinely attended the dying of loved ones in their bedchambers.[56]

By the early 1990s, however, it was a much different story than in the 1960s and 1970s, with a new chapter in the American way of dying being written. Millions of people had signed living wills, for one thing, and a good many were fluent in the emotional stages of dying, courtesy of Kübler-Ross. Derek Humphry and Jack Kevorkian had made suicide a popular subject in the media if not an acceptable topic for dinner conversation. A couple of states were considering making medical-assisted suicide legal; this, too, helping to bring death back into the discourse of everyday life. How and why did death, marginalized throughout much of the twentieth century in the West, become such a ubiquitous feature on the American scene? Jeanne Guillemin, a professor of sociology at Boston College, offered some good answers in "Planning to Die," a 1992 article for *Society*. The aging of the population had a lot to do with it, Guillemin explained, as did the AIDS epidemic. But it was the opportunity to turn death into a highly individualized affair that was shifting society's focus to the end of life, she posited, the very thing that had contained it now bringing it out into the open.[57]

It was, more than anyone else, the Me Generation that was rewriting the rules of death in the early 1990s. "You might think no one ever died before," noted Debra Goldman of *Adweek* in 1992, commenting that baby boomers' rather sudden obsession with death was a result of having "entered the springtime of their mortality." One could argue that boomers' determination to look and feel young via gym memberships, eating healthy, and plastic surgery was at its core an effort to slow the aging process and delay the inevitable. Boomers were, in short, trying to control death just as they loved to control every other aspect of life, this line of thought went, something that no generation in history had attempted to do (or even considered doing).[58] Not that long ago almost unmentionable, death had become, much in part to baby boomers, "popular." Just as they were transforming the concept of "middle-aged" from "over the hill" to "prime of life," so were they transforming the prospect of the end of life. "We thought it was a trip to the void, but it turns out to be a growth experience," quipped Barbara Ehrenreich in *The Nation* in 1993, believing that "death is looking more and more attractive."[59]

As a rule a big advertising no-no, death had even become the unique selling proposition for a number of marketers in the early 1990s. A new cable channel was running a commercial with the tagline, "We're all going to die. Watch Comedy Central," for example, while Pepe Jeans had adopted in the United Kingdom a similar message in its television advertising: "Because one day you'll die." Cunard, too, had joined the ranks of the better-do-it-now-while-you-can, running a print ad with the headline, "Life Is Short." How had death snuck into the normally happy talk of advertising? "There's a sense of disquietude pervading people's lives, like you could get hit by a car any moment," explained Maureen Berman, a market researcher, the recession and general malaise of the early 1990s making "seize the day" a popular advertising platform.[60] "The 1990s are clearly an age of loss," echoed *Psychology Today* in 1992, the time ripe for marketers to capitalize on whatever psychic malady was ailing Americans.[61]

If consumer culture had been sprinkled with death, popular culture was positively strewn with it. Death reared its ugly head in many novels, the more gruesome the better for sales, it seemed. While Elisabeth Kübler-Ross was the undisputed Queen of Death, novelist Stephen King could claim all rights to the title of king, rather fittingly. An expert in all things King, Stephen J. Spignesi estimated that the man had by 1992 described in his books more than seven hundred "deaths, tortures, and mutilations," a feat not easy to achieve. Just a few of the more interesting ways characters had met their end in King's novels included: decapitation by werewolf, consumption by giant maggots, collision with UPS truck, suffocation by own vomit, sacrificial crucifixion, overinflation by air compressor, explosion by (living) toy soldiers, execution by townsfolk, and, last but not least, self-cannibalization. Who said Americans did not like to be reminded of death?[62]

Whether the cause was "disquietude" or something else, death certainly seemed to be on Americans' mind as the millennium approached. Death was certainly not taking a holiday in Hollywood, which both shaped and reflected the trend. Two movies of late 1993—*Fearless* and *My Life*—were centered around mortality, with a handful more—*Philadelphia*, *Schindler's List*, *Heaven & Earth*, and *Shadowlands*—on the way. That some filmmakers and studio executives themselves were hitting the half-century mark was likely part of the reason for death becoming a kind of genre all its own, but the self-reflection that typically attended the end of a century seemed to also be playing a role.[63] These movies were also a lot darker than typical Hollywood films dealing with death or the afterlife. Just a couple of years earlier, in fact, films such as *Field of Dreams*, *All Dogs Go to Heaven*, *Always*, *Ghost*, and *Ghost Dad* hit the screen, these much more in the tradition of Hollywood when it came to, as one 1936 movie was called, "the green pastures." Reaching heaven typically required the use of an elevator or escalator in these films, as Richard Corliss noted in *Time*, and God was either black or George Burns. "Some dignified gent—Claude Rains or James Mason—will serve as celestial flight attendant for a poignant trip to earth, where you will perform the one deed that makes your life fulfilled and your death noble," Corliss wrote, the afterlife not a dead end but "an angelic resort spa."[64]

Although critics hated *Ghost* (Corliss considered it "exasperatingly capricious"), the movie turned out to be a blockbuster, leading other Hollywood producers to jump on the death bandwagon. A dozen films featuring the afterlife were released in 1991, the thematic range going from the sublime (*The Rapture*) to the ridiculous (*Bill & Ted's Bogus Journey*). Cinematic death appeared to be part of the larger trend of middle-agers' search for spirituality and the meaning of life in the early 1990s, as well as a backlash against the greed-is-good 1980s. "Death is hot," said Bruce Joel Rubin, writer of *Ghost*, the ex-hippie who studied Buddhism in India using some of his metaphysical insights to inform the film's script. With the exception of *The Rapture* (whose story involved events of literal biblical proportions), dying and death were decidedly fluffy in these films, not unlike "mov[ing] to a new neighborhood," as Martha Smilgis of *Time* described it. That the film industry was based in Los Angeles certainly played a role in Hollywood's preoccupation with the afterlife, that city still the New Age capital of the world.[65]

By 1994, it was safe to say that death had become a principal theme in American pop culture. Besides *How We Die*, the best seller list included *The Tibetan Book of Living and Dying* and two books on near-death experiences, Betty Eadie's *Embraced by the Light* and Dannion Brinkley's *Saved by the Light*. Movies such as *Serial Mom*, *Four Weddings and a Funeral*, *Corrina, Corrina*, *Lassie*, and *Angels in the Outfield* all had something to do with death, and widowed dads was a theme in no less than four television shows (*Full House, The Nanny, Me and the Boys*, and *Earth 2*). "All this morbidity taps a deep psychological nerve," noted *Newsweek*, the creators of such entertainment knowing full well that death was a reliable plot device. (Dead moms not only pervaded Disney movies but also television since the birth of the medium; one researcher documented no less than fifty television families without mothers while another study found that television families were seven times more likely to have a dead mother than those in real life.)[66]

Indeed, while the ante of death had been raised in the early 1990s, both television and movies had always relied heavily on the subject for dramatic effect. Children were often exposed to death in entertainment as much as adults, the psychological implications of such not fully clear. It was believed the average American fifteen-year-old had witnessed thirteen thousand fictional murders on television, quite a statistic if true.[67] Movies were just as violent, adding to teenager's observational death toll. Some of the greatest heroes of the silver screen such as James Cagney, Edward G. Robinson, and Humphrey Bogart were famous for their death scenes, which kids since the 1930s had eagerly replicated in backyards and school playgrounds. War movies and Westerns were also visual feasts of death, offering matinee audiences Hollywood interpretations of killing that typically had little to do with the real thing. Film historian David Thomson noted that one movie, *The Godfather*, alone included seventeen deaths (one of them the result of getting shot 612 times), the MPAA's "R" rating probably not keeping many young adults from seeing the bloodbath.[68]

While it would be hard to match *The Godfather* (or its two sequels) for murder on a pound-for-pound basis, the end of the twentieth century was turning out to be a golden age of death in America. Pico Iyer of *Time* made note of the country's preoccupation with death, arguing that most of us were missing the point. "One of the liveliest topics of the moment seems, improbably, to be death, even as life expectancies increase," he observed in the magazine, his local bookstore having an entire section devoted to the subject (right next to Recovery and Affirmations). While thinking it was an interesting cultural phenomenon, Iyer was skeptical that all this musing about death was being used for constructive purposes. "Thinking about death is useful only if it makes us concentrate on life," he astutely wrote, that all of us were dying every moment the thing to take away from it all.[69] If there was any doubt at all that death had become a "lively" topic, a new Roper poll offered quantitative proof. Death and dying—perhaps the most difficult subjects to talk about—were becoming the stuff of normal conversation, Roper found (on behalf of its client, FTD, the flower people), with two-thirds of respondents saying they could talk about death and dying and do so more easily than ever before.[70] As the nation headed into the final turn of the century and millennium, however, another twist in the story of death in America lay in store.

Chapter Six

Design for Dying

"Dying is easy. Parking is hard."
—Art Buchwald

On St. Patrick's Day, 1996, a disparate collection of people gathered at the bedside of Timothy Leary, the famous psychologist, writer, and counterculture guru. The seventy-five-year-old Leary was dying of prostate cancer and was treating his death much as he lived his life—an exercise in creativity. Making visits that day included a grandchild, a group of Rastafarians, filmmaker Oliver Stone, an assortment of slackers, and Perry Farrell, the frontman for the alternative rock band Jane's Addiction. In recent weeks, an equally eclectic list of people—Yoko Ono, Winona Ryder (his goddaughter), former Mamas and the Papas singer Michelle Phillips, Laura Huxley (Leary had attended her husband, Aldous's, deathbed vigil in 1963), and Ram Dass (aka Richard Alpert, Leary's old friend from Harvard)—had also stopped by his Beverly Hills home to pay their respects. (Susan Sarandon and Tim Robbins had dropped off a tape of *Dead Man Walking*, in a bit of gallows humor.) Surrounding Leary were not just friends and relatives but also a stack of bills, bouquets of flowers, a collection of medical journals, a giant tank of laughing gas (nitrous oxide), a computer, and a lava lamp. Painkillers, hallucinogens, cigarettes, liquor, and a number of vials of unidentified white powder were also within easy reach.[1]

The months-long "Irish wake," as reporters called it, would end in a similarly celebratory way, Leary had announced. His stated intent was "to die on the World Wide Web" and leave behind a virtual tour of his home, this consistent with his recent fascination with the Internet. Although this did not happen when he died a couple of months later, it could not be said that Leary did not go out of this life with a bang. "The key to dying well is for you to decide where, when, how and whom to invite to the last party," he told a visiting reporter, the man certainly living up to his words.[2] Despite being "deanimated," as he referred to death, a few months after his St. Patrick's Day party, Leary continued to make his presence felt. His book, *Design for Dying*, in which he outlined how to take charge of one's own death, was published the following year, and for years he, or at least part of him, was kept in literal circulation.[3] Some of Leary's remains were part of the first "space burial" the following year, in which the ashes of a few dozen people, including those of *Star Trek* producer Gene Roddenberry, were put in tiny capsules and launched into low earth orbit.[4]

Although Timothy Leary perhaps had some advantages many of us do not have—a big house in Beverly Hills, loads of famous friends, and plenty of options to kill the pain—we should all die as well as he did. Dying well has been on Americans' minds a lot in recent years, the turning of a new century and millennium, 9/11, and a graying population just a few of the reasons explaining why. Death is gradually becoming the proverbial elephant in the room as it becomes increasingly evident we can no longer just ignore it. Too many forces are pushing death and dying to the forefront of America's consciousness whether we are ready for it or not. The last decade or so has shown that while some progress has been made, death remains, in many respects, our last taboo. Time will tell if we can design our dying as Leary did, but America is on the brink of major social turmoil unless and until we accept death for the natural event it is and has always been.

A SACRED EVENT

As we entered the final stretch of the twentieth century, it was clear that Americans were less comfortable with the idea of death than when the century began. And despite the "coming out" of death over the past two or three decades, most Americans still wanted to have little or nothing to do with it. Except in entertainment, especially television dramas and the movies, death remained, for the most part, an off-limits subject. Magazines and television talk shows continued to steer away from the topic, knowing that readers and viewers would prefer lighter fare or practical advice in their leisure hours. Any number of subjects—how to handle moving to a new city, advance in a career, take care of a baby, get along with one's in-laws, manage one's money and invest wisely, or have great sex—were fair game, but death and dying were generally not. Americans were still sensitive to and uncomfortable about death much the way many had felt about sex decades ago, our two great taboos going in reverse directions. Much about sex was or could be known, however, something that could not be said about death. That death was an abstraction, a full (or even partial, perhaps) understanding of it impossible, explained why so many of us preferred to spend our time thinking about more graspable matters. "Our values are challenged when we dabble with the unknown or unfamiliar," wrote Lois Greene Stone in *The Humanist* in 1996, our multicultural society also discouraging a strong, common narrative of death in America.[5]

When presented in a heartwarming, uplifting, and life-affirming way, however, the subject of death could be very popular. That was the case with Mitch Albom's 1997 number-one best seller, *Tuesdays with Morrie*. In the book, Albom told the true story of the time he had spent in the 1970s with his college professor, Morrie Schwartz. Albom learned a lot from Professor Schwartz's sociology classes at Brandeis University, more about life than anything else. Albom promised to stay in touch with his favorite professor after graduation but did not, too occupied in his career for much of anything else. Watching the television show *Nightline* one evening nearly twenty years after the two last talked, Albom was very surprised to see that Schwartz was featured in a segment. Schwartz was dying of ALS but was writing and talking about his approaching death, something so unusual it caught the attention of the *Boston Globe* and then *Nightline*. Albom promptly telephoned his old professor and then paid a visit, the first of many that would come. Conveniently out of work for a while, Albom flew from Detroit to Boston to see Schwartz every Tuesday for the next fourteen weeks, the inspiration for the book. Albom gained the same kind of wisdom that he got from Schwartz twenty years earlier as an undergraduate, the most valuable being the tools with which to reunite with his estranged brother. *Tuesdays with Morrie* (as well as the television movie based on the book) struck a chord with many Americans, its fundamental message ("love always wins") making death seem almost warm and fuzzy.[6]

Hollywood was having a much tougher time dealing with the reality of death in the late 1990s, however. David Ansen of *Newsweek* did not like the ending of the new movie *Stepmom* at all, feeling the audience had been somehow cheated. In the film, Susan Sarandon's character is dying of cancer, but the last thing we see is her happily smiling in a family portrait, this analogous to not seeing the championship match in *Rocky*. "Death just isn't what it used to be," he wrote, plenty of violent killings in movies but natural expiration seemingly off-limits. A similar thing happened at the end of the recent film *Meet Joe Black*, when the "Cute Reaper," as Ansen called Brad Pitt's character, takes Anthony Hopkins's character for a pleasant stroll to "the next place," as it is referred to. And in *What Dreams May Come* starring Robin Williams, a whole family dies but finds heaven to be even better than what they imagined, death not unlike a five-star resort. "Somebody has taken death out of the Death Movie," Ansen continued, thinking that if they saw these films the old Hollywood moguls would be rolling in their graves, so to speak. Greta Garbo's last gasp in the 1936 *Camille* and Bette Davis's performance in the 1939 *Dark Victory* were prime examples of cinematic death, even the sappy *Love Story* giving audiences the emotional jolt they deserved. *Titanic* was the rare exception, the tragic death of Leonardo DiCaprio's character harkening back to the good old days of Hollywood. Ansen suggested that Hollywood's skittishness about death could be related to baby boomer's denial of it, the new moguls not ready to face their own mortality. Ghosts, angels, and other supernatural visitors from the other side were also popping up in a number of recent films, perhaps evidence that middle-aged moviemakers were not prepared for the long good-bye.[7]

However death was presented in popular culture, the sheer volume of it increased steadily through the 1990s. "The past five years or so have seen a swirling controversy surrounding the way Americans think about death," thought the editors of *Utne Reader* in 1998, crediting both Jack Kevorkian's assisted suicides and the "death with dignity" movement for the louder conversation about the end of life. A flurry of books about dying, including Marilyn Webb's *The Good Death: The New American Search to Reshape the End of Life*, Stephen Levine's *A Year to Live: How to Live This Year as If It Were Your Last*, Ira Byock's *Dying Well: The Prospect for Growth at the End of Life*, Tim Brookes's *Signs of Life: A Memoir of Dying and Discovery*, Merrill Collett's *Stay Close and Do Nothing: A Spiritual and Practical Guide to Caring for the Dying at Home*, and Patricia Weenolsen's *The Art of Dying: How to Leave This World with Dignity and Grace, at Peace with Yourself and Your Loved Ones*, had recently been published; this, too, suggested that death was in the air. Aging baby boomers were the underlying reason for the higher profile of dying at the end of the twentieth century, the editors sensibly proposed, "this particularly self-possessed generation" trying to redefine death as they did with pregnancy a couple of decades earlier. Just as boomers recast giving birth from a medical condition to a natural and healthy part of life, this line of thinking went, so could dying be "depathologized." "People can become healthy in their dying," said Byock, sounding a lot like proponents of "death awareness" and "death consciousness" in the 1970s.[8]

Optimists like Byock had faith that Americans—specifically older, wiser baby boomers—could master the art of dying as many cultures had done throughout history. Although there was precious little evidence to support such a claim and the United States was a relatively young country, other great civilizations had shown that death did not have to be the enemy. Jews' Kabbalah and Zohar; the shamanistic rituals of some Native Americans, Africans, Aborigines, and Latin Americans; and Tibetans' and Egyptians' *Book of the Dead* all proved that death could be seen as an integral part of life rather than its evil twin. Could the most powerful nation on earth, led by the largest, best-educated, and most affluent generation in history, remake dying as they remade living thirty years earlier?[9]

Cobbling together some Native American philosophy, Buddhism, and Eastern mysticism, second-generation New Agers put forth bits of wisdom to "make death come to life," as Pythia Peay expressed it. The physical act of dying was now a "transformation," the weariness that came with it reconceived as "deep relaxation." "The look of pained concentration . . . slowly changed to wonder" as a "pearly translucence . . . radiated softly around him," Peay, an editor of *Common Boundary*, recalled after watching her father die. "I felt I was witnessing a sacred event, perhaps even a miracle," she continued, such a description a far cry from the kind of institutional deaths that many Americans experienced. A team of hospice workers, plus a compassionate priest and a dedicated family, made this miracle possible, she explained, plenty of morphine of considerable value as well.[10]

Was this sort of death the modern version of the Zohar or *Book of the Dead*, our shamanistic rituals a combination of spirituality, therapy, and narcotics? It certainly seemed so, different times and different places calling for different modalities but the goal—a peaceful death—much the same. Dying was presented as not the ultimate form of decline but a time of growth, a host of positive things—completion, closure, learning, love, acceptance, self-discovery, transcendence, and surrender—to come of it. Much growth could come from the dying making a final act of sacrifice, death reformers believed, the donating of an organ, correcting a bad character trait, asking forgiveness, or giving money to a worthy cause adding meaning to one's life.[11] Likewise, death was not a state of nothingness but one of "impermanence" or a "disunity of body and spirit," a necessary transition from life to afterlife. Interestingly, some of this school of thought believed it was better to die alone, there being less distraction and fewer people to complicate matters. "Go to a cave by yourself [or] die like a deer in the forest," suggested Rick Fields, the editor-in-chief of *Yoga Journal*, who had been diagnosed with inoperable lung cancer in 1995 at age fifty-three.[12]

Music, too, was increasingly being seen as a way to bring about a peaceful death. Music as therapy was nothing new, of course, but few Americans in recent times had used it to comfort the dying, something Therese Schroeder-Sheker fully embraced via her Missoula, Montana–based Chalice of Repose Project. A professional harpist, Schroeder-Sheker began playing for patients as part of death vigils, an idea that hearkened back to medieval days. The music often lowered patients' pulse and respiration rate (even if they were unconscious), also reducing their need for painkillers. Schroeder-Sheker became an evangelist for what she called *music thanatology*, helping the dying realize what monks a half millennium ago called "a blessed death." By the late 1990s, more than a hundred doctors had referred patients to

Schroeder-Sheker, her staff of harpists on duty for twelve hours a day, 365 days a year.[13]

Other theories and practices that could help lead to "a good death" were put forth in the late 1990s. Psychotherapists were drawing on the work of Carl Jung and transpersonal psychologists to develop a "trans-egoic" model of intervention for use by caregivers to the dying. A healthy self-identity was a good thing to have for most of one's life, this theory went, but "ego disattachment" was valuable while dying. Letting go of the roles one had played in life allowed an individual to achieve a higher self, these psychologists proposed, the ability to distance oneself from one's body another benefit. Based on various cultures' belief that it took minutes, hours, or even days for the soul to withdraw itself from the body, caregivers were also instructed to meditate, recite prayers and spiritual teachings, and play music after the dying person had drawn his or her last breath. All of this guidance was believed to provide the deceased with a kind of map of consciousness to and through the afterlife, this inspired by ancient Tibetan, Egyptian, and medieval European manuscripts. As in this world, it was helpful to know where and where not to go in the next one, spiritually speaking.[14]

In millennial America, all kinds of theories recasting death as a "sacred event" were entertained. In her *Dreaming beyond Death*, for example, Patricia Bulkeley reported that many people have powerful dreams as they approach the end of life, these experiences helping them cope with their fears and find closure. Bulkeley saw a lot of people die while working as a hospice chaplain for ten years in Marin, California, a good number of them sharing their dreams with her in their final days and weeks. Soaring birds and butterflies was a common image, the dreamer feeling a sense of freedom as they saw them fly through the air. Embarking on a journey was another frequent theme, the dreamer happy to know that an exciting trip could be waiting for him or her. Seeing dead family members also often wove through predeath dreams, the ones who went before hugging them or offering words of comfort. Although little previous research had been done in this area, many brilliant minds of the past (including Confucius, Socrates, and Carl Jung) had described having such dreams shortly before they died. Although tempting to assume these were premonitions of what lay beyond (visions of a divine entity also sometimes appeared), it was important to keep in mind that people often experience vivid, intense dreams at acute stages of crisis and transition in their lives.[15]

THE BEST THING THAT EVER HAPPENS TO YOU

All this outpouring of death and dying in fin de siecle America was directly related to baby boomers' confronting the fact that they were indeed mortal.

Not just the parents of boomers were dying but older siblings and friends, sometimes only a personal connection with death making the inevitable real. Some funeral parlors, however, were not willing to wait for midlifers to come to this realization. More marketing-savvy morticians began targeting baby boomers in direct mail campaigns, encouraging them to invest in their services while they were relatively young. Many homeowners were no doubt surprised to see in their mailbox an offer to attend an open house at a funeral home, the fact that refreshments would be served and a prize given away not sweetening the deal. Morticians had traditionally kept a low profile, rarely advertising and, when doing so, doing it as simply and tastefully as possible. But now funeral parlors were increasingly eager to show off their services to a generation that had been aggressively sold to throughout their lives. Those choosing to attend such an opening would be encouraged to take a look at the caskets and cremation urns on display, the experience not all that different from shopping for a new car. Embalmers, too, would typically be on hand to answer any questions, the goal to take some of the mystery and ghoulishness out of a service that one day everyone would need.[16]

Morticians were naturally eager to sign baby boomers up because it meant very big business. The average funeral service in the United States in 1996 cost about $4,600 ($2,100 for the casket, $1,000 for the funeral home, $500 for embalming and other preparation, and $1,000 for the hearse and memorial service), according to the National Funeral Directors Association. The cost of a cemetery plot and marker was $1,500 or so, putting the price of a soup-to-nuts burial over $6,000. It was thus no wonder more Americans were opting for cremation, which cost only about $500, including disposal of the ashes. The market share of cremation rose from 17 to 21 percent between 1990 and 1995, with 43 percent of Americans saying in 1995 that is how they wanted their body to be disposed. Our discomfort with reminders of death no doubt also had something to do with the popularity of cremation. "People don't want to be in the presence of a body," stated Sandra M. Gilbert, professor of English at the University of California and author of *Death's Door: Modern Dying and the Ways We Grieve*, nothing making death more real than a corpse.[17] Interestingly, more often than not (54 percent of the time), the ashes of a cremated body were left at the funeral home. Ashes were returned to families 23 percent of the time, buried or stored in a cemetery 16 percent of the time, and scattered over land or water 6 percent of the time. Morticians expected more creative dispersals of ashes in the years ahead, however. Rock star Kurt Cobain's ashes were molded into small sculptures in a Buddhist monastery and sent to his friends, for example, while those of labor organizer Joe Hill were placed in envelopes and mailed to union locals around the world. Who knew where the remains of the most individualistic generation in history would end up?[18]

Meanwhile, it was "the greatest generation" who were dying in consider-able numbers at the end of the twentieth century. Millions of baby boomers (myself included) were facing the death of their parents, the event often the most difficult of their lives. Many boomers had not previously experienced the death of a loved one, making the experience a surreal one. (*Men's Health* felt the need to publish an article called "How to Bury Your Father.")[19] Watching once hale and hearty bodies wither away was profoundly sad, the final days of one's mother or father not any easier despite the sense of relief. Many still had trouble sleeping or recurring nightmares years after the funer-al, any number of things bringing back vivid reminders of their parent. Smelling a particular brand of perfume or hearing a certain song could elicit a sea of memories, a flood of tears often following. Emotionally speaking, fortysomethings were briefly transformed into four-year-olds, simply want-ing their mom or dad to be there for them. Those who were on bad terms with a parent when he or she died often felt great guilt and remorse. For boomers whose parents were not well, a call late at night could be terrifying, the first thought that they had taken a turn for the worse or had already died. The statistics bore out their fears. By the time they turned fifty, a quarter of Americans had lost their mothers and a half their fathers. Depression, family conflict, or a midlife crisis could follow the death of a parent, the full realiza-tion that one was also mortal another part of the challenging experience.[20]

Other issues added to the stress of a parent dying. Children often lived hundreds or thousands of miles away, meaning they had to "commute" to the bedside vigil or plan the burial remotely. At the peak of their careers and frequently holding high-pressure jobs, boomers found it tough to devote the proper time and energy to the situation. As well, three-day bereavement leaves, the norm at many companies, were simply not long enough to take care of what had to get done. Balancing work and mourning, like work and childraising, often meant something had to give. Well-known for their self-awareness, to put it kindly, boomers were also apt to be not quite emotionally prepared for the death of a parent regardless of its likelihood. In the case of both parents now being dead, feeling suddenly alone in the world was com-mon, as was the sense that one's biggest supporters were gone. No more stories from childhood, some were sorry to realize, or, much more important, grandparents for one's children. Hosting family events and holidays was now the domain of the next generation; this, too, a difficult thing to accept.[21] More practical considerations, like clearing up problems with the estate or the disposing of belongings, added to the strain. If there was any consolation, it was that many people were going through the process. Some friends and siblings were seeing each other just at funerals, the unfortunate occasion the only reason for very busy baby boomers to find the time to get together with people with whom they had once been close.[22]

As with most of their other activities, however, boomers were known to throw themselves into the funeral of a parent, sometimes customizing the event to honor the unique individual that was their mother or father. Funerals had become, relatively suddenly, "celebrations of life," infused with New Age philosophy and self-help positivism. Playing old home movies or having "guests" write personal notes to the departed and put them in a "memory box" were not unusual.[23] Things that a generation earlier would have been considered odd—releasing butterflies, putting cremation ashes into lockets, or incorporating something the parent loved in the ceremony—were no longer so, virtually any twist considered in good taste as long it was true to the memory of the deceased. Setting a Harley alongside the casket of a motorcycle enthusiast was perfectly acceptable, as was holding a memorial at a local stable for a horse (or horse racing) lover. Rifles and fishing poles were standing in for flowers at the funerals of some hunters and anglers; this, too, appreciated by mourners who knew the deceased best. Given baby boomers' inclination to personalize everything they hold dear, one can only imagine the kind of funerals that will be held over the next few decades.[24]

Some, however, have recently proposed that a parent's death can be not just a sad experience but also a positive one. "The death of your parents can be the best thing that ever happens to you," said Jeanne Safer, a Manhattan psychotherapist, in 2008, believing that the circumstances, as painful as they are, are ideal for great personal growth. Safer, author of *Death Benefits: How Losing a Parent Can Change an Adult's Life—For the Better*, argued that "nothing else in adult life has so much unrecognized potential to help us become more fulfilled human beings—wiser, more mature, more open, less afraid." While her thesis (based on case studies of sixty of her patients, as well as her own experience) was controversial, Safer was part of a new wave of thinking about parental death. A new genre of books about and for "midlife orphans" had emerged, in fact, the list including *Losing Your Parents, Finding Yourself: The Defining Turning Point of Adult Life*; *Never the Same: Coming to Terms with the Death of a Parent*; *Nobody's Child Anymore*; *Midlife Orphan: Facing Life's Changes Now That Your Parents Are Gone*; *The Orphaned Adult: Understanding and Coping with Grief and Change after the Death of Our Parents*; and *Death of a Parent: Transition to a New Adult Identity*.[25]

With longer life spans and extended adolescence, parental death was now a major maturational milestone, some felt, the marker of adulthood not having a child but losing one's mother and father. Although many in the past had proposed that the death of one's parents was an existential crisis, the idea took on special resonance when applied to "forever young" baby boomers.[26] Growing up in an era of broad prosperity and good health care, many boomers simply had not faced major adversity in their lives, making the death of parents all the more shocking. Some baby boomers, upon their parents' death, finally felt able to pursue the career they really wanted to pursue rather than the one they had to make their mother and father happy. Divorce, too, was common after the death of one's parents, the loss of unconditional love making some look for a replacement for it outside their marriage. Relationships among siblings could go either way; some brothers and sisters grew closer after the death of their parents while some drifted further apart, the glue keeping them together no longer there.[27]

ON OUR OWN TERMS

Complicating things for baby boomers were the ways in which their parents were dying. "We don't die well in America," said journalist Bill Moyers in 2000, his own mother's recent death a perfect example. (She died after three grueling years of illness.) Despite many saying throughout their life they wanted a "natural" death in familiar surroundings, most ended up having little choice and control over the circumstances. Moyers interviewed over a dozen dying Americans for his four-part PBS documentary *On Our Own Terms: Moyers on Dying*, which aired in September of that year. Moyers hoped the series would lead to steps that would improve the end-of-life experience and prompt Americans to better prepare for their own deaths. Discussing the options with one's family was vital, the interviews clearly illustrated, especially if or when to choose relieving physical pain and emotional distress over curative measures. The death of a loved one was always sad, the series showed, but there were ways to make the last good-bye a relatively good one.[28]

Interviewed by *Money* magazine about the series, Bill and Judith Moyers explained why they felt the need to address what they called "the last taboo." "Once it's on the table, then I think things will change," said Judith, a variety of factors—a growing movement to improve end-of-life care, the AIDS epidemic, the Kevorkian controversy, and baby boomers' gradual recognition of the existence of mortality—stirring up interest in death and dying. With Americans still reluctant to raise the topic with their doctors, clergy people, or spouses, however, there was a long way to go before it could be said to be "on the table." "We are a nation of the future, and we don't like to think that there are limits and boundaries to that future," explained Bill, hitting the nail on the head when it comes to our culture of denial. Americans had, in Freudian terms, a neurosis about death, they believed, the knowledge that there was a boundary to life repressed in our collective subconscious. Accepting that choices could be made regarding the parameters of one's death would go a long way in addressing these psychological issues, the simple acknowledgment that life had an ending a good beginning.[29]

A contributing factor to Americans not dying well was that most were very misinformed about what was likely to kill them. In a 2000 survey, for example, 34 percent of women twenty-five-years or older listed breast cancer as the greatest threat to their health, 7 percent listed heart disease, and just 1 percent listed stroke. The reality, however, was that heart disease accounted for more than five times the number of deaths of women as breast cancer, and stroke more than twice the number. In fact, more Americans died as a result of medical errors than breast cancer (or than motor vehicle accidents or AIDS, for that matter), illustrating low little we knew (or wanted to know) about what was likely to kill us. Deaths by diabetes was rising fast, this also not something most Americans were too worried about.[30] Canadians were equally overconcerned about certain things killing them and underconcerned about other things that were more likely. Thirty Canadians had died from the much-feared SARS "epidemic" by June 2003, for example, and eighteen from the similarly dreaded West Nile virus. Some 6,714 people died from diabetes in that country in 2000, however, the disease there not getting the attention it deserved. More Canadians were killed at railway crossings or from falling off ladders in 2000 than people who would die from SARS, in fact; our sensible neighbors to the north are as mixed up as we are when it comes to cause of death.[31]

Dying on one's own terms went much further than a familiarity with government statistics on cause of death. It was tempting to believe that the division between life and death was a nice, clean break, but the hard truth was that dying was often a messy business. With the rise of technologically extended life, a host of ethical dilemmas had sprung up that were highly problematic to patients, their families, doctors, and hospital administrators. Most large hospitals across the country had formed on-staff ethics teams to deal with such challenges, many of them addressing the gray zone between life and death. Such teams, which usually consisted of physicians, bioethicists, social workers, chaplains, and legal experts, helped patients and families understand a prognosis, evaluate treatment alternatives, and act as mediators when there was some kind of conflict. Typical cases were what to do when siblings disagreed about a parent's end-of-life care, whether a girlfriend should be able to retrieve her dying boyfriend's sperm, and if the family of a man dying of AIDS had to be informed of the cause of death. Other cases included whether dying homeless people should be forced to receive treatment if they refused it and what to do with suicide cases who were clinging to life. Such real-life situations illustrated how complex dying could be, making it somewhat understandable why so many people had difficulty just discussing it.[32]

There were other completely nonmedical ethical issues to consider when it came to death. For example, what to do with an apartment or home for sale in which there had been a violent death? Real estate brokers occasionally faced this quandary, with no real consensus on the matter. Saying as little as possible to potential buyers about the situation was the typical way to go, although some agents were amenable to revealing what had taken place there. ("Are you aware of the history of the building?," was a gentle way to break the news.) A middle ground was to disclose that a death had occurred in the dwelling but not go into the sordid details (i.e., that it had been a murder, suicide, or both). Those from Chinese ancestry were especially suspect of buying a place where someone had died, even if the death had been a peaceful one. (Given that most people used to die at home, it was of course highly likely that many houses going back one, two, or three centuries had a death occur within its walls.) Some homes with a gruesome past sat on the market much longer than they normally should have, the sense that there could be lingering bad karma keeping the place from selling despite a very attractive price.[33]

DYING WELL

It was ironic, given that death was one of the few certainties in life, that few of us spent much time planning for it. Americans' reluctance to give much thought to the end of their lives seemed to support Freud's theory that others' deaths were understandable but that one's own was unimaginable. Americans spent more time planning their annual two-week vacation than their last two weeks alive, studies showed, the knowledge that the former would probably be a lot more fun than the latter certainly having something to do with this. Statistics at the beginning of the twenty-first century revealed that Americans had clearly not mastered the art of dying. Seven out of ten people said they wanted to die at home, according to a 2000 Time/CNN poll, but more than that actually died in medical institutions. More than a third of dying Americans spent at least ten days in intensive-care units hooked up to IVs and monitors, this certainly not the way most people wanted to leave this earth. As well, the dying were more often than not treated by strangers and frequently in a drug-induced fog or in pain (the latter almost always unnecessary given available medications like fentanyl), this, too, not an ideal way to end one's life. Worse, all this undesired unpleasantness was extremely expensive. One-third of Americans bankrupted their families by dying, rather incredibly, this fact alone making it clear something had gone very wrong when it came to death in this country. Why did we spend years planning for retirement and virtually no time planning for death, one had to ask?[34]

Ira Byock, the author of *Dying Well*, felt that we simply did not demand enough when it came to our own deaths. "Our expectations as a culture for end-of-life care are too low," he told *Time* magazine in 2000, thinking it was time for us to insist that physicians approach dying in a different way. Seeing how their parents were dying, many baby boomers—a group notorious for wanting to get their way and, usually, getting it—felt similarly. Dying comfortably should not be just a nice idea but one of our basic rights, some progressive physicians, caregivers, and academics agreed, a "death reform" movement beginning to bubble up. Physicians' fear of legal scrutiny or that they would get patients addicted or kill them was behind their decision to prescribe weaker medications, something that had to change, reformers felt. Medical schools had begun teaching pain management to future doctors, encouragingly, and the AMA now offered continuing education on the subject.[35]

The problem of dying in America went well beyond effective pain management, however; it was our general attitudes toward death that was the larger issue. Safer surgery and the invention of antibiotics, each going back to the 1930s, had made combating disease the focus of medicine, the dying patient often getting lost in the process. As dying increasingly became the province of modern medicine, in other words, death was removed from everyday life, this the real reason why Americans were so bad at it. Not only did we not want to talk about death, most of us had not made it clear what kind of care we wanted when it was near. In 2000, only 55 percent (an all-time high) of those over sixty-five years old had an advance directive specifying the kind of medical decisions to be made while one was dying, the number significantly lower for younger Americans. Religious leaders also found it difficult to offer guidance to the dying, studies showed, not too surprising given that a fair share of the clergy had little or no training in end-of-life care.[36]

Given that those with a fatal illness typically spent a couple of years with it (as much time as they spent as toddlers, one could say), more attention to dying was clearly needed, death reformers sensibly explained. How to live with a disease that was going to kill you—and live well with it—was the principal issue, hardly an easy one to face. Giving up rescue medicine and life-prolonging treatments (such as chemotherapy) for comfort care was the key if the chances of a cure were tiny, with getting out of the hospital the first order of business. Hospice care, focused on managing the physical pain and helping patients address the emotional aspects of dying, was next, with doctors, social workers, and therapists members of one's team. Simply helping out with things that had to get done around the house was another part of hospice care. Much more patient-focused than nursing homes and a lot cheaper than hospitals (less than a fourth of being in an ICU), hospice seemed to be the best option for the dying not interested in taking their chances with a traditional medical approach.[37]

Despite all the apparent benefits, just 17 percent of dying Americans were choosing hospice care in 2000, however, partly because of Medicare's tight restrictions. (Two doctors had to certify that a patient had less than six months to live, something many were reluctant to do.) The average length of hospice care was just two to three weeks, this hardly enough time for the dying to die well. But many patients voluntarily turned down hospice care, preferring to fight on and hope for a miracle. Experimental clinical trials offering a remote possibility of a cure were and are routinely offered, a carrot dangling in front of terminal patients. Many dying patients thus had to make the tough choice between hospice and bankruptcy, the cost of prescriptions often not covered by Medicare. Giving up procedures that alleviated symptoms of diseases, such as dialysis, was another cost of choosing hospice care, this, too, keeping the numbers down. Insurance companies were doing the dying no favors, refusing to reimburse hospice patients for such procedures (despite providing coverage for more expensive, unlikely-to-cure chemotherapy). Lawmakers were considering ways to make hospice care more accessible, but it was clear that all parties involved—cities, states, graduate schools, doctors, and patients themselves—could do a better job of improving the state of dying in America as we began a new century.[38]

Dying at home may have been the choice of many Americans, even if most ended up dying in hospitals, but there could be problems in doing so. A death at home was more likely to be calm and peaceful, but it often got complicated after the last breath of the departed. First, it was required that a licensed professional determine that a person was indeed dead, meaning one had to go out to the home where the death took place. Doctors had a way of not being available for such duties, making the bereaved have to call an ambulance—for a dead person—to get the job done. Other requirements caused further difficulties when someone died at home. Death certificates had to be completed in black ink (listing only approved diagnoses), an undertaker had to be specified, and it was necessary for the police to be called to make sure no crime had taken place. Hospitals and even hospice care centers certainly had their faults but were masters of bureaucracy and efficiency, including the handling of the administrative details for a death.[39]

AN INSULAR EXPERIENCE

The death reform movement, the result in large part of an unprecedented demographic phenomenon, helped to trigger a greater awareness of and interest in the end of life at the turn of the twenty-first century. E. Annie Proulx wondered why looking at death so intrigued us now, whether it was via a wreck on the highway, a person lying stone, cold dead on the sidewalk, or slasher films. Will this be the way we died? How do we protect ourselves from such a fate? These questions, plus the reminder that we were safe and sound, accounted for some of our mortal rubbernecking. Mary Roach's 2003 *Stiff: The Curious Lives of Human Cadavers* was a prime example of our fascination with death, especially its more grisly side. Over the past couple of decades, photographs of dead people had also become quite popular, with morgue shots, crime scenes, skeletons, and preserved body parts some of the images we found fascinating. Memorial photographs went back over a century, of course, but these were intended just for the bereaved family, unlike more recent ones that were for public consumption. Images from the Vietnam War had a lot to do with the coming out of death photography, Proulx thought, the scourge of AIDS in the 1980s also removing some of the taboo surrounding the art form. Interestingly, there was no real equivalent in literature, she pointed out, only the novel *American Psycho* depicting the same kind of voyeuristic peek into the darker side of death.[40]

Death could definitely be found in contemporary movies and television, much of it courtesy of Alan Ball. Ball wrote the screenplay of the 1999 movie *American Beauty* and created the HBO series *Six Feet Under*, each of these heavily steeped in the harsh reality of death and dying. "*Six Feet Under* . . . goes for the jugular, reminding us that death is as arbitrary and unexpected as it is inevitable," thought *New York* magazine as the series ended its five-year run in 2005.[41] The show was set in a funeral home, a place with which Ball was intimately familiar. Ball's sister died in an automobile accident when he was thirteen (he was in the car), his father, grandfather, grandmother, and great-aunt also dying over the next two years. Going to all these funerals while a teenager "taught me that death exists and it just comes out of nowhere," Ball said, finding our end-of-life rituals "weird and creepy." Besides his dead sister not looking much as she had in life and the strange music that was played at her funeral, actual grief was discouraged. (His mother was whisked away when she broke down and started sobbing.) America's immaturity had a lot to do with our denial of mortality, Ball believed, our focus on youth also a key factor in our repression of death. Hiding the reality of death and dying was "profoundly unhealthy," he felt, something quite apparent in his television show and movie (which won five Oscars, including Best Screenplay and Best Picture). "When you pretend death doesn't exist, you just give it that much more power over you," Ball explained, America's phobia of mortality speaking for itself.[42]

Literature, too, was strewn with death in the 2000s. Joan Didion's *The Year of Magical Thinking* had sold six hundred thousand copies in the first couple of years since its release in 2005 and won a National Book Award, the 2007 Broadway show based on it also a big hit. Death, at least a memoir about it, had rarely been so popular, making one wonder what about it made it so compelling. Calvin Trillin's tribute to his late wife, *About Alice*, was also a best seller, suggesting that the subject of grief and, specifically, the death of a spouse was becoming an area Americans wanted to explore. There was also Donald Hall's *The Best Day the Worst Day*, a "grief memoir" about his late wife, Jane Kenyon. That Didion's daughter died shortly after the book was finished helped make *The Year of Magical Thinking* a cultural phenomenon, however, her double loss seemingly too much for one person to bear. Like others who had lost their spouse, Didion refused to believe her husband of thirty-nine years was really gone (this the "magical thinking"), that she was unable to get rid of his clothes just one example of her denial. Readers and theatergoers were invited into Didion's slightly mad universe of grief, a rare opportunity to share an individual's close and personal encounter with the death of a loved one. In 2011, Didion followed up *The Year of Magical Thinking* with *Blue Nights*, which told the story of the death of her daughter, Quintana. Two other "grief memoirs" written by notable authors were published that same year, Joyce Carol Oates's *A Widow's Story* and Meghan O'Rourke's *The Long Goodbye*. Why were so many authors rather suddenly writing books about the death of a spouse or parent and, more importantly, why did so many people want to read them? Although dying is a natural and inevitable part of life, it is clear we are simply not very well prepared to face the death of a loved one, making both the writing and the reading of such books cathartic experiences.[43]

Philip Roth's 2006 novel *Everyman*, about a man's approach toward death, also struck a nerve with its candor. (The book begins with the protagonist's funeral.) Some rightly felt that both Didion's book and Roth's were more about each writer's personal sense of grief or self-pity than the broader significance of death, however. "It's not surprising that two of our most important writers are telling us that death is an insular experience that transcends social circumstance," wrote Richard Goldstein in *The Nation*, feeling that self-obsession was at the root of both works. These works were a far cry from Tolstoy's *The Death of Ivan Ilyich*, Goldstein thought, that novel presenting dying as "a supremely social event." Literature about AIDS a decade or two earlier had also located suffering within the larger community, revealing something about life, but, according to Goldstein, "this concept no longer seems plausible." Goldstein traced this new, more self-absorbed attitude toward death to Sherwin Nuland's 1994 *How We Die* and Jim Crace's 1999 novel *Being Dead*, the latter about the decay of a couple's bodies on a beach. "Social detachment breeds a rigid narrowness," Goldstein concluded, these two books prime examples of our prevailing "I-Me-Mine" attitude.[44] Interestingly, Lakshmi Chaudhry said much the same thing about the Harry Potter series of books and films in the same publication about a year later. There was lots of death in the hugely popular franchise (including the Hogwarts ghosts, who celebrated their "Deathday"), "but [J. K.] Rowling is oddly coy when it comes to telling us what to die for," Chaudhry thought. It was just Harry's life, along with those of his friends and family, that seemed to matter, this writer along with author A. S. Byatt suggested, here, too, a no larger social or cultural significance of an individual's death.[45]

Given the self-absorption of death in American popular culture, it was no wonder that newspaper obituary notices had recently become lengthy tributes to the dearly departed, although it was not quite clear who was intended to read them. The deceased were often courageous in death ("Suddenly but peacefully, without a word of complaint," went the opening line of one from 2007), their lives almost always "rich" and "vibrant." Children were inevitably "beloved" and grandchildren "wonderful" (or vice versa). After such an introduction, death announcements in your average American newspaper were apt to go on and on, describing the childhood, education, career, achievements, and even extraordinary beauty of the dead man or woman. Everyone had the right to his or her fifteen minutes of fame, it seemed, even if one was dead. Likewise, eulogies had become overly self-important and self-serving, not for the deceased but for the eulogizer. The trend was for speakers to relate a personal story that revealed a particular insight about the one being eulogized, the net result often being that attendees of a funeral learned more about the person at the podium than the one lying in the coffin.[46] It was Cher's speech at the funeral of ex-husband Sonny Bono in 1998 that made the eulogy an acceptable literary art form for family and friends rather than just clergy, Cyrus M. Copeland argued. After hearing Cher's rhetorical masterpiece, many thought to themselves, "I could do that," Copeland wrote in his book *Farewell, Godspeed: The Greatest Eulogies of Our Time.*[47]

Much less self-absorbed, ironically, was Kathleen Kennedy Townsend's account of her experience with death. As Robert Kennedy's daughter, Townsend had been around death since she was child, her family's many tragedies part of the nation's story. Townsend, who was lieutenant governor of Maryland from 1995 to 2003, was named for her aunt, Kathleen, who died in a plane crash three years before she was born. Her aunt's husband was killed in World War II, as was her uncle Joe, all of them under age thirty when they died. Although she had never met them, her parents talked about these three often, something that would prove to be valuable for the rest of her life. "Immunity was not possible," she remembered in *Reader's Digest* in 2008, death making no distinctions in whom it claimed.[48]

Townsend's grandparents (Ethel's parents) were killed in a plane crash when she was four, the beginning of an incredible series of personal encounters with death. Her uncle, President John F. Kennedy, was killed when she was twelve, this followed a few years later by the death of another uncle (Ethel's brother) and one of her father's best friends (again in a plane crash). Just nine months later, the widow of Ethel's brother choked on a piece of food and died, her four orphaned children sent to live with other family members. Townsend was sixteen (the oldest of ten children) when her father was killed (another sister was born six months after the assassination of her dad). Death would continue to make itself known to Townsend. In college, one of her best friends committed suicide, another friend beaten into a coma and dying thirty years later. Townsend's brother, David, died of a drug overdose in 1984, another brother, Michael, killed in a freak skiing accident thirteen years later. Her cousin John, along with his wife and sister-in-law, were killed in a plane crash in 1999, the end to Townsend's unimaginable acquaintance with death.[49]

Rather than Didion's, Roth's, and Rowling's "It's-all-about-me" treatment of death and grief, however, Townsend framed hers in a larger, more socially aware context. "We acknowledge the pain and the loss, we develop rituals, . . . and we remember," she wrote in her fittingly titled article "Beyond Tragedy," this simple formula the only real way to get through such devastating loss. People often sympathized that her family's tragic history was public knowledge, but she considered it a blessing. Many of the dead were quickly forgotten, after all, but millions fondly remembered her relatives, their spirit very much alive. Turning outward, not inward, was the key to dealing with death when it struck close to home. "The worst confronts us, and the question for each of us is, 'How do we respond?,'" her response something we all could and should learn from.[50]

Similar lessons had been learned after 9/11, lessons that continued to resonate years after the attacks. The event of 9/11 shifted the narrative of death in America, the collective "near-death experience," as some referred to it, making us all feel more vulnerable. Besides the sheer number of people who died (2,977, not including the nineteen hijackers), it was the way they died—a jet airplane flying into a building, being blown up or stabbed on an airplane, or falling ninety floors—that was so disturbing. Violent, impersonal, and seemingly senseless, this kind of death was difficult to comprehend.[51] Many thousands lost husbands, wives, parents, children, friends, and colleagues, the loss lingering years following the terrorists' strikes. Jill Goldstein, the wife of a Cantor Fitzgerald employee who was killed at the World Trade Center, told her story in *Good Housekeeping* in 2003, describing her pain as "becom[ing] more intense every day." Routinely asked by family and friends what they could do, Goldstein felt the need to offer ten "Don'ts," her suggestions designed to help others in similar situations. Don't try to fix us or tell us to snap out of it, she advised, offering pity or compliments on their strength or trying to assume the role of a surrogate parent for their children also not desired. Don't be afraid to talk about their loved ones, don't be put off by their moodiness, and please don't ask about their financial situation, she continued, adding that it was not personal if they did not return phone calls. Most important, however, don't abandon them, Goldstein urged others when the worst happens, their need for friendship as great now as ever.[52]

THE MOST IMPORTANT TOOL

American death culture again entered a new trajectory in 2007 with the case of Randy Pausch. Because of the reach and speed of the Internet, arguably no dying person in the world was more famous than the Carnegie Mellon professor after he gave his final speech to his class. "The Last Lecture" became an Internet sensation (it reportedly received ten million hits on YouTube), with a best-selling book cowritten with Jeffrey Zaslow based on the talk soon published. Going (extremely) public with his terminal condition allowed millions of people to think seriously about dying and to confront their own mortality, a rare thing in our death-phobic culture. That "The Last Lecture" and the book of the same name was upbeat and filled with jokes made it all the more remarkable, its underlying message (like Professor Morrie Schwartz's) that love should be the center of one's life. Pausch received ten thousand e-mails saying, "Your lecture bettered my life" or the equivalent, this part of the legacy he knew he was leaving behind. Pausch likened himself to the dying Lou Gehrig who, when he bade farewell to his fellow players in Yankee Stadium in 1939, famously called himself "the luckiest man on the face of this earth." "It's not the years, it's the mileage," he told *Reader's Digest* in May 2008, not happy to be dying at forty-seven but grateful for the life he had lived.[53]

Three months before Pausch died, *Time* magazine invited readers to ask him a question, with people from New York City to Tokyo seizing the unusual opportunity to have a personal exchange with a stranger who was dying. The questions ranged from the spiritual ("Do you believe you were chosen to deliver a message of hope?") to the personal ("Have you given your wife permission to remarry?") to the medical ("Have you looked at alternative remedies?"), a clear sign of the curiosity surrounding the circumstances of impending death. Of the ten published, however, one question, or series of questions, from a fifty-four-year-old man from Indianapolis also with terminal cancer, stood out. Always wanting to be an artist but ending up working in information technology, the man asked Pausch what he thought he should do with the remainder of his life. "Do I keep working till I die?" "Do I quit and go to art school?" "Do I travel the world?" "What the hell am I supposed to do?" Such questions illustrated how unprepared most of us are when death approaches, an unfortunate thing given the certainty it will happen to everyone. "Everybody's situation is unique [but] I'd bet on art school," Pausch responded, pretty good advice from someone who knew of which he spoke.[54]

Townsend's, Goldstein's, and Pausch's stories showed that the best thinking about death linked dying to living, the two not opposing forces but rather complementary, symbiotic ones. Denying death, as most of us did, was thus denying a big part of life, only the awareness that our life would one day end enabling us to get the most out of it.[55] "Remembering that I'll be dead soon is the most important tool I've ever encountered to help me make the big choices in life," Steve Jobs, cofounder of Apple, had told a recent graduating class, his bout with cancer making him realize he had little to lose both professionally and personally by taking chances.[56]

An even more important authority—science—was making the case that there was actually an upside to death, at least at an evolutionary level. The idea that evolution should not be blamed but rather credited for death gained additional currency in recent years. Cells and, perhaps, entire organisms (like you and me) self-destruct to benefit the species, some biologists continued to argue, death at its root a clever evolutionary strategy. There was no dispute that human cells continually committed suicide via apoptosis, a process that got rid of mutations that would otherwise kill us (as by cancer). Some evolutionary biologists went further, however, by suggesting that we had an inbuilt genetic aging program that kept a cap on longevity. All of us living forever or even more than a century and a half would overpopulate the human species and create a much older population, making death a very good thing from a biological point of view. Despite all the incredible scientific advances that had been made over the last century, however, no one really knew why people died from old age, this one of the biggest stories still being told in the history of death.[57]

The death reform movement, now a decade or so old, continued to percolate as more Americans sought ways to turn dying into a more positive experience. Some couples, for example, were deciding to "go public" with the news that one of them was dying. Going directly against the pervasive denial of death, these couples were overtly open about it, holding special gatherings with family and friends to escort the dying individual on his or her journey. The process was on occasion streamed on the Internet, with viewers from around the world invited to be part of the event (just as Timothy Leary had imagined his would be). Welcoming death rather than hiding from it was the key, with visitors encouraged to ask the person making the trip any question they would like. Such conversations were in fact all too rare in American society, few people willing or able to talk frankly about their death and few people wanting to hear about it. Most couples choosing this option were already well acquainted with death, the loss of a previous partner giving them a less fearful, more spiritual attitude toward the end of life. A friend or family member sometimes was asked or volunteered to build the casket, another way to personalize the passing and avoid the assembly-line approach of the modern funeral industry. Washing the dead body could also be a communal affair, this a popular tradition before the professionalization of death. Likewise, holding a vigil around the deceased for a few days hearkened back to earlier times, a much different thing than the current custom of whisking the body away before it even was cold.[58]

Ethical wills were another way to add meaning and purpose to death and dying. Rooted in Western religion, ethical wills went back thousands of years, a means for the dying to express and hopefully pass on their values to children. Usually in the form of letters, ethical wills also often were an opportunity to document family history. Just as someone bestowed physical and financial assets to others in a legal will, an ethical will allowed the leaving of one's philosophical and spiritual assets, these considered as or even more valuable than material objects or money. Ethical wills had become a useful tool for hospice workers in the 1970s, one of various therapies to help the dying achieve a conscious or "mindful" death. Now, with the popularity of home video cameras and the Web, the dying were able to deliver their messages through multiple media and to a much larger audience, the ancient practice reinvented for the twenty-first century.[59]

The Web was changing the culture of death in other ways. At its best (and worst) when it allows people to do things they cannot do in "real" life, the Internet was increasingly becoming a place for the bereaved to express their grief. Griefnet.org was one website that had been launched in the mid-1990s to help midlifers deal with the loss of their parents. Public, anonymous, and informal, the online universe was in many ways an ideal setting for people to say what they wanted to say and feel what they wanted to feel. The number of funeral-related websites thus not surprisingly grew steadily through the 2000s. Funeralcast.com was reportedly the first site to show webcasts of services, while sites such as VirtualMemorials.com, AngelsOnline.com, and LifeRecorded.com allowed users to create their own websites dedicated to a dead person. Today, there is Legacy.com, a website "where life stories live on." Through obituaries and guest books (to "celebrate a loved one's life"), memorial sites (to "remember shared legacies"), and even an "ObitMessenger" for "free obituary alerts," Legacy.com is a one-stop shop for keeping the memory of a loved one, friend, or complete stranger alive. More than eighteen million visitors from all around the world visit the site each month, clear evidence that it serves a real need.[60]

Was the shifting of grief and, more generally, death online a good or bad thing? A solid case could be made either way, reflecting the ambivalent nature of the Internet in general. From one respect, attending a funeral service through a monitor, posting a comment about the deceased on a blog, or even building a virtual shrine to a loved one can be viewed as poor substitutes for the real, face-to-face thing. Virtual grieving is enabling our denial of death rather than helping us overcome it, this argument goes, our underlying problem with mortality in no way resolved through technology. On the other hand, any and all opportunities to vent grief and other strong emotions related to the death of someone close is probably a good thing, especially given our discomfort, fear, and embarrassment surrounding the end of life. Letting it all out online is no different than Victorian-style weeping and wailing, one might say, the venue merely moved from a stuffy parlor room to a one gigabyte PC.[61]

Not everything about death and dying was moving in a positive direction, however. Possibly the worst view of death was that of the financial community. "Death bonds" were the latest exotic investment to pique the interest of Wall Street, seen as an opportunity to make big money by betting people would die sooner than later. Death bonds, or life settlement–backed securities, were created when investors agreed to continue paying the premium of life insurance policies when the original owners (usually people over sixty-five) wanted to cash out because they were too expensive. When a seller died, the new owner of the policy (who often paid just a third of its value) collected, meaning the quicker the death the bigger the profit. As it did with subprime mortgages, Wall Street planned to package the policies into bundles and then sell them as bonds to investors, a process called "securitization." Hedge funds had been buying "life settlements" for some time, but now firms such as Deutsche Bank, Merrill Lynch, UBS, and Wells Fargo were thinking of getting in on the action. The market for unwanted life insurance policies had grown from $8 billion in 2005 to $15 billion in 2008, this the kind of thing that investment bankers dream about. Goldman Sachs even created a "mortality index" that predicted the life expectancy of sixty-five-year-olds with insurance policies. Death bonds were expected to return about 8 percent, not too bad in the shaky economic climate of the late 2000s. The life settlement industry had a sketchy past, but that did not stop the heavy hitters from seeing if and how they could get into the death business.[62]

Almost as evil was direct marketers' targeting the dead with their junk mail. It was not unusual for a person to receive direct mail a decade or longer after he or she died, this one of the many costs of our technological and impersonal age. This was hard on families, to say the least, especially when the addressee was a child. Parents of a child who died but still received offers to buy something in the mail often rushed to the mailbox to intercept the offensive letter before his or her spouse saw it. People who thought they had over the years gotten over the experience, knowing it was just the result of a misinformed computer, were apt to break out in tears when a piece of mail addressed to their dead child arrived. That solicitations were often timed with birthdays, especially the eighteenth, did not help matters, an offer for graduation pictures or a limousine service a heartbreaking piece of mail to receive.[63]

AN INFINITE PROCESS OF
TRANSFORMATION AND IMPROVEMENT

Technology was also allowing for some to continue living, in a manner of speaking, despite having already died. By the mid-2000s, there were reports of dead people both collecting and dispensing money just as if they were alive, the miracle achieved not through a magic potion but automated banking. Pensions were being automatically deposited to bank accounts and condominium fees and utility bills deducted, no one the wiser that the payee and payer was dead (for two years, in the case of a Winnipeg man who was estranged from his family). "New technologies like electronic banking have created a system in which it's possible to become so physically disengaged from the day-to-day administration of your own affairs that your life can effectively go on without you, perhaps indefinitely," noted Lianne George in reporting the story for *Maclean's*, such a possibility quite disturbing.[64] More people are also continuing to live on in the virtual world after they die in this one, their online identities not obeying the physical laws of nature. Through blogs, tweets, Facebook pages, YouTube videos, or Flickr accounts, very dead people remain, or at least appear to remain, as alive as ever. "Social media sites, emails and digital records are replacing the photo albums, letters and papers of the past and should be considered in estate planning," wrote Pam Greenberg in *State Legislatures* in 2012, with even the Library of Congress now offering advice on how to preserve digital memories. Avatars in role-playing games such as *Second Life* or *World of Warcraft*, too, enjoy a busy afterlife; what will happen to all these ghosts in the machine is not exactly clear.[65]

For some, however, technological immortality was not nearly enough. Only the real thing would do, a growing contingent of "radical life extension" supporters declared, man's ultimate dream within reach. Since the late 1990s, in fact, a number of scientists and entrepreneurs had openly stated that dramatic life extension was both feasible and desirable, the possibility of eliminating death also not completely out of the question. Millennial fever and the decoding of the human genome further stirred up interest in immortality, a confluence of forces encouraging the challenging of accepted beliefs about life and death. It was thus not too surprising that thousands of Americans began seriously pursuing immortality or something close to it, doing whatever they could to live well beyond one hundred years. Some started to take a hundred pills a day or endured daily injections of supplemental solids and liquids in the belief that doing so would add many decades to their life span. Others were restricting their caloric intake to 1,200 calories a day based on research showing that doing so would extend one's life span by 30 percent. Books such as *Why Die? A Beginner's Guide to Living Forever*, *Immortality: How Science Is Extending Your Life Span—and Changing the World*, and *Gary Null's Ultimate Anti-Aging Program* appeared on bookshelves, the latter's videocassette "How to Live Forever" so popular it was given away by National Public Radio as a pledge premium. Although so-called experts had different opinions regarding how to "de-age," as radio host Null called it (cloning, stem cells, gene therapy, and computer chips inserted into the brain were just a few), it was clear that immortality was in the air as we turned the century and millennium.[66]

Over the next decade, the radical life extension and immortality movement picked up steam but, at the same time, drew critics. Leon Kass believed the conquest of disease, aging, and death has long been "the unstated but implicit goal of modern medical science," suggesting that all of us have essentially served as guinea pigs for a larger, future cause. For Kass and others, radical life extension was not only impossible but also a very disturbing development, antithetical to basic humanism. The full-fledged pursuit of immortality would create considerable anguish, he and others argued, not at all the Holy Grail many believed it would be. Daniel Callahan made a similar case, with virtually every aspect of society—from marriage to education to the economy—to be much altered, and not for the better. Market forces were driving the pursuit for dramatic life extension, he felt, with biotechnology companies the ones to gain the most from it.[67]

Critics of radical life extension also pointed out the obvious fact that the issue of age would be much transformed. The prospect of a ninety-year-old being considered an adolescent was very alarming, such a scenario throwing our entire social order out of whack. A worldwide divide between a new class of "immortals" and those unable to become one would create conflict right out of H. G. Wells's or Philip Dick's science fiction, Francis Fukuyama has argued, with philosopher Hans Jonas adding that the presence of fewer young people would make humans a stagnant, not very interesting species. Sheila Jasanoff felt that we were already a split society on many levels, a much grayer population to only exacerbate the problem.[68] Finally, Howard L. Kaye pointed out that, with so much more life to lose, our fear of death would be even greater, the possibility of being killed by an accident positively terrifying.[69]

Supporters of radical life extension thought otherwise, of course. Freed from the looming apprehension about death, we would become much more creative and productive, people like "anti-aging activist" Aubrey de Grey of the University of Cambridge claimed, viewing children as more distracting than anything else. Continual treatments to repair the body would allow us to never fear dying of old age, perhaps the ultimate dream of mankind.[70] Bill Andrews, a top molecular biologist, has spent the last twenty years researching the cellular causes of aging; his mission is to extend the human life span to 150 years.[71] With such a life span or, better yet, a couple of centuries or even more, self-fulfillment would not be a dream but a reality; humans would finally be able to achieve everything they wanted in life. "We can look forward to an infinite process of transformation and improvement with no fear of an inevitable boredom and meaninglessness," Max More, a leading member of the immortality movement wrote, with mind-altering drugs available should things get a little repetitive.[72] A bit Orwellian, perhaps, but the fact was that humans had already undergone radical life extension, with longevity nearly doubling over the past century. If antibiotics, better nutrition, and cleaner water were responsible for dramatically extending life in the twentieth century, what was wrong with biotechnology doing it in the twenty-first?[73]

While having especially high stakes, the debate over radical life extension was the latest in a long line of critical social issues involving death and dying in America. For almost a century, the nation had struggled with the "problem" of death, the end of life antithetical to many of our defining cultural values. Over the last decade and a half, the issues surrounding death and dying had risen in intensity, an attempt to make "the last taboo" an integral part of the national conversation. The conversation is destined to grow only louder over the next few decades, as Americans try to come to terms with the psychological, philosophical, and spiritual consequences of death.

Conclusion

In April 2008, Michael Kinsey mused over the intersection between death and baby boomers for *The New Yorker*. Kinsey, the well-known journalist and pundit, was one of the few critics to recognize the social upheaval that is fast approaching as death approaches for this generation on a massive scale. "He Who Dies with the Most Toys Wins," the popular bumper sticker of the 1980s, may have aptly described boomers' values then, he proposed, but no longer. Now "He Who Dies Last" reflected the generation's driving ethos, longevity a better measure of success than a nice car or big house. "What good are the toys if you're dead?," Kinsey sensibly asked, many sixtysomethings beginning to ask the very same question. "The only competition that matters, in the end, is about life itself," he stated, the title of his article, "Mine Is Longer Than Yours," the emerging mantra for baby boomers.[1]

Kinsey's bold thesis was grounded in baby boomers' well-known habit of assessing their lives not in absolute terms but rather against those of their peers. Boomers' values may have changed over the course of a couple of decades, he believed, but their notorious competitive streak remained as strong as ever. Staying alive would be the ultimate game for this generation, with beating the statistical odds (75.2 years for men and 80.4 years for women in 2004) the first victory. Factors one could control and those one could not would determine the winners and losers in the coming years, with boomers to be just as proud of having made it to ninety or one hundred as they were about their brand new Beamer during the Reagan years. How one aged, too, would be part of the competition, Kinsey predicted. Those seeming to be younger than their chronological age would enjoy higher status than those appearing to be older. How one looked, felt, and thought would matter even more, he envisioned; how much hair someone had left or the pace of his or her walk would be carefully scrutinized. (That such criteria varied considerably in one's later years made them all the more important; a seventy-five-year-old could be highly active in all dimensions of life or institutionalized.) "Contrasts like these will be common," Kinsey foresaw, with distinctions to be made between those in "independent living" situations versus those in "assisted living" and those in the bottom of the geriatric barrel, nursing homes. "Entering one of these places is entering a new phase of life as clearly as going away to college," he suggested, a cruel, Darwinian fate awaiting the Woodstock generation.[2]

Enduring a form of peer pressure more intense than that in high school is just one of many potential scary scenarios as the proverbial pig works its way though the demographic python. Ten thousand baby boomers will celebrate their sixty-fifth birthday *every day* for the next nineteen years, a remarkable statistic that poses huge consequences for the future. Many of these boomers "have no intention of ceding to others what they consider rightfully theirs: youth," wrote Dan Barry on New Year's Day 2011 in the *New York Times*, envisioning heaven (or hell) for them to perhaps be "a place where the celestial Muzak plays a never-ending loop of the Doobie Brothers."[3] Unless our best and brightest really do come up with a way to turn us all into modern-day Methuselahs, however, baby boomers will eventually be forced to concede they are no longer the eternally young generation. Along with the harsh realities of old age and chronic disease will come that of mortality, this even further off boomers' current radar. Should baby boomers not go through some kind of radical transformation over the next couple of decades, America may be destined for a crisis of, without too much exaggeration, biblical proportions.

Some progress has admittedly been made in recent years to increase the likelihood that Americans will "die well." Doctors have shown some flexibility in their commitment to the Hippocratic oath, for one thing, with consideration given to the many costs involved with interventionist or rescue medicine. The "conspiracy of silence," too, appears to be gradually breaking down, with physicians, nurses, and family members more likely to let the dying know the truth of their condition. Other trends, such as the hospice movement, virtual bereavement, and "green" funerals also point the way to more of us having the opportunity to realize a "good death." Larger, stronger forces are working against the prospect of death being seen as a natural part of life, however. Death remains our principal cultural taboo, for example, with no signs of this changing. Edward Zuckerman recently wrote in the *New York Times* magazine, for example, that he could not erase the names and contact information of those people he knew were dead from his cell phone, a sign of our persistent apprehension surrounding death. "Deleting the entries of the dead feels wrong, an irrevocable step toward forgetting them entirely," he explained, viewing such a harmless action as "almost akin to killing them a second time."[4] The fundamental problem of death and dying being "un-

American" also persists, our national identity still heavily steeped in values relating to youth and beauty. As well, the modern death industry has not wavered much from its priorities of efficiency and standardization, making it easier to die in the hospital than at home. Finally, traditional religion continues to decline, this also discouraging a wholesale making of peace with the Grim Reaper.

On a positive note, more attention is being paid to death in America, perhaps as a result of more baby boomers dying. The definition of death continues to shift, for one thing, and writers from various disciplines are addressing some of the fundamental, existential aspects of the subject. *New Scientist* recently dedicated an issue to death, for example, examining how, as the magazine's deputy editor wrote, the knowledge that life would one day end for all of us "perhaps the defining feature of the human condition." That humans are, it appears, the only species able to reflect upon our own approaching deaths leads to all kinds of fascinating questions, such as whether it is good or bad to fear the inevitable.[5] As well, the idea that death is not an event but rather a process continues to gain currency, something that also takes one down some interesting paths. In his *Erasing Death*, Sam Parnia, a physician at Cornell Medical Center, explored the implications of bringing people back to life after being in a state in which they would have previously been pronounced dead. Is death "reversible" in certain situations, he and others are asking? As the boundaries of life and death get increasingly blurry, near-death or after-death experiences are deservedly attracting more interest, pushing the subject further toward a religious or spiritual realm.[6]

Meanwhile, grief memoirs continue to be written, as those missing their loved ones try to process their deep emotional pain. Roger Angell, the essayist, recently wrote a piece for *The New Yorker* about losing his wife, Carol, and Armen Bacon and Nancy Miller's *Griefland* told the story of how the two women found each other and shared the loss of their respective children.[7] Guides to navigating the tricky legal waters of death, such as Scott Taylor Smith's *When Someone Dies*, are also increasingly popular, with a growing audience of readers in search of advice for how to manage that often difficult process.[8] Finally, efforts such as the University of California, Riverside-based The Immortality Project continue to prosper, as scientists, philosophers, and theologians tackle what they believe is the possibility of surviving bodily death altogether.[9]

Something much bigger, however, needs to happen for us to avert the social crisis surrounding death that I believe is fast approaching. Simon Critchley, a British philosopher who teaches at the New School in New York, has a keen understanding of Westerners' aversion to all things death and the changes in beliefs, attitudes, and behavior that are required for us to become better acquainted with the topic. Critchley is comanager of the International Necronautical Society, an "avant-garde network" attempting to make death not just an acceptable subject but also a popular one. "Our culture denies death in a massive, systemic way," he told *Psychology Today* in 2011, believing that "we don't know how to deal with it, we don't have rituals around it, [and] we don't know what to do, [or] what to say." More than anyone else, perhaps, Critchley recognizes the sorry state of death and dying in America today, specifically how the quest for longevity has made the end of life, in his words, "obscene, invisible, and an embarrassment." Proponents of immortality are doing much more damage than good, further ingraining the idea of death as "something we can catch, like a cold." The subject of death, as uncomfortable as it is, should be more integrated into everyday life, not limited to its most popular expression—books, movies, and television shows about vampires and zombies. "There is no radical contrast between life and death," he concludes, precisely the concept that Americans should embrace as more of us than ever begin to die.[10]

Such a revolutionary shift in the way we think and act is admittedly unlikely given our widespread phobia of death and dying. As history has shown over and over, however, it is folly to try to predict the future based on present circumstances. Underestimating the capabilities of Americans, especially baby boomers—the most ambitious and prosperous generation in history—also is unwise, their third and perhaps greatest act still to come. Boomers and American society as a whole has the opportunity to integrate death into everyday life as great civilizations of the past did, this the only real way to avoid the cultural upheaval that is looming. A revolution is hopefully waiting in the wings, with death in America to one day be no different from life in America.

Notes

INTRODUCTION

1. Jessica Mitford, *The American Way of Death* (New York: Simon & Schuster, 1963).

2. Geoffrey Gorer, "The Pornography of Death," *Encounter* (October 1955): 49–52; Geoffrey Gorer, *Death, Grief, and Mourning* (Garden City, NY: Doubleday-Anchor, 1967); Herman Feifel, ed., *The Meaning of Death* (New York: McGraw-Hill, 1959); Jacques Choron, ed., *Death and Western Thought* (New York: Macmillan, 1963); Arnold Toynbee, *Man's Concern with Death* (New York: McGraw-Hill, 1969); Richard G. Dumont and Dennis C. Foss, *The American View of Death: Acceptance or Denial?* (Cambridge, MA: Schenkman Publishing Company, 1972); Ernest Becker, *The Denial of Death* (New York: Free Press, 1973); Philippe Aries, *Western Attitudes toward Death: From the Middle Ages to the Present* (Baltimore: Johns Hopkins University Press, 1974); Philippe Aries, *The Hour of Our Death* (London: Allen Lane, 1981); James J. Farrell, *Inventing the American Way of Death, 1830–1920* (Philadelphia: Temple University Press, 1980); John S. Stephenson, *Death, Grief, and Mourning: Individual and Social Realities* (New York: Free Press, 1985); Christine Overall, *Aging, Death, and Human Longevity: A Philosophical Inquiry* (Berkeley: University of California Press, 2003); Gary Laderman, *Rest in Peace: A Cultural History of Death and the Funeral Home in Twentieth-Century America* (New York: Oxford University Press, 2003); Lucy Bregman, *Preaching Death: The Transformation of Christian Funeral Sermons* (Waco, TX: Baylor University Press, 2011).

3. Michael K. Bartalos, ed., *Speaking of Death: America's New Sense of Mortality* (Santa Barbara, CA: Praeger, 2008).

4. Susan Jacoby, *Never Say Die: The Myth and Marketing of the New Old Age* (New York: Pantheon, 2011).

5. Jill Lepore, *The Mansion of Happiness: A History of Life and Death* (New York: Alfred A. Knopf, 2012).

6. Louis LaGrand, *Healing Grief, Finding Peace* (Naperville, IL: Sourcebooks, 2011); Jennifer Collins Taylor, *Living Life Dying Death: A Guide to Healthy Conversations about Death and Dying to Inspire Life and Living* (Scottsdale, AZ: MyRehab, 2011); Lani Leary, *No One Has to Die Alone: Preparing for a Meaningful Death* (New York: Atria, 2012); Barbara Okun and Joseph Nowinski, *Saying Goodbye: How Families Can Find Renewal through Loss* (New York: Berkley, 2011); Jon Katz, *Going Home: Finding Peace When Pets Die* (New York: Villard, 2012); Jessica Pierce, *The Last Walk: Reflections on Our Pets at the End of Their Lives* (Chicago: University of Chicago Press, 2012).

7. Janet Boyanton, *Alone and Alive: A Practical Guide for Dealing with the Death of Your Husband* (Lyons, NJ: Shafer, 2011); Joshua Slocum and Lisa Carlson, *Final Rights: Reclaiming the American Way of Death* (Hinesburg, VT: Upper Access, 2011); Bernd Heinrich, *Life Everlasting: The Animal Way of Death* (New York: Houghton Mifflin Harcourt, 2012).

8. David Shields and Bradford Morrow, eds., *The Inevitable: Contemporary Writers Confront Death* (New York: W. W. Norton, 2011); Lee Gutkind, ed., *At the End of Life: True Stories about How We Die* (Pittsburgh: Creative Nonfiction, 2012); Cheryl Eckl, *A Beautiful Death: Facing the Future with Peace* (Littleton, CO: Flying Crane Press, 2010); Philip Gould, *When I Die: Lessons from the Death Zone* (New York: Little Brown, 2012); Christopher Hitchens, *Mortality* (New York: Twelve, 2012).

9. Ptolemy Tompkins, *The Modern Book of the Dead: A Revolutionary Perspective on Death, the Soul, and What Really Happens in the Life to Come* (New York: Atria, 2012); Eben Alexander, MD, *Proof of Heaven: A Neurosurgeon's Journey into the Afterlife* (New York: Simon & Schuster, 2012); Todd Burpo, *Heaven Is for Real: A Little Boy's Astounding Story of His Trip to Heaven and Back* (Nashville, TN: Thomas Nelson, 2010).

10. Future Trends 2010 Conference Catalog, Institute of International Research, New York City.

11. Diane Umansky, "The Good Goodbye," *Good Housekeeping* (September 2000): 88–90.

12. Allen Verhey, "Still Dying Badly: A Christian Critique," *Christian Century* 128, no. 22 (November 1, 2011): 22.

13. Nancy Isenberg and Andrew Burstein, eds., *Mortal Remains: Death in Early America* (Philadelphia: University of Pennsylvania Press, 2002), 1, 13.

14. Drew Gilpin Faust, *This Republic of Suffering: Death and the American Civil War* (New York: Alfred A. Knopf, 2008), 4.

15. Hereward Carrington, *Death: Its Causes and Phenomena* (New York: Funk & Wagnalls, 1912).

16. Elisabeth Kübler-Ross, *On Death and Dying* (New York: Macmillan, 1970).

17. Aries, *Western Attitudes toward Death.* See Howard Ball's *At Liberty to Die: The Battle for Death with Dignity in America* (New York: New York University Press, 2012) for a full legal history of the death with dignity (or right to die) movement.

18. James W. Green, *Beyond the Good Death: The Anthropology of Modern Dying* (Philadelphia: University of Pennsylvania Press, 2008), 30.

19. Isenberg and Burstein, *Mortal Remains*, 13.

CHAPTER 1

1. Vernon Kellogg, "The Biologist Speaks of Death," *The Atlantic* (June 21, 1921): 774–87.

2. Kellogg, "The Biologist Speaks of Death."

3. H. A. Dallas, "What Is Death?," *The Living Age* 332 (February 15, 1927): 354–59.

4. Dallas, "What Is Death?"

5. Sarah N. Cleghorn, "Changing Thoughts of Death," *The Atlantic* (December 1923): 808–12.

6. Anonymous, "Good-Night, All," *The Atlantic* (November 1925): 596–600.

7. M. E. B., "Death as a Dream Experience," *The Atlantic* (February 1924): 208–10.

8. M. E. B., "Death as a Dream Experience."

9. M. M. G., "What Death Is Like," *The Atlantic* (April 1924): 537–39.

10. "How Death May Feel," *The Atlantic* (January 1930): 135–37.

11. "How It Feels to Die," *The Living Age* (February 1931): 647–48.

12. Lester Howard Perry, "Death Has No Terrors," *The Reader's Digest* (May 1938): 33–36.

13. W. Henry, "The Contributor's Column," *The Atlantic* (June 1930): 861–62.

14. Hermine Kane, "The End," *The American Mercury* (April 1930): 458–61.

15. Kane, "The End."

16. Kane, "The End."

17. Kane, "The End."

18. Kane, "The End."

19. Gertrude Carver, "Early Holiday," *The Atlantic* (October 1931): 438–42.

20. Carver, "Early Holiday."

21. Carver, "Early Holiday."

22. Carver, "Early Holiday."

23. Carolyn Wells, "Two Years to Live," *Saturday Evening Post* (January 14, 1933): 29.

24. Anonymous, "The Art of Dying," *The Atlantic* (April 1935): 459–62.

25. Anonymous, "The Art of Dying."

26. Anonymous, "The Art of Dying."

27. Anonymous, "The Art of Dying."

28. Stephen Dirck, "I Set My House in Order," *The Atlantic* (January 1936): 5–9.

29. Dirck, "I Set My House in Order."

30. Dirck, "I Set My House in Order."

31. Anonymous, "We Who Have a Rendezvous with Death," *The Forum* (September 1937): 141–42.

32. Anonymous, "We Who Have a Rendezvous with Death."

33. Anoymous, "We Who Have a Rendezvous with Death."

34. Anonymous, "One Year to Live," *The Forum* (May 1938): 266–68.

35. "Under Sentence of Death," *Scribner's Magazine* (October 1934): 233–36.

36. Jeannette Wilcox, "Prelude to Death," *The Forum* (June 1939): 296–300.

37. "Under Sentence of Death."

38. Mina Curtiss, "To My Lost Husband," *The Reader's Digest* (February 1938): 85–91.

39. Anonymous, "What Can We Believe?," *The Atlantic Monthly* (June 1939): 744–48.

40. A Believer, "The Living Presence," *The Atlantic Monthly* (May 1938): 615–17.

41. "Why Do We Die?," *The Literary Digest* (September 3, 1921): 26.

42. "Are Our Bodies Immortal?," *The Literary Digest* (August 22, 1925): 21–22.

43. H. Munro Fox, "Is Death Inevitable?," *The Forum* (September 1926): 421–24.

44. Vernon Kellogg, "The Evolutionist and Death," *Scribner's Magazine* (July 1928): 31–36.

45. "Live Hearts in Dead Bodies," *The Literary Digest* (July 7, 1928): 23.

46. "Heart-Beats after Death," *The Literary Digest* (August 15, 1931): 28.

47. "From beyond the Styx," *The Literary Digest* (February 23, 1935): 26.

48. "Only One Sure Sign of Death," *The Literary Digest* (August 30, 1930): 27.

49. William Marias Malisoff, "Death Is Not a Necessity," *The Forum* (March 1938): 153–55.

50. Alexis Carrel, MD, "The Mystery of Death," *Vital Speeches of the Day* (December 30, 1935): 188–91.

51. Edward S. Martin, "A Matter of Importance," *Harper's Monthly Magazine* (December 1923): 133–36.

52. Anonymous, "Good-Night, All," 596–600.

53. Bertrand Russell, "Your Child and the Fear of Death," *The Forum* (March 1929): 174–78.

54. Russell, "Your Child and the Fear of Death."

55. Arthur Styron, "Do People Fear Death?," *Scribner's Magazine* (March 31, 1931): 319–21.

56. Lee Wilson Dodd, "The Sixth Decade," *The Forum* (October 1931): 228–31.

57. Clarence C. Little, "Let Us Face Death," *Scribner's Magazine* (June 1931): 599–602.

58. Little, "Let Us Face Death."

59. Milton Waldman, "America Conquers Death," *The American Mercury* (February 1927): 216–21.

60. Waldman, "America Conquers Death."

61. Waldman, "America Conquers Death."

62. M. Beatrice Blankenship, "Death Is a Stranger," *The Atlantic* (December 1934): 649–57.

63. Sir W. Beach Thomas, "Animals and Death," *The Atlantic* (September 1926): 347–51.

64. Blankenship, "Death Is a Stranger."

65. Blankenship, "Death Is a Stranger."

66. Blankenship, "Death Is a Stranger."

67. Blankenship, "Death Is a Stranger."

68. Blankenship, "Death Is a Stranger."

CHAPTER 2

1. "What Is Death?," *Time* (June 2, 1941): 64.

2. "Dies as He Predicted," *New York Times* (July 29, 1940): 30.

3. "Death of Last Veteran of World War Set for '96," *New York Times* (May 31, 1940): 13.

4. "Traffic Death Toll 8,110 for Quarter," *New York Times* (April 30, 1941): 21.

5. "Auto Deaths Increase to 14,740 in 6 Months; Safety Board Cites 'War Jitters' as Factor," *New York Times* (July 31, 1940): 19.

6. "Home Fatalities Equal Road Toll," *New York Times* (November 3, 1940): 5.

7. "Safety Mark Set in Private Flying," *New York Times* (March 30, 1941): 34.

8. "8 Battleships Hit," *New York Times* (December 6, 1942): 1.

9. "8 Battleships Hit."

10. "Dying U.S. Captain Stayed at His Post," *New York Times* (February 26, 1942): 4.

11. "Army Death List Increased by 145," *New York Times* (November 28, 1942): 7.

12. "Army Death List Increased by 145."

13. "Army Death List Increased by 145."

14. "Dying Flier Downs 2 Japanese Planes," *New York Times* (August 10, 1943): 8.

15. "Read Bible to Crew on Doomed Bomber," *New York Times* (May 18, 1944): 5.

16. "Our Casualties Now Total 91,644," *New York Times* (July 4, 1943): 8.

17. "Army Death Rate Sets Low Record," *New York Times* (July 9, 1943): 8.

18. Louis I. Dublin, "War's Heavy Impact on Population," *New York Times* (March 14, 1943): SM14.

19. "Death-Claim Rise in War Is Forecast," *New York Times* (August 25, 1943): 11.

20. "Soldier Deaths Cost Equitable $3,275,000," *New York Times* (July 26, 1944): 27.

21. "Quick Care Saves American Troops," *New York Times* (July 2, 1944): 5.

22. Alan Devoe, "Down to Earth," *The American Mercury* (September 1942): 371–75.

23. "De Mortuis," *Time* (May 13, 1946): 61. See Suzanne E. Smith's *To Serve the Living: Funeral Directors and the African American Way of Death* (Cambridge: Belknap Press of Harvard University Press, 2010) for an excellent history of African American death and the significant role of funeral directors within the black community.

24. Devoe, "Down to Earth."

25. Ellen J. O. Leary, "In the Midst of Life," *Parents' Magazine* (September 1945): 22–23.

26. Leary, "In the Midst of Life."

27. Leary, "In the Midst of Life."

28. Sophia L. Fahs, "When Children Confront Death," *Parents' Magazine* (April 1943): 34.

29. Fahs, "When Children Confront Death."

30. Fahs, "When Children Confront Death."

31. Catherine MacKenzie, "Children Must Be Told," *New York Times* (June 17, 1945): SM14.

32. MacKenzie, "Children Must Be Told."

33. Polly McKeethers, "Death Is an Old Gray Shadow," *Parents' Magazine* (November 1943): 37.

34. McKeethers, "Death Is an Old Gray Shadow."

35. McKeethers, "Death Is an Old Gray Shadow."

36. "Letters to Bob," *Rotarian* (May 1944): 12–13.

37. "Letters to Bob."

38. John C. McManus, *The Deadly Brotherhood: The American Combat Soldier in World War II* (New York: Random House, 2003), 176; Emily Yellin, *Our Mothers' War: American Women at Home and at the Front during World War II* (New York: Free Press, 2004).

39. Lieutenant Commander Leslie B. Hohman, "The War Department Regrets . . .", *Ladies Home Journal* (January 1945): 102–3.

40. Hohman, "The War Department Regrets . . ."

41. John Wright Buckham, "They Did Not Die in Vain," *Christian Century* (August 22, 1945): 954.

42. Leary, "In the Midst of Life."

43. Fahs, "When Children Confront Death."

44. Mary McBurney Green, "When Death Came to School," *Parents' Magazine* (April 1947): 20.

45. Fahs, "When Children Confront Death."

46. Winnifred Ariel Weir, "We Faced Death Together," *Parents' Magazine* (February 1948): 32.

47. Fahs, "When Children Confront Death."

48. Fahs, "When Children Confront Death."

49. Fahs, "When Children Confront Death."

50. Robert D. Potter, "The Closer Ol' Man Death Comes the Less We Fear Him," *Science Digest* (January 1944): 61–64.

51. Potter, "The Closer Ol' Man Death Comes the Less We Fear Him."

52. Potter, "The Closer Ol' Man Death Comes the Less We Fear Him."

53. Sam Boal, "Three Anecdotes on a Theme," *The New Yorker* (December 30, 1944): 50–51.

54. Captain Eddie Rickenbacker, "When a Man Faces Death," *The American Magazine* (November 1943): 20–21.

55. Rickenbacker, "When a Man Faces Death."

56. "Birth Gains Bring Population Record," *New York Times* (October 16, 1944): 30.

57. "Twelve Births Offset Each Battle Death in This War to Date, Says Census Official," *New York Times* (March 4, 1945): 28.

58. "U.S. Births Fell 140,060 in 1944," *New York Times* (September 26, 1945): 20.

59. "Low Record Is Set by Infant Deaths," *New York Times* (October 30, 1945): 14.

60. "Maternity Toll Seen Much Too High," *New York Times* (November 16, 1945): 20.

61. "Maternity Toll Seen Much Too High."

62. Halbert L. Dunn, "Get Married and Live Longer!," *Science Digest* (January 1946): 1–5.

63. Dunn, "Get Married and Live Longer!"

64. Brigadier General David Sarnoff, "'Science for Life or Death' Discussed by Sarnoff," *New York Times* (August 10, 1945): 6.

65. "Dead Dogs Brought Back to Life," *Science Digest* (January 1944): 5–6.

66. "Russian Report 12 'Dead' Revived," *Science Digest* (December 1944): 50–51; Albert Deutsch, "Dead Are Brought Back to Life," *Forum* (October 1945): 165–66.

67. "Traffic Toll Put at 29,000 Deaths," *New York Times* (December 29, 1945): 18.

68. "Accident Toll Up in 1946," *New York Times* (December 28, 1946): 18.

69. Thomas C. Desmond, "Prediction for 1948: 30,000 Auto Deaths," *New York Times* (January 25, 1948): SM16.

70. "Deplores Accidental Deaths of Children," *New York Times* (January 31, 1947): 27.

71. "Labor's Accidents Lead to U.S. Drive," *New York Times* (May 16, 1948): 37.

72. Lucy Freeman, "100,000 U.S. Deaths Held Preventable," *New York Times* (November 4, 1948): 31.

73. "1,000 Doctors Urge 'Mercy Death' Law," *New York Times* (December 15, 1947): 30.

CHAPTER 3

1. John Steinbeck, "The Easiest Way to Die," *Saturday Review* (August 23, 1958): 12.

2. Steinbeck, "The Easiest Way to Die."

3. Enid W. Dearborn, "The Hardest Question of All," *Parents' Magazine* (July 1951): 95.

4. Dearborn, "The Hardest Question of All."

5. Marguerita Rudolph, "Do the Children Have to Know?," *Woman's Home Companion* (October 1951): 98–99.

6. Rudolph, "Do the Children Have to Know?," SM40.

7. Mary Margaret Kern, "Should Children Go to Funerals?," *Parents' Magazine* (February 1957): 54.

8. Kern, "Should Children Go to Funerals?"

9. "On Death as a Constant Companion," *Time* (November 12, 1965): 62.

10. Adeline Bullock, "The Day Granddad Died," *Parents' Magazine* (May 1953): 40–41.

11. Rudolph, "Do the Children Have to Know?"

12. Anonymous, "Our Child Walks in the Valley of the Shadow," *Parents' Magazine* (September 1952): 38–39.

13. Joe E. Brown, "The Lessons of Sorrow," *Better Homes and Gardens* (November 1952): 109.

14. Brown, "The Lessons of Sorrow."

15. Brown, "The Lessons of Sorrow."

16. Marguerite Higgins, "Thoughts on the Death of a Five-Day-Old Child," *Good Housekeeping* (August 1954): 26–27.

17. Zelda Popkin, "If Tragedy Comes . . .," *Coronet* (March 1953): 61–64.

18. Mary Alson, "I'll Go on Working after Death," *McCall's* (May 1953): 22.

19. Bertram B. Moss, MD, "Autopsy: An Important Medical Aid," *Today's Health* (May 1966): 65.

20. Moss, "Autopsy: An Important Medical Aid."

21. Moses, "Autopsy: An Important Medical Aid."

22. Moses, "Autopsy: An Important Medical Aid."

23. Don Wharton, "Why Women Die," *McCall's* (July 1953): 48.

24. Wharton, "Why Women Die."

25. Anonymous, "A Way of Dying," *The Atlantic Monthly* (January 1957): 53–55.

26. Anonymous, "A Way of Dying."

27. Joseph G. Hoffman, "The Importance of Death," *Saturday Review* (August 3, 1957): 42.

28. Joseph W. Still, MD, "Why Can't We Live Forever?," *Better Homes and Gardens* (August 1958): 36–37.

29. Still, "Why Can't We Live Forever?"

30. Still, "Why Can't We Live Forever?"

31. D. E. Koshland Jr., "The Research Frontier," *Saturday Review* (June 1, 1963): 46.

32. Robert C. W. Ettinger, "New Hope for the Dead," *Esquire* (May 1965): 63–65.

33. "New Hope for the Dead." Recently, Valerie Barbaro suggested that cryonics is "an afterlife for atheists," an interesting explanation for why some

people want their bodies or brains frozen after they die. Valerie Barbaro, "Heaven for Atheists," *The Humanist* (July–August 2011): 25.

34. V. A. Negovskii, "The Reversal of Death," *Saturday Review* (August 4, 1962): 44.

35. "Five Slices of Life," *Saturday Review* (April 20, 1957): 20.

36. "The Meaning of Death," *Time* (January 11, 1960): 54.

37. Harry S. Meserve, "The Undiscovered Country," *Saturday Review* (March 4, 1961): 43–44.

38. "A Lonely Business," *Newsweek* (May 22, 1961): 56.

39. Sanford Gifford, MD, "Death and Forever: Some Fears of War and Peace," *Atlantic Monthly* (March 1962): 88–92.

40. Norman Vincent Peale, "How to Rise above the Fear of Death," *Reader's Digest* (April 1963): 103–6.

41. "The Death of Death," *Newsweek* (January 24, 1966): 53.

42. Felix Marti-Ibanez, MD, "A Doctor Looks at Death," *Reader's Digest* (March 1964): 145–46.

43. "What Americans Die Of . . . Where Smoking Fits In," *U.S. News & World Report* (February 10, 1964): 62.

44. M. Renate Dische, MD, "The Enigma of Sudden Infant Death," *Ladies Home Journal* (March 1965): 48.

45. "Safety in the Home," *Today's Health* (June 1965): 35–42.

46. William Kitay, "Let's Retain the Dignity of Dying," *Today's Health* (May 1966): 62–64.

47. Kitay, "Let's Retain the Dignity of Dying."

48. Kitay, "Let's Retain the Dignity of Dying."

49. Malcolm Muggeridge, "Books," *Esquire* (July 1966): 24–25.

50. Muggeridge, "Books."

51. David Sudnow, "The Logistics of Dying," *Esquire* (August 1967): 102–3.

52. Edwin Diamond, "Are We Ready to Leave Our Bodies to the Next Generation?," *New York Times* (April 21, 1968): SM26.

53. Sudnow, "The Logistics of Dying."

54. Sudnow, "The Logistics of Dying."

55. Sudnow, "The Logistics of Dying."

56. Sudnow, "The Logistics of Dying."

57. Sudnow, "The Logistics of Dying."

58. "When Are You Really Dead?," *Newsweek* (December 18, 1967): 87.

59. Lawrence Lader, "Who Has the Right to Live?," *Good Housekeeping* (June 1968): 84–85.

60. Lader, "Who Has the Right to Live?"

61. "Scorecard for Death," *Newsweek* (July 1, 1968): 61.

62. Fred Anderson, "Who Will Decide Who Is to Live?," *New Republic* (April 19, 1969): 9–10; Leonard A. Stevens, "When Is Death?," *Reader's*

Digest (May 1969): 225–32. See Dick Teresi's *The Undead: Organ Harvesting, the Ice-Water Test, Beating-Heart Cadavers: How Medicine Is Blurring the Line between Life and Death* (New York: Pantheon, 2012) for a fascinating study of organ harvesting and a vitriolic attack on the 1968 Ad Hoc Committee of Harvard Medical School and its definition of brain death.

63. "Death, When Is Thy Sting?," *Newsweek* (August 19, 1968): 54.

64. Webster Schott, "A Bold Plan to Abolish Death," *Life* (July 4, 1969): 8.

65. Howard Luck Gossage, "Will I Be Active Right Up to the Last?," *The Atlantic Monthly* (September 1969): 55–57.

66. Gossage, "Will I Be Active Right Up to the Last?"

67. "On Death as a Constant Companion," *Time* (November 12, 1965): 62.

CHAPTER 4

1. Leon R. Kass, "Problems in the Meaning of Death," *Science* (December 11, 1970): 1235–36.

2. Kenneth L. Woodward, "How America Lives with Death," *Newsweek* (April 6, 1970): 81–89.

3. William Saroyan, "Last Words of the Great," *The Nation* (September 24, 1973): 282–83.

4. "Death, Not Sex, Called Newest Forbidden Topic," *New York Times* (March 28, 1971).

5. Woodward, "How America Lives with Death."

6. Woodward, "How America Lives with Death."

7. Woodward, "How America Lives with Death."

8. Thomas Powers, "Learning to Die," *Harper's Magazine* (June 1971): 72–74.

9. Powers, "Learning to Die."

10. Powers, "Learning to Die."

11. "Defining Death," *Time* (March 10, 1975): 84.

12. Powers, "Learning to Die."

13. Stewart Alsop, "Stay of Execution," *Saturday Review/World* (December 18, 1973): 20–23.

14. Powers, "Learning to Die."

15. "Toward a Better Death," *Time* (June 5, 1972): 68.

16. Barney G. Glaser and Anselm L. Strauss, *Awareness of Dying* (Piscataway, NJ: Aldine Transaction, 1965).

17. Powers, "Learning to Die."

18. David Dempsey, "Learning How to Die," *New York Times* (November 14, 1971): SM58.

19. Dempsey, "Learning How to Die."

20. Dempsey, "Learning How to Die."

21. Joan Arehart-Treichel, "Teaching Doctors How to Care for the Dying," *Science News* (March 15, 1975): 176–77.

22. Jerry Avorn, "Beyond Dying," *Harper's Magazine* (March 1973): 56–60.

23. "Toward a Better Death."

24. Dempsey, "Learning to Die."

25. Dempsey, "Learning to Die."

26. Dempsey, "Learning to Die."

27. Robert S. Morison, "Death: Process or Event?," *Science* (August 20, 1971): 694–98.

28. Leon R. Kass, "Death as an Event: A Commentary on Robert Morison," *Science* (August 20, 1971): 698–702.

29. "Death with Dignity: The Debate Goes On," *Science News* (August 19, 1972): 118.

30. "AMA Passes 'Death with Dignity' Resolution," *Science News* (December 15, 1973): 375.

31. John Fischer, "The Easy Chair," *Harper's Magazine* (February 1973): 25–27.

32. Fischer, "The Easy Chair."

33. Avorn, "Beyond Dying."

34. Stewart Alsop, "Stay of Execution," *Saturday Review/World* (December 18, 1973): 20–23.

35. Avorn, "Beyond Dying."

36. Avorn, "Beyond Dying."

37. Avorn, "Beyond Dying."

38. Avorn, "Beyond Dying."

39. Avorn, "Beyond Dying."

40. Avorn, "Beyond Dying."

41. Avorn, "Beyond Dying."

42. Avorn, "Beyond Dying."

43. Avorn, "Beyond Dying."

44. "A Bliss before Dying," *Newsweek* (May 6, 1974): 63–64.

45. Leonard C. Lewin, "What to Do with the Old Folks," *The Nation* (April 23, 1973): 538–40.

46. William Hamilton, "Regard the End," *The New Republic* (November 24, 1973): 30.

47. Hamilton, "Regard the End."

48. Lewin, "What to Do with the Old Folks."

49. Daniel C. Maguire, "Death by Chance, Death by Choice," *Atlantic Monthly* (January 1974): 56–65.

50. Daniel C. Maguire, "Death, Legal and Illegal," *Atlantic Monthly* (February 1974): 72–74.

51. Melvin Moddocks, "Waiting for the End," *Time* (January 7, 1974): 95.

52. Malcolm Muggeridge, "Books," *Esquire* (March 1974): 52.

53. Robert Boyers, "Brief Tour," *The New Republic* (August 24, 1974): 30–31.

54. Giles Gunn, "End of It All," *The New Republic* (September 21, 1974): 28.

55. Michael J. Arlen, "The Cold, Bright Charms of Immortality," *The New Yorker* (January 27, 1975): 73–77.

56. Arlen, "The Cold, Bright Charm of Immortality."

57. John Wren-Lewis, "Breaking the Final Taboo," *Psychology Today* (May 1975): 14–15.

58. J. P. Donleavy, "The Gentleman's Guide to Death," *Esquire* (June 1975): 46–57.

59. "Death Watch," *Time* (May 3, 1976): 79.

60. "Death without Dignity," *Time* (July 1, 1974): 64; Gilbert Cont, "Deciding When Death Is Better Than Life," *Time* (July 16, 1973): 40.

61. "States Debate Death with Dignity Bills," *Science* (December 26, 1975): 1272.

62. "'Right to Die' Case: Will Anything Change?," *U.S. News & World Report* (November 24, 1975): 31.

63. "The Right to Die: Should a Doctor Decide?," *U.S. News & World Report* (November 3, 1975): 53–54.

64. Phyllis Battelle, "'Let Me Sleep': The Story of Karen Ann Quinlan," *Ladies Home Journal* (September 1976): 69–76.

65. Harold Rubin, "The Right to Die Decently," *The Nation* (February 4, 1978): 114–16.

66. "First 'Right-to-Die' Law Passes," *Science* (November 5, 1976): 588.

67. Barbara J. Culliton, "Helping the Dying Die: Two Harvard Hospitals Go Public with Policies," *Science* (September 17, 1976): 1105–6.

68. Daniel Goleman, "We Are Breaking the Silence about Death," *Psychology Today* (September 1976): 44–47.

69. Daniel Goleman, "The Child Will Always Be There. Real Love Doesn't Die," *Psychology Today* (September 1976): 48–52.

70. "Death Companionship," *Time* (February 17, 1975): 74.

71. Daniel Goleman, "Help for the Dying and Their Friends," *Psychology Today* (March 1978): 34–36.

72. Stanley N. Wellborn, "Death in America: No Longer a Hidden Subject," *U.S. News & World Report* (November 13, 1978): 67–70. See Lucy Bregman's *Death and Dying, Spirituality and Religions: A Study of the Death Awareness Movement* (New York: Peter Lang, 2003) as well as her

Beyond Silence & Denial: Death and Dying Reconsidered (Louisville, KY: Westminster John Knox Press, 1999) for full studies of the death awareness movement.

73. Thomas H. Middleton, "Light Refractions," *Saturday Review* (December 1978): 10. See Alan Swedlund's *Shadows in the Valley: A Cultural History of Illness, Death and Loss in New England, 1840–1916* (Amherst: University of Massachusetts Press, 2009) for much more on death in the nineteenth century.

74. Wellborn, "Death in America: No Longer a Hidden Subject."

75. Wellborn, "Death in America: No Longer a Hidden Subject."

76. "Why Americans Are Healthiest Ever: A New Size-Up," *U.S. News and World Report* (October 29, 1979): 63–66.

77. "Why Americans Are Healthiest Ever: A New Size-Up."

78. Wellborn, "Death in America: No Longer a Hidden Subject."

CHAPTER 5

1. Kirkpatrick Sale, "A Perfect Enemy," *The Nation* (May 23, 1994): 689.

2. Thomas J. Cottle, "Mama's Boy," *Psychology Today* (June 1980): 110.

3. Anthony Brandt, "Last Words for My Father," *Psychology Today* (April 1982): 72–77.

4. Michael Novak, "Tomorrow and Tomorrow," *National Review* (June 13, 1980): 734.

5. Bruce Duffy, "Feeling Something," *Harper's Magazine* (June 1990): 70–75.

6. Marian Osterweis, "Bereavement and the Elderly," *Aging* (January 1985): 8.

7. Philippe Bouvard, "Maybe the Ostrich Was Right," *World Press Review* (January 1990): 42.

8. "Death Is Painless, Quiet for Most," *Aging* 363/364 (1992): 4.

9. Thomas W. Clark, "Death, Nothingness, and Subjectivity," *The Humanist* (November 1994): 15–20.

10. Gwen Gilliam, "The Anguish of Accidental Killers," *Psychology Today* (September 1980), 22–23.

11. Ronald K. Siegel, "Accounting for 'Afterlife' Experiences," *Psychology Today* (January 1981): 65–75.

12. Siegel, "Accounting for 'Afterlife' Experiences."

13. Ann Rae Jonas, "Surviving a Relative's Murder," *Psychology Today* (May 1983): 14–15.

14. "Happy Birthday, and So Long," *Science News* (October 10, 1992): 237.

15. Robert Bobrow, "The Choice to Die," *Psychology Today* (June 1983): 70–72.

16. "Grief Is No Killer," *Time* (September 5, 1988): 55.

17. Jean Seligmann, "The Death of a Spouse," *Newsweek* (May 9, 1994): 57.

18. "Loss," *Psychology Today* (July–August 1992): 64–67.

19. "Visions of the Afterlife," *Omni* (November 1992): 39–44.

20. Ron Rosenbaum, "Turn on, Tune in, Drop Dead," *Harper's* (July 1982): 32–42.

21. Rosenbaum, "Turn on, Tune in, Drop Dead."

22. Patricia Blake, "Going Gentle into That Good Night," *Time* (March 1983): 107.

23. Daniel Goleman, "Coping with Death on a Long-Distance Line," *Psychology Today* (September 1982): 43–48.

24. Goleman, "Coping with Death on a Long-Distance Line."

25. Goleman, "Coping with Death on a Long-Distance Line."

26. Michael Kramer, "Pulling the Plug," *Time* (October 4, 1993): 36.

27. Mary Catherine Bateson, "Death: The Undiscovered Country," *Omni* (April 1992): 8.

28. Herbert and Kay Kramer, "Conversations at Midnight," *Psychology Today* (March–April 1993): 26–28.

29. Terence Monmaney, "Counting the AIDS Victims," *Newsweek* (February 23, 1987): 65.

30. Michael Zimecki, "Filling Out the Last Form," *Harper's Magazine* (October 1988): 50–51.

31. Harold Brodkey, "To My Readers," *The New Yorker* (June 21, 1993): 80–82.

32. Richard Howard, "Almost Classic," *The New Republic* (July 12, 1993): 10–11.

33. Harold Brodkey, "Dying: An Update," *The New Yorker* (February 7, 1994): 70–84.

34. Fergus M. Bordewich, "Mortal Fears," *The Atlantic Monthly* (February 1988): 30–34.

35. Bordewich, "Mortal Fears."

36. Bordewich, "Mortal Fears."

37. Bordewich, "Mortal Fears."

38. Graham Turner, "The Lost Art of Dying," *World Press Review* (June 1989): 37–38.

39. Turner, "The Lost Art of Dying."

40. Turner, "The Lost Art of Dying."

41. Bill Bryson, "Living Dangerously," *Saturday Evening Post* (September 1988): 30–32.

42. Bryson, "Living Dangerously."

43. Bernard L. Cohen, "How to Assess the Risks You Face," *Consumers' Research Magazine* (June 1992): 11–16.

44. Jim Holt, "Sunny Side Up," *The New Republic* (February 21, 1994): 23–27.

45. Mark Dowie, "The Biomort Factor," *American Health* (October 1990): 18–19.

46. Kathleen Stein, "Last Rights," *Omni* (September 1987): 59–66.

47. Dowie, "The Biomort Factor."

48. Stein, "Last Rights."

49. Elisabeth Rosenthal, "Dead Complicated," *Discover* (October 1992): 28–30.

50. Sharon Begley, "Choosing Death," *Newsweek* (August 26, 1991): 42–46.

51. Daniel Callahan, "Our Fear of Dying," *Newsweek* (October 4, 1993): 67.

52. Michele Ingrassia, "Should We Not Go Gentle?," *Newsweek* (February 7, 1994): 54–56.

53. George F. Will, "Facing the Skull beneath the Skin of Life," *Newsweek* (March 7, 1994): 74.

54. Anne Ricks Sumers, "I Want to Die at Home," *Newsweek* (April 4, 1994): 14.

55. "Death Is Painless, Quiet for Most."

56. Jeanne Guillemin, "Planning to Die," *Society* (July/August 1992): 29–33.

57. Guillemin, "Planning to Die."

58. Debra Goldman, "In My Time of Dying," *Adweek* (March 2, 1992): 18.

59. Barbara Ehrenreich, "The Ultimate Chic," *The Nation* (December 6, 1993): 681.

60. Joshua Levine, "Dr. Pangloss, Meet Ingmar Bergman," *Forbes* (March 30, 1992): 96.

61. "Loss."

62. Stephen Spignesi, "Means to an End," *Harper's Magazine* (August 1992): 28–30.

63. Betsy Sharkey, "Death Scene," *Adweek* (December 13, 1993): 21.

64. Richard Corliss, "Giving Up the Ghosts," *Time* (July 16, 1990): 86–87.

65. Martha Smilgis, "Hollywood Goes to Heaven," *Time* (June 3, 1991): 70.

66. Melinda Beck, "Movies without Mothers," *Newsweek* (August 29, 1994): 56.

67. Bordewich, "Mortal Fears."

68. David Thomson, "Death and Its Details," *Film Comment* (September 1993): 12–17.

69. Pico Iyer, "Death Be Not a Stranger," *Time* (August 8, 1994): 68.

70. "Changing Attitudes toward Death and Dying," *USA Today (Magazine)* (April 1994): 16.

CHAPTER 6

1. Jeffrey Ressner, "Dr. Tim's Last Trip," *Time* (April 29, 1996): 72–73.

2. Ressner, "Dr. Tim's Last Trip."

3. Douglas Rushkoff, "Leary's Last Trip," *Esquire* (August 1996): 62–66.

4. Lane Jennings, "Finding Better Ways to Die," *The Futurist* (March–April 2005): 43–47.

5. Lois Greene Stone, "Dealing with Death and Parents," *The Humanist* (May–June 1996): 40–41.

6. Mitch Albom, "Tuesdays with Morrie," *Reader's Digest* (April 1998): 9–17.

7. David Ansen, "Death Takes a Hike," *Newsweek* (December 28, 1998–January 4, 1999): 81.

8. The Editors, "A Good Death," *Utne Reader* (March–April 1998): 67.

9. The Editors, "A Good Death."

10. Pythia Peay, "Mastering the Natural Art of Dying," *Utne Reader* (March–April 1998): 68–72.

11. Peay, "Mastering the Natural Art of Dying"; More Americans, both healthy and dying, were now donating organs because of more publicity about the cause. In 1997, the country held its first National Organ and Tissue Donor Awareness Week, the event led by three members of Congress who had a personal connection with the issue. (Senator Mike DeWine had to make the difficult decision when his twenty-two-year-old daughter was killed in a car crash, Senator Bill Frist was a surgeon who did transplants, and Representative Joe Moakley actually had a donated liver.) As well, seventy million Americans received donor cards along with their tax refunds that year, making it a lot more likely there would be organs available for people who needed them. In a situation like the one DeWine had faced, many families refused to allow their loved one's organs to be harvested, their grief just too great to permit such a thing. Margaret Carlson, "A Dead Issue," *Time* (April 28, 1997): 26.

12. Helen Tworkov, "Slow Dancing with the Rhino," *Utne Reader* (March–April 1998): 73–76.

13. Joshua Simon, "A Song for the Dying," *Life* (December 1998): 108–12.

14. Peay, "Mastering the Natural Art of Dying."

15. Anne Underwood, "A Dream before Dying," *Newsweek* (July 25, 2005): 50–51.

16. Jane O'Hara, "The Baby Boomers Confront Mortality," *Maclean's* (July 1, 1996): 64.

17. Joseph Hart, "Grief Goes Online," *Utne* (March–April 2007): 88–89.

18. Brad Edmondson, "Trends in How We Die," *Current* (June 1997): 26.

19. C. McEnroe, "How to Bury Your Father," *Men's Health* (September 1999): 62.

20. Daniel McGinn and Julie Edelson Halpert, "Final Farewells," *Newsweek* (December 14, 1998): 60–62.

21. Wendy Lichtman, "Nobody's Daughter," *Good Housekeeping* (February 2002): 64.

22. McGinn and Halpert, "Final Farewells."

23. Leslie Billera, "Saying Goodbye to Mom," *Good Housekeeping* (January 2006): 120.

24. McGinn and Halpert, "Final Farewells."

25. Anne Kingston, "Finally, It Is All about You," *Maclean's* (June 16, 2008): 44–46.

26. Kingston, "Finally, It Is All about You."

27. Sharon Begley, "When You're Nobody's Child," *Newsweek* (April 3, 2000): 75.

28. Diane Umansky, "The Good Goodbye," *Good Housekeeping* (September 2000): 88–90.

29. "On Their Own Terms," *Money* (October 2000): 128–30.

30. "Top 10 Causes of Death in the U.S. by Age," *Discover* (July 2003): 42–43.

31. "What Are the Chances?," *Maclean's* (June 9, 2003): 23.

32. Janelle Nanos, "Can One Sibling Pull the Plug If the Others Don't Want To?," *New York* (June 16, 2008): 64–70.

33. Carl Swanson, "Death and the Salesman," *New York* (December 4, 2000): 24.

34. John Cloud, "A Kinder, Gentler Death," *Time* (September 18, 2000): 60–74.

35. McCloud, "A Kinder, Gentler Death."

36. McCloud, "A Kinder, Gentler Death."

37. McCloud, "A Kinder, Gentler Death."

38. McCloud, "A Kinder, Gentler Death."

39. Kent Sepkowitz, "Dignity in Dying," *Newsweek* (October 5, 2009): 13.

40. "Returning Death's Gaze," *Harper's Magazine* (April 1998): 31–35; Mary Roach, *Stiff: The Curious Lives of Human Cadavers* (New York: W. W. Norton, 2003).

41. Heather Havrilesky, "Did Nate Fisher Die for Our Sins?," *New York* (August 22, 2005): 61.

42. "Kickin' It," *Utne* (September–October 2005): 51–53.

43. Cathleen McGuigan, "Death Becomes Her," *Newsweek* (March 26, 2007): 82.

44. Richard Goldstein, "Death Trip," *The Nation* (October 23, 2006): 7–9.

45. Lakshmi Chaudhry, "Harry Potter and the Half-Baked Epic," *The Nation* (August 13–20, 2007): 5–6.

46. John Fraser, "The Way We Mourn," *Maclean's* (September 3, 2007): 50–52.

47. Laine Bergeson, "Death and Grieving Explored in Print," *Utne* (September–October 2005): 56.

48. Kathleen Kennedy Townsend, "Beyond Tragedy," *Reader's Digest* (November 2008): 183–95.

49. Townsend, "Beyond Tragedy."

50. Townsend, "Beyond Tragedy."

51. Richard Ford, "Love Lost," *New York Times Magazine* (September 23, 2001): 17.

52. Jill Goldstein, "Don't Be Afraid to Talk about My Husband," *Good Housekeeping* (January 2003): 43.

53. "A Father's Farewell," *Reader's Digest* (May 2008): 188–96. Randy Pausch and Jeffrey Zaslow, *The Last Lecture* (New York: Hyperion, 2008).

54. "10 Questions," *Time* (April 21, 2008): 4.

55. Laine Bergeson, "Good Life, Good Death," *Utne* (September–October 2005): 48–50.

56. Karen Olson, "Time to Say Goodbye," *Utne* (September–October 2005): 4.

57. Bob Holmes, "Death, the Upside," *Utne* (September–October 2005): 53.

58. Nina Utne, "To Live with No Regrets," *Utne* (September–October 2005): 54–56.

59. Paul O'Donnell, "Some Parting Advice," *Utne* (September–October 2005): 57–59.

60. Joseph Hart, "Grief Goes Online," *Utne* (March–April 2007): 88–89; www.Legacy.com.

61. Hart, "Grief Goes Online."

62. Matthew Goldstein, "Profiting from Mortality," *BusinessWeek* (July 30, 2007): 44–51; Matthew Goldstein, "Why Death Bonds Look So Frail," *BusinessWeek* (February 25, 2008): 40.

63. Gary Wiener, "Dear Junk Mailers: Leave My Son Alone," *Newsweek* (February 19, 2007): 26.

64. Lianne George, "A High-Tech Ghost Story," *Maclean's* (September 20, 2004): 32–33.

65. Rob Walker, "Things to Do in Cyberspace When You're Dead," *New York Times Sunday Magazine* (January 9, 2011): 30–37; Pam Greenberg, "Life after Death Online," *State Legislatures* (June 2012): 8.

66. Richard Dooling, "Immortal Man," *Esquire* (May 1999): 88–89; "It's Such a Simple Thing," *Esquire* (May 1999): 88–89.

67. Daniel Callahan, "Life Extension: Rolling the Technological Dice," *Society* (March 31, 2009): 214–20.

68. Sheila Jasanoff, "The Past as Prologue in Life Extension," *Society* (March 27, 2009): 232–34.

69. Howard L. Kaye, "Death and Us," *Society* (March 27, 2009): 237–39.

70. Aubrey de Grey, "A Thousand Years Young," *The Futurist* (May–June 2012): 18–23.

71. Joseph Hooper, "The Man Who Would Stop Time," *Popular Science* (August 2011): 51.

72. Kaye, "Death and Us."

73. Frank Furedi, "Extending a Life with Meaning," *Society* (March 31, 2009): 235–36. See Jonathan Weiner's *Long for This World: The Strange Science of Immortality* for more on the search for the fountain of youth.

CONCLUSION

1. Michael Kinsey, "Mine Is Longer Than Yours," *The New Yorker* (April 7, 2008): 38–43.

2. Kinsey, "Mine Is Longer Than Yours"; The longevity numbers were a bit misleading. If one made it to sixty, life expectancy jumped up to 80.8 for men and 84.0 for women, quite a nice bonus.

3. Dan Barry, "Boomers Hit Another Milestone of Self-Absorption: Turning 65," *New York Times* (January 1, 2011): A1.

4. Edward Zuckerman, "They Won't Call Back," *New York Times Magazine* (December 15, 2012): 62.

5. Graham Lawton, "Death," *New Scientist* (October 20, 2012): 3.

6. Sam Parnia and Josh Young, *Erasing Death: The Science That Is Rewriting the Boundaries between Life and Death* (New York: HarperOne, 2013).

7. Roger Angell, "Over the Wall," *The New Yorker* (November 19, 2012): 46; Armen Bacon and Nancy Miller, *Griefland: An Intimate Portrait of Love, Loss, and Unlikely Friendship* (Guilford, CT: Skirt! Books, 2012).

8. Scott Taylor Smith, *When Someone Dies: The Practical Guide to the Logistics of Death* (New York: Scribner, 2013).

9. www.sptimmortalityproject.com.

10. Ross Simonini, "The Terminator," *Psychology Today* (May–June 2011): 28.

Bibliography

Albom, Mitch. *Tuesdays with Morrie: An Old Man, a Young Man, and Life's Greatest Lesson.* New York: Doubleday, 1997.

Alexander, Eben, MD. *Proof of Heaven: A Neurosurgeon's Journey into the Afterlife.* New York: Simon & Schuster, 2012.

Alsop, Stewart. *Stay of Execution: A Sort of Memoir.* Philadelphia: Lippincott, 1973.

Aries, Philippe. *Western Attitudes toward Death: From the Middle Ages to the Present.* Baltimore: The Johns Hopkins University Press, 1974.

———. *The Hour of Our Death.* London: Allen Lane, 1981.

Bacon, Armen, and Nancy Miller. *Griefland: An Intimate Portrait of Love, Loss, and Unlikely Friendship.* Guilford, CT: Skirt! Books, 2012.

Ball, Howard. *At Liberty to Die: The Battle for Death with Dignity in America.* New York: New York University Press, 2012.

Bartalos, Michael K., ed. *Speaking of Death: America's New Sense of Mortality.* Santa Barbara, CA: Praeger, 2008.

Bartocci, Barbara. *Nobody's Child Anymore.* Notre Dame, IN: Sorin Books, 2000.

Barton, Betsey. *As Love Is Deep.* New York: Duell, Sloan and Pierce, 1957.

de Beauvoir, Simone. *A Very Easy Death.* New York: G. P. Putnam, 1966.

Becker, Ernest. *The Denial of Death.* New York: Free Press, 1973.

Bova, Ben. *Immortality: How Science Is Extending Your Life Span—and Changing the World.* New York: William Morrow, 1998.

Bowie, Herb. *Why Die? A Beginner's Guide to Living Forever.* Scottsdale, AZ: Power Surge Publishing, 1998.

Boyanton, Janet. *Alone and Alive: A Practical Guide for Dealing with the Death of Your Husband.* Lyons, NJ: Shafer, 2011.

Bregman, Lucy. *Beyond Silence & Denial: Death and Dying Reconsidered.* Louisville, KY: Westminster John Knox Press, 1999.

———. *Death and Dying, Spirituality and Religions: A Study of the Death Awareness Movement.* New York: Peter Lang, 2003.

———. *Preaching Death: The Transformation of Christian Funeral Sermons.* Waco, TX: Baylor University Press, 2011.

Brinkley, Dannion. *Saved by the Light: The True Story of a Man Who Died Twice and the Profound Revelations He Received.* New York: Villard, 1994.

Brookes, Tim. *Signs of Life: A Memoir of Dying and Discovery.* New York: Crown, 1997.

Brooks, Jane. *Midlife Orphan: Facing Life's Changes Now That Your Parents Are Gone.* New York: Berkley Trade, 1999.

Bulkeley, Patricia. *Dreaming beyond Death: A Guide to Pre-Death Dreams and Visions*. Boston: Beacon Press, 2005.

Burpo, Todd. *Heaven Is for Real: A Little Boy's Astounding Story of His Trip to Heaven and Back*. Nashville, TN: Thomas Nelson, 2010.

Byock, Ira. *Dying Well: The Prospect for Growth at the End of Life*. New York: Riverhead, 1997.

Callahan, Daniel. *The Troubled Dream of Life: Living with Mortality*. New York: Simon & Schuster, 1993.

Carrel, Alexis. *Man, the Unknown*. New York: Harper & Brothers, 1935.

Carrington, Hereward. *Death: Its Causes and Phenomena*. New York: Funk & Wagnalls, 1912.

Choron, Jacques, ed. *Death and Western Thought*. New York: Macmillan, 1963.

Collett, Merrill. *Stay Close and Do Nothing: A Spiritual and Practical Guide to Caring for the Dying at Home*. Kansas City: Andrews McMeel, 1997.

Copeland, Cyrus M. *Farewell, Godspeed: The Greatest Eulogies of Our Time*. New York: Crown, 2003.

Cote, Richard N. *In Search of Gentle Death: The Fight for Your Right to Die with Dignity*. Mt. Pleasant, SC: Corinthian, 2012.

Crace, Jim. *Being Dead: A Novel*. New York: Farrar, Straus and Giroux, 2000.

Curtin, Sharon R. *Nobody Ever Died of Old Age*. New York: Little, Brown, 1972.

Didion, Joan. *The Year of Magical Thinking*. New York: Alfred A. Knopf, 2005.

———. *Blue Nights*. New York: Alfred A. Knopf, 2011.

Dumont, Richard G., and Dennis C. Foss. *The American View of Death: Acceptance or Denial?* Cambridge, MA: Schenkman Publishing Company, 1972.

Eadie, Betty J. *Embraced by the Light*. Detroit: Gold Leaf Press, 1992.

Eckl, Cheryl. *A Beautiful Death: Facing the Future with Peace*. Littleton, CO: Flying Crane Press, 2010.

Eissler, Kurt. *The Psychiatrist and the Dying Patient*. Madison, CT: International Universities Press, 1955.

Ellis, Bret Easton. *American Psycho*. New York: Vintage, 1991.

Ettinger, Robert C. W. *The Prospect of Immortality*. Palo Alto, CA: Ria University Press, 2005.

Fahs, Sophia L., and Elizabeth Skelding Moore Manwell. *Consider the Children, How They Grow*. Boston: The Beacon Press, 1940.

Farrell, James J. *Inventing the American Way of Death, 1830–1920*. Philadelphia: Temple University Press, 1980.

Faust, Drew Gilpin. *This Republic of Suffering: Death and the American Civil War*. New York: Alfred A. Knopf, 2008.

Feifel, Herman, ed. *The Meaning of Death*. New York: McGraw-Hill, 1959.

Fontana, A., and J. Keene. *Death and Dying in America*. Cambridge, UK: Polity Press, 2009.

Gabrielson, Catherine. *The Story of Gabrielle*. Cleveland: World Publishing Company, 1956.

Gesell, Arnold, and Francis L. Ilg. *The Child from Five to Ten*. New York: Harper Brothers, 1947.

Gilbert, Sandra M. *Death's Door: Modern Dying and the Ways We Grieve*. New York: W. W. Norton, 2006.

Glaser, Barney G., and Anselm L. Strauss. *Awareness of Dying*. Piscataway, NJ: Aldine Transaction, 1965.

Gorer, Geoffrey. *Death, Grief, and Mourning*. Garden City, NY: Doubleday-Anchor, 1967.

Gould, Philip. *When I Die: Lessons from the Death Zone*. New York: Little, Brown, 2012.

Green, James W. *Beyond the Good Death: The Anthropology of Modern Dying*. Philadelphia: University of Pennsylvania Press, 2008.

Gunther, John. *Death Be Not Proud*. New York: Harper & Row, 1959.

Gutkind, Lee, ed. *At the End of Life: True Stories about How We Die*. Pittsburgh: Creative Nonfiction, 2012.

Hall, Donald. *The Best Day the Worst Day: Life with Jane Kenyon*. New York: Houghton Mifflin Harcourt, 2005.

Harlow, S. Ralph. *Life after Death*. New York: Doubleday, 1961.

Harrington, Alan. *The Immortalist: An Approach to the Engineering of Man's Divinity.* New York: Random House, 1969.

Heinrich, Bernd. *Life Everlasting: The Animal Way of Death.* New York: Houghton Mifflin Harcourt, 2012.

Hendin, David. *Death as a Fact of Life.* New York: W. W. Norton, 1973.

Hitchens, Christopher. *Mortality.* New York: Twelve, 2012.

Howarth, Glennys. *Death and Dying: A Sociological Introduction.* Cambridge, UK: Polity Press, 2007.

Humphry, Derek. *Let Me Die before I Wake.* Eugene, OR: Hemlock Society, 1984.

———. *Final Exit: The Practicalities of Self-Deliverance and Assisted Suicide for the Dying.* Secaucus, NJ: Carol Publishing, 1991.

Isenberg, Nancy, and Andrew Burstein, eds. *Mortal Remains: Death in Early America.* Philadelphia: University of Pennsylvania Press, 2002.

Jacoby, Susan. *Never Say Die: The Myth and Marketing of the New Old Age.* New York: Pantheon, 2011.

Katz, Jon. *Going Home: Finding Peace When Pets Die.* New York: Villard, 2012.

Keleman, Stanley. *Living Your Dying.* New York: Random House, 1975.

Kellehear, A. *A Social History of Dying.* Cambridge, UK: Cambridge University Press, 2007.

Kramer, Herbert, and Kay Kramer. *Conversations at Midnight: Coming to Terms with Dying and Death.* New York: William Morrow & Co., 1993.

Krant, Melvin J. *Dying and Dignity: The Meaning and Control of a Personal Death.* Springfield, IL: Charles C. Thomas Publishers, 1974.

Kübler-Ross, Elisabeth. *On Death and Dying.* New York: Macmillan, 1970.

———. *Questions and Answers on Death and Dying.* New York: Scribner, 1974.

———. *Death: The Final Stage of Growth.* New York: Simon & Schuster, 1980.

———. *Living with Death and Dying.* New York: Macmillan, 1981.

Laderman, Gary. *Rest in Peace: A Cultural History of Death and the Funeral Home in Twentieth-Century America.* New York: Oxford University Press, 2003.

LaGrand, Louis. *Healing Grief, Finding Peace: 101 Ways to Cope with the Death of Your Loved One.* Naperville, IL: Sourcebooks, 2011.

Langone, John. *Vital Signs: The Way We Die in America.* New York: Little, Brown, 1974.

Leary, Lani. *No One Has to Die Alone: Preparing for a Meaningful Death.* New York: Atria, 2012.

Leary, Timothy. *Design for Dying.* San Francisco: HarperOne, 1997.

Lepore, Jill. *The Mansion of Happiness: A History of Life and Death.* New York: Alfred A. Knopf, 2012.

Levine, Stephen. *A Year to Live: How to Live This Year as If It Were Your Last.* New York: Harmony, 1997.

Levine, Stephen, and Ondrea Levine. *Who Dies? An Investigation of Conscious Living and Conscious Dying.* New York: Anchor, 1989.

Levy, Alexander. *The Orphaned Adult: Understanding and Coping with Grief and Change after the Death of Our Parents.* New York: Perseus Books, 1999.

Lifton, Robert Jay, and Eric Olson. *Living and Dying.* London: Wildwood House, 1974.

Mack, Arien, ed. *Death in American Experience.* New York: Schocken Books, 1973.

Maguire, Daniel C. *Death by Choice.* New York: Doubleday, 1974.

Mannes, Marya. *Last Rights: A Case for the Good Death.* New York: Signet Books, 1973.

McManus, John C. *The Deadly Brotherhood: The American Combat Soldier in World War II.* New York: Random House, 2003.

Mitford, Jessica. *The American Way of Death.* New York: Simon & Schuster, 1963.

Moody, Raymond. *Reflections on Life after Life.* New York: Bantam Books, 1977.

———. *Life after Life: The Investigation of a Phenomenon-Survival of Bodily Death.* New York: Bantam Books, 1979.

Negovskii, V. A. *Resuscitation and Artificial Hypothermia.* New York: Consultants Bureau, 1962.

Nuland, Sherwin. *How We Die: Reflections on Life's Final Chapter.* New York: Alfred A. Knopf, 1994.

Null, Gary. *Gary Null's Ultimate Anti-Aging Program.* New York: Kensington Books, 1999.

Oates, Joyce Carol. *A Widow's Story: A Memoir.* New York: Ecco, 2011.

Okun, Barbara, and Joseph Nowinski. *Saying Goodbye: How Families Can Find Renewal through Loss.* New York: Berkley, 2011.

O'Rourke, Meghan. *The Long Goodbye: A Memoir.* New York: Riverhead, 2011.

Overall, Christine. *Aging, Death, and Human Longevity: A Philosophical Inquiry.* Berkeley: University of California Press, 2003.

Parnia, Sam. *What Happens When We Die : A Groundbreaking Study into the Nature of Life and Death.* Carlsbad, CA: Hay House, 2006.

Parnia, Sam, and Josh Young. *Erasing Death: The Science That Is Rewriting the Boundaries between Life and Death.* New York: HarperOne, 2013.

Pausch, Randy, and Jeffrey Zaslow. *The Last Lecture.* New York: Hyperion, 2008.

Pelikan, Jaroslav. *The Shape of Death: Life, Death, and Immortality in the Early Fathers.* Nashville: Abingdon Press, 1961.

Pierce, Jessica. *The Last Walk: Reflections on Our Pets at the End of Their Lives.* Chicago: University of Chicago Press, 2012.

Rinpoche, Sogyal. *The Tibetan Book of Living and Dying.* San Francisco: HarperOne, 1992.

Roach, Mary. *Stiff: The Curious Lives of Human Cadavers.* New York: W. W. Norton, 2003.

Roth, Philip. *Everyman.* New York: Houghton Mifflin Harcourt, 2006.

Safer, Jeanne. *Death Benefits: How Losing a Parent Can Change an Adult's Life—for the Better.* New York: Basic Books, 2008.

Salzberger, Cyrus. *My Brother, Death.* New York: Harper Brothers, 1961.

Sankar, Andrea. *Dying at Home: A Family Guide for Caregiving.* Baltimore: The Johns Hopkins University Press, 1991.

Schuurman, Donna. *Never the Same: Coming to Terms with the Death of a Parent.* New York: St. Martin's Press, 2003.

Secunda, Victoria. *Losing Your Parents, Finding Yourself: The Defining Turning Point of Adult Life.* New York: Hyperion, 2000.

Shields, David, and Bradford Morrow, eds. *The Inevitable: Contemporary Writers Confront Death.* New York: Norton, 2011.

Slocum, Joshua, and Lisa Carlson. *Final Rights: Reclaiming the American Way of Death.* Hinesburg, VT: Upper Access, 2011.

Smith, Scott Taylor. *When Someone Dies: The Practical Guide to the Logistics of Death.* New York: Scribner, 2013.

Smith, Suzanne E. *To Serve the Living: Funeral Directors and the African American Way of Death.* Cambridge: Belknap Press of Harvard University Press, 2010.

Stephenson, John S. *Death, Grief, and Mourning: Individual and Social Realities.* New York: Free Press, 1985.

Still, Joseph W. *Science and Education at the Crossroads: A View from the Laboratory.* New York: Public Affairs Press, 1958.

Swedlund, Alan. *Shadows in the Valley: A Cultural History of Illness, Death and Loss in New England, 1840–1916.* Amherst: University of Massachusetts Press, 2009.

Taylor, Jennifer Collins. *Living Life Dying Death: A Guide to Healthy Conversations about Death and Dying to Inspire Life and Living.* Scottsdale, AZ: MyRehab, 2011.

Teresi, Dick. *The Undead: Organ Harvesting, The Ice-Water Test, Beating-Heart Cadavers: How Medicine Is Blurring the Line between Life and Death.* New York: Pantheon, 2012.

Tompkins, Ptolemy. *The Modern Book of the Dead: A Revolutionary Perspective on Death, the Soul, and What Really Happens in the Life to Come.* New York: Atria, 2012.

Toynbee, Arnold. *Man's Concern with Death.* New York: McGraw-Hill, 1969.

Trillin, Calvin. *About Alice.* New York: Random House, 2006.

Umberson, Debra. *Death of a Parent: Transition to a New Adult Identity.* New York: Cambridge University Press, 2003.

Webb, Marilyn. *The Good Death: The New American Search to Reshape the End of Life.* New York: Bantam Books, 1997.

Weenolsen, Patricia. *The Art of Dying: How to Leave This World with Dignity and Grace, at Peace with Yourself and Your Loved Ones.* New York: St. Martin's Press, 1996.

Weiner, Jonathan. *Long for This World: The Strange Science of Immortality*. New York: Ecco, 2010.

Weisman, Avery. *On Dying and Denying*. New York: Human Sciences Press, 1972.

Wertenbaker, Lael Tucker. *Death of a Man*. New York: Bantam Books, 1957.

Yellin, Emily. *Our Mothers' War: American Women at Home and at the Front during World War II*. New York: Free Press, 2004.

Index

Ackerman, Diane, xiii

afterlife: after-death experiences, 157; Eben Alexander on, xiv; and avatars in role-playing games, 150; belief in while dying, 8; Thomas W. Clark on, 106; and the Death and Dying II project, 110; interest in the 1920s, 2; Kubler-Ross on, 111; in movies of the 1990s, 126; portrayals of, xiv; possibilities of, 68; John Puckering on, 18; relationship with death, x; and the religious, 15, 43; and scientists, 18; Ronald K. Siegel on, 107; and "trans-egoic" model of intervention, 134; as transition from life, 133

AIDS: and Harold Brodkey, 115; as cause of death, 139; as contributor to "death education", 116; and death in the early 1990s, 124; and death in the 1980s, xx, 103; and death photography, 142; and death in 2000, 138; and hospital ethics teams, 139; and *How We Die*, 122; and *The Inevitable*, xiii; and literature, 144; and misreporting on death certificates, 114–115

Albom, Mitch, 131

American Medical Association (AMA), xv, xix, 75, 88, 94, 120, 140

autopsies, 59–61, 71–72, 73, 83

baby boomers: aging of, 156; confronting their mortality, xxii, 103, 105, 125, 138; and death and dying at end of twentieth century, 132; and death and dying in the 1980s, xx; and death of parents, 136–137, 140; denial of death, 131; dying, 157; Michael Kinsey on, 155; as masters of the art of dying, 132; as most ambitious and prosperous generation in history, 158; and the "prodeath movement", 111; as target of morticians, 134–135; as unprepared for death, xi, xii, xxi; George Will on, 123

Ball, Alan, 143

Benny, Jack, 96–97

Bono, Sonny, 145

Brodkey, Harold, 115

Brown, Joe E., 58

cemeteries (graveyards): caretakers, 115; and children, 35, 40, 56; cost of plot and marker in 1996, 135; and "death education", 116; in England, 117; and *The Inevitable*, xiii; located outside of cities, 81; in the Middle Ages, 95; and modernity, 34; during the Renaissance, 124; and Carson C. Surles, 28

Cher, 145

children: accidental deaths, 50; Gertrude Carver on, 10; and death in postwar years, 54–57; and death during World

About the Author

Lawrence R. Samuel is the founder of Culture Planning LLC, a Miami- and New York-based resource offering cultural insights to Fortune 500 companies. He holds a PhD in American studies and was a Smithsonian Institution Fellow.

His previous books include *Pledging Allegiance: American Identity and the Bond Drive of World War II*; *Brought to You By: Postwar Television Advertising and the American Dream*; *The End of the Innocence: The 1964-1965 New York World's Fair*; *Future: A Recent History*; *Rich: The Rise and Fall of American Wealth Culture*; *Freud on Madison Avenue: Motivation Research and Subliminal Advertising in America*; *Supernatural America: A Cultural History*; *The American Dream: A Cultural History*; *Sexidemic: A Cultural History of Sex in America* (Rowman & Littlefield); *Shrink: A Cultural History of Psychoanalysis in America*; and *The American Middle Class: A Cultural History*.